Women's Ventures

Women's Ventures
Assistance to the Informal Sector in Latin America

Editors

Marguerite Berger

Mayra Buvinić

Kumarian Press, Inc.

*This book is dedicated to all of the women borrowers in the
Ecuadorian Development Foundation's credit program.*

Printed in the United States of America, 1990
94 93 92 91 90   5 4 3 2 1

Cover design by Marilyn Penrod

Phototypeset by The Type Galley, Boulder, Colorado

Library of Congress Cataloging-in-Publication Data

Women's ventures: assistance to the informal sector in Latin America
  /   editors, Marguerite Berger, Mayra Buvinić.
      p.   cm. — (Kumarian Press library of management for
  development)
    Includes bibliographical references.
    ISBN 0-931816-79-3
    1. Women in business—Latin America.   2. Women-owned business
  enterprises—Latin America.   3. Informal sector (Economics)—Latin
  America.   I. Berger, Marguerite.   II. Buvinić, Mayra.   III. Series.
  HD6054.2.L29W66   1989
  331.4'81381—dc20   89-39190
                                                             CIP

Contents

List of Tables

Contributors

Luz María Abreu is a graduate of the School of Sociology, Universidad Autónoma de Santo Domingo, in the Dominican Republic. She currently serves as director of Mujeres en Desarrollo Dominicana Inc. (MUDE). Ms. Abreu cofounded various associations that work with small farmers (1970–80) and has published several papers dealing with rural development. In addition, she has aided in the formation of numerous rural development efforts.

María Eugenia Arias is presently working with the Instituto de Estudios de Posgrado en Administración de Negocios in Guayaquil, Ecuador, where she is a professor of Business Administration. Previously she worked as a teaching assistant while completing her Master's and Ph.D. at the Yale University School of Organization and Management. Her publications include: "La Vida A," a case on the takeover of a plant in a Latin American country by a large multinational firm; and "Loans to Women," a case on loans to small entrepreneurs in Peru, which was published in *Gender Roles in Project Development,* edited by Catherine Overholt and James Austin.

Marguerite Berger, an economist with the International Center for Research on Women (ICRW), specializes in credit, microenterprise, and employment issues. Since joining the Center in 1983, she has provided technical assistance to government and private agencies in project design, monitoring, and evaluation in Ecuador, Indonesia, Peru, Guatemala, and Bangladesh. She has also conducted policy-oriented research on diverse topics related to women's participation in development, including housing, agriculture, and technical education. During 1986, Ms. Berger was a visiting scholar at the Instituto Latinoamericano de Investigaciónes Sociales (ILDIS) in Quito, Ecuador. Prior to joining ICRW she worked as an economic analyst for the Small Business Administration and the Corporation for Enterprise Development. Ms. Berger is a Ph.D. candidate in economics at American University in Washington, D.C.

Mayra Buvinić is the founder and director of the International Center for Research on Women. She is past president of the Association for Women in Development and a current member of the Board of Trustees of the International Institute for Tropical Agriculture in Lagos, Nigeria. Among her best known publications are *Women and Poverty in the Third World* (Johns Hopkins University Press, 1983) and "Women's Projects in the Third World: Explaining their Misbehavior" (*World Development*, May 1986). Dr. Buvinić holds a doctorate in social psychology from the University of Wisconsin, Madison, and a degree in psychology from the Catholic University of Santiago, Chile.

María Clemencia Castro, administrative director of the Banco Mundial de la Mujer in Colombia, is responsible for the Bank's administration, operations, planning, and research. Her work there helps provide aid to individuals and solidarity groups in Colombia through credit and management training programs. Her last three papers, entitled "Impacto Financiero en el Programa de Grupos Solidarios" (May and November 1986 and May 1987) documented the progress and shortcomings of the solidarity groups. Ms. Castro received her Master's degree in business administration from Universidad del Valle in Cali.

Silvia Escobar de Pabon is a researcher at the Centro de Estudios para el Desarrollo Laboral y Agrario (CEDLA), where she works in the Unit for Urban Studies. In this position she is responsible for research projects on economic activities and development in the urban informal sector. She received her degree in sociology from the Universidad Mayor de San Andres (La Paz, Bolivia). Ms. Escobar is presently involved in a project aimed at the development, publication, and diffusion of a report on the urban informal sector, and is working on the design and implementation of programs to increase income and employment of workers in the urban informal sector.

Stephen Gross is ACCION International's associate director for Latin American operations. With ACCION for over ten years, Mr. Gross has spent seven of these in Latin America initiating microbusiness projects as a resident advisor to local institutions in the Dominican Republic and Ecuador. He has also assisted in program start-up in Paraguay, Bolivia, and Honduras. With a field staff of eleven residential advisors/directors, he presently collaborates in support efforts for some thirty microbusiness programs throughout Latin America.

María Margarita Guzman is a consultant for Women's World Banking in Colombia. Her work with WWB has involved her in many important projects including the extension of lines of credit to solidarity groups and the supply of capital resources to women with small businesses. She has served on the board of directors of many organizations, including the Fundación para el Desarrollo Social/FUNDES (vice president), Women's World Banking (representative for Latin America and the Caribbean), and Banco Mundial de la Mujer in Cali (president). Ms. Guzman received her degree in economics from Universidad del Valle in Cali.

Cecilia Jaramillo, Executive Manager, is responsible for the financial planning and project management of the International Center for Research on Women. Since 1984, she has also provided technical assistance to the Fundación Ecuatoriana de Desarrollo, a private foundation in Quito, Ecuador, that makes loans to men and women entrepreneurs. In addition, she organized ICRW's 1986 seminar on women and credit in Latin America. She is also the coauthor of a paper on low-income housing for urban women. Ms. Jaramillo has a Master's degree in City Planning and Community Development from Howard University.

Jorge F. Landivar is the executive president of the Ecuadorian Development Foundation (Fundación Ecuatoriana de Desarrollo), where he has executed a variety of functions since its founding in 1968. He has also worked with the Counsel for Development Foundations in Latin America (Consejo de Fundaciones de Desarrollo de America Latina) and served as a promoter and manager with over seventeen foundations in various countries. His interest in the field of socioeconomic development is a long standing one, focusing on the creation of programs and institutions whose main objectives center around the augmentation of self-management skills. Mr. Landivar received his B.A. in business administration with a specialization in marketing. He also holds a Master's degree in economics, and is working toward his Ph.D. in development at the University of Wales in Great Britain.

Margaret Lycette is deputy director of the International Center for Research on Women. She is an economist with extensive experience in providing technical services to development agencies, conducting applied research on women in developing countries, and managing projects. She specializes in low-income housing, small enterprise credit, basic education, and vocational training. Ms. Lycette directs ICRW's major technical services work with the U.S. Agency for International Development. Her fieldwork has involved technical assistance in Ecuador, Indonesia, Jordan, Morocco, and Pakistan. A graduate of Boston University, Ms. Lycette earned an M.A. in economics at the Johns Hopkins University, and is now a Ph.D. candidate in that program. She is currently working on the Gender Resource Awareness in National Development Project, which involves the development of computer simulation models of women's participation in key economic sectors for eight developing countries.

Cressida McKean has recently joined the U.S. Agency for International Development's Program Policy Evaluation Division where she works as a senior social scientist in the Center for Development Information and Evaluation. Previously, her work has involved managing, designing and evaluating projects, primarily those supporting small and microenterprise development for US AID, the ILO, the Inter-American Foundation, and other institutions. Her field experience includes work in the Dominican Republic, Ecuador, the Philippines, and the Caribbean. Ms. McKean received a Master's of Philosophy in development studies from the University of Sussex, England. She also holds a Master's of Science in international relations/economics concentration from the London School of Economics, England, and a B.A. in Latin American studies from Stanford University.

Jaime Mezzera is Regional Advisor on the Informal Sector with the International Labor Organization's Regional Employment Program of Latin America and the Caribbean (PREALC). In this capacity he has conducted policy research and assisted in the creation of small and microenterprise development programs in different Latin American countries including Peru, Venezuela, and Ecuador. He holds a Master's degree in Economics from Boston University and is a candidate for the Ph.D. at the same institution. His recent publications include: "Un modelo de mercados laborales segmentados," published in the PREALC volume, *Modelos de Empleo y Política Económica,* and "Labor Market Segmentation without Policy-Induced Labor Market Distortions," in *World Development.*

María Otero, a native of Bolivia, is the country director in Honduras for ACCION International/AITEC. In this position she provides long-term technical assistance to Honduran organizations, particularly ASEPADE in the implementation of its microenterprise development program. Prior to joining ACCION/AITEC, Ms. Otero worked with the Inter-American Foundation, the Center for Development and Population Activities, and the U.S. Agency for International Development. She holds a Master's degree from the Johns Hopkins University School of Advanced International Studies. Her most recent publications include *The Solidarity Group Concept: Its Characteristics and Significance for Urban Informal Sector Activities*, for Private Agencies Collaborating Together (PACT).

María Mercedes Placencia is a sociologist who founded and directs the Center for Study and Promotion of the Urban Informal Sector (CEPESIU) in Guayaquil, Ecuador. She has served as advisor to the International Labor Organization and to numerous microenterprise projects in Latin America. She was the first Director of the National Office of Women in the Ecuadorian Ministry of Social Welfare.

Rebecca Lynn Reichmann is a program officer with the Ford Foundation in Brazil. Prior to joining the Foundation she was the director of training, research and evaluation for ACCION International where she was responsible for the coordination and management of numerous tasks related to microenterprise development projects. She has also worked with corporations in development education, as a consultant for various development organizations, and as part of a support team to develop and implement an educational awareness program in Andean Peru. Her most recent publication is "Solidarity in Development: The Tricicleros of Santo Domingo," in *Grassroots Development.* Ms. Reichmann received her Ed.D. degree in counseling and consulting psychology from the Harvard Graduate School of Education. She also holds a B.A. in English from Yale University, New Haven.

Karen White currently serves as the information director of PRITECH, a project designed to introduce oral rehydration therapy to developing countries. In this capacity, she provides technical support to PRITECH field representatives and counterparts in developing countries and manages the Information Center. Prior to joining PRITECH, Ms. White worked for the International Center for Research on Women, first as information specialist and later as development officer. She is the author of several reports and bibliographies in the women-in-development field. Ms. White holds an M.L.S. and an M.A. from the University of Maryland.

Acknowledgments

T
he idea for this book and much of its contents emerged from an international meeting on "Women's Access to Credit in Latin America: Suggestions for Development Programs," which took place in Quito, Ecuador, in 1986. The meeting was co-sponsored by the United States Agency for International Development (USAID), the Latin American Institute for Social Research/ILDIS (Friedrich Ebert Foundation) in Ecuador, and the Ecuadorean Interinstitutional Committee for Microenterprise Development. The International Center for Research on Women organized the event. The editors wish to express their appreciation to ILDIS, the Ecuadorean Development Foundation (FED), and the Women in Development Office of USAID for their support throughout the project. Special thanks go to Alexander Kallweit, Santiago Escobar, Galo Chiroboga, and the administrative staff of ILDIS who worked on the conference and this book; to Joan Wolfe of the Women in Development Office of USAID; and to Miriam Carillo and the credit extensionists of the FED.

Sonia Guerra at the FED contributed to the research done in-country and the organization of the meeting; K. Lee Martinez at ICRW supervised the translation, editing, and preparation of this manuscript. The translation was done by Charlie Roberts, Amalia Cabib, and Rene Otero. Libby Lopez typed the manuscript in English and Spanish with great patience and efficiency. Our deepest gratitude goes to them.

1

An Introduction

MARGUERITE BERGER

Women entrepreneurs seem to be invisible in Latin America. Their specific characteristics and needs are often overlooked by policymakers and project implementors despite the development community's increased interest in microenterprise. Among the wealth of materials written on the informal sector and microenterprise in the region, we generally find only passing reference to the importance of women's contribution. Reviews of assistance programs targeted to this sector of the urban or rural economy tend to limit their analysis of women's participation to an obligatory mention of the number of women beneficiaries or a paragraph about their businesses.

Women entrepreneurs are not really invisible, however, not even to the casual observer. Nor are many of them true entrepreneurs, at least in the classical sense of the term. Some of the most common types of women-owned businesses in Latin America (such as selling) are openly operated on the same streets where government and international agency offices are located. These activities and others undertaken by women are not considered to be "entrepreneurial" by many observers, even though women are risking their own capital—limited though it may be—and creating new jobs in the process. Their businesses are often survival activities with modest prospects for growth or a dynamic effect on the macroeconomy. However, while other informal-sector business operators are considered to be "micro-entre-preneurs," activities dominated by women tend to be overlooked, and women remain invisible or two-dimensional in much of the discussion of microenterprise.

This book seeks to enhance the visibility of women microentre-preneurs by bringing their concerns into the arena of empirical inquiry and policy and program review. It addresses the subject of women and microen-

1

terprise in a manner that reflects the reality of their participation: integral to an important and growing segment of the Latin American economies. It is based largely on papers presented at an international seminar on the subject held in Quito, Ecuador.[1] The seminar and this volume bring together two topics that are usually defined as complementary but separate: women's employment and microenterprise assistance. The articles extend beyond the boundaries that separate the realms of activity of scholars, policymakers, and program implementors, and therefore provide insights that will allow policymakers, planners, and project managers to improve their own policies and projects, or to design new ones.

The collection of readings in this volume is organized around four broad subject areas: an overview of the informal sector, specifically the microenterprise segment of that sector, and policies and programs designed to provide assistance to it; training and technical assistance activities targeted to the sector; case studies of credit programs for small and microenterprise; and the gender-disaggregated evaluation of assistance programs. This introductory chapter provides a common ground to frame the discussion that follows in the individual contributions. The purpose of the chapter is threefold: to consider the context of women's work in the informal sector and the reasons for highlighting women's participation; to establish characteristics of women's activities in the informal sector and relate them to the different ways of conceptualizing the sector that have been put forward by various observers; and finally, to examine some of the policies and projects directed to the informal sector and their significance for women.

THE IMPORTANCE OF A FOCUS ON WOMEN

Why is the role of women in the informal sector so important? Why does it merit special attention? One answer is the major change that has occurred in the labor force in Latin America over the past two decades: the increasing participation of women in the labor market. The 1980-1981 Annual Report of the Inter-American Development Bank (IDB) noted that a "subtle revolution" was taking place in Latin America, in the form of an increasing entrance of women into the labor market. Figures cited in the IDB's latest Economic and Social Progress Report (IDB 1987) again highlight this trend, showing that although women were only 17.9 percent of the labor force of the region as a whole in 1950, this percentage will rise to 27.5 percent by the year 2000. The economic activity of women as measured by these statistics, which are undoubtedly understating their economic participation, has been increasing much faster than that of men. While the male labor force doubled between 1950 and 1980, the female labor force grew by more than three times. Between 1980 and the year 2000 the female labor force is projected to nearly double again as an additional 22 million women enter the labor force in Latin America. In certain regions the period 1980 to 2000 will be even more important in terms of rising participation of women, particularly in Central America and other areas where urbanization has lagged behind other countries in the region (IDB 1987).

Women's increased participation is due in part to four important changes that have taken place in the past twenty years. The first is related to the changing structure of the Latin American economies associated with urbanization. In Latin America, women's migration to the cities has often been higher than that of men, especially among young women who have gone to the city seeking economic opportunity. Urbanization and associated changes in production have also transformed work that women used to do at home into work that is done for pay in the marketplace. In addition, although the traditional economic activities of rural women were often home-based and inextricably linked to their reproductive responsibilities in the household, a lack of access to land and other productive resources, along with modernization of agricultural production, has forced women to orient their activities more directly to the market, making them more visible.

At the same time, the distribution of educational benefits in Latin America has shown a tendency toward equalization between the sexes. In many countries today the levels of educational enrollment are nearing equality for men and women. This equality, nevertheless, still evades a number of the poorer countries, particularly those in Central America and the Caribbean, and there still exists a large sex-related gap in the educational attainments of the older population. However, increasing educational opportunities for young women have led to expanded economic opportunities for them.

A third factor that helps to explain the rise in women's economic participation is their increased need to bring a monetary income into the household. This need exists in traditional, nuclear families as well as among the rising number of female-headed households in Latin America. On the one hand, the deterioration in real levels of earnings during the 1980s has made it necessary for married women to enter the labor force as secondary earners. There is evidence that their entrance into the labor market, fueled by the need to earn an income, has a countercyclical character. In other words, the number of women who are looking for work, particularly poor women, increases as economic growth declines. For example, a recent report by the International Center for Research on Women (Buvinic and Horenstein 1986) cited the following situation in Costa Rica: women's share of the labor force increased from 24.8 percent in 1980 to 26.2 percent in 1982, the peak economic crisis year, and leveled off at 25.4 percent in 1983, which was a year of slight recovery. At the same time, women's open unemployment rate in the country increased from 7.8 percent in 1980 to 11.4 percent in 1982 and then fell to 9.6 percent in 1983. Male unemployment continued to rise over the entire period, increasing from 5.3 to 8.6 percent between 1980 and 1982, and again to 8.8 percent in 1983.

Another case, in Santiago, Chile, showed a paradoxical outcome in changes in female employment. However, this paradox can be explained by disaggregating women's participation in the labor force by household income level. Whereas the activity rates of women in the lowest quintile of the household income distribution increased sharply from 18 to 22.4 percent during the economic crisis of 1974-75, among high-income women the opposite trend occurred. Women in the medium-low income group showed a declining participation rate from 22.6 to 19.5 percent, medium-high income women decreased their participation rate from 25.8 to 23.0 percent, and the participation of high-income women fell most dramatically from 34.3 to 31.9 percent over that period (Rosales 1979).

Another element in augmenting women's need to work for pay is the rising proportion of households where women are the primary income earners. Household surveys conducted in five Latin American cities in 1982 revealed that women headed between 18 and 38 percent of all households, with the highest rates apparent among the lowest income groups (CEPAL 1984). In all the cities surveyed except Bogota, female headship rose between 1982 and 1985, the year for which the most recent data are available (Arriagada 1987).

The phenomenon of increasing female headship is important for the analysis of changes in the informal sector because of three factors. Firstly, according to even official statistics, economic participation rates are higher for female heads of household than they are for women in general. In six major Latin American cities, female heads of household between the ages of fifteen and forty-four have a participation rate that fluctuates between 44.7 and 88.2 percent, which is roughly equivalent to male rates for that age group (CEPAL 1986, p. 39).

Secondly, the participation of female household heads is economically motivated. Available data on incomes of households by sex of household head show that woman-headed households are poorer than those headed by men. Households headed by women are not any more likely to be part of extended households than those headed by men and, therefore, do not have additional sources of economic support. Also, there is generally a higher dependency ratio in female-headed households; in other words, there are fewer income earners in relation to the total number of household members, a situation that contributes to women's need to work for pay to support the household.

Finally, the occupations of women heads of household often yield very low earnings. A high proportion of women who are heads of household work in the informal sector. Data from Colombia, for example, show that women who are heads of household are more likely to be self-employed than other women (Arriagada 1987). And a study in Belo Horizonte, Brazil, found that one of the major factors explaining differences in income between male and female heads of household was their occupation. The study found that 53 percent of the female heads worked in the informal sector as compared to only 13 percent of the males. Furthermore, women heads of household working in the informal sector tended to earn significantly less than male heads working in the same sector (Merrick and Schmink 1983).

WOMEN IN THE INFORMAL SECTOR

Where do women who are new entrants into the labor force, or even those who had been employed previously, go to look for jobs in order to sustain their families or to contribute to household income? The answer lies, in part, in the concentration of women in small-scale service and commerce or trading activities. Faced with increasing economic need, and unable to find employment in modern-sector firms, women are forced to create their own jobs. They are joining the so-called informal economy, where wages and working conditions are generally worse than those in regularized wage employment.

In general, the representation of women in the informal sector is higher than their rate of participation in the economy as a whole, a fact that observers of the sector have unanimously pointed out. Women account for a major portion of informal-sector workers in Latin America by a number of measures and often approach, or even surpass, half of this population.

According to studies conducted by the Programa Regional de Empleo para América Latina y el Caribe (PREALC) in the 1970s, women comprised between 51 and 62 percent of those employed in the informal sector in major Mexican cities if domestic service is included as part of the informal sector. If domestic service is excluded, women still accounted for 32 to 37 percent of those in the informal sector in these cities. In the two principal cities of Ecuador, women made up 39 percent of the informal sector labor force excluding domestic service, and in Honduras they comprised 40 percent of this population. Exceptions are Costa Rica and Panama, where the participation of women was lower in the informal than the formal sector. In Costa Rica, for example, women accounted for 24 percent of informal-sector workers, but they made up 31 percent of formal-sector workers. In Panama, women accounted for 20 percent of those employed in the informal sector and 38 percent for those in the formal sector. According to PREALC, the low percentage of women in the informal sector in these last two countries may be due largely to greater educational opportunities that permitted women to obtain more desirable jobs in the modern sector (PREALC 1981).

Describing the Informal Sector

The term "informal sector" has a certain attraction for describing a phenomenon that seems to be evident to most observers of economic development in the Third World, and perhaps is even more evident when one speaks of women's employment. But when it comes to formal application of this term, in order to identify the group quantitatively or to specify the object of policies and programs of assistance for the sector, it becomes clear that the term embodies many contradictions (Kannappan 1985; Peattie 1987).

In part, the "informal sector" is a popular label because it allows us to put a name to and legitimize a vaguely defined target population for which policies and programs have been developed (Peattie 1987). For purposes of this volume, we can use the term if we restrict it to focus on the economic units (establishments) that make up the informal sector—microenterprises. If self-employed professionals, such as doctors and lawyers, are excluded, we can roughly define informal-sector microenterprises as businesses employing no more than five workers and having assets valued at less than the equivalent of US$20,000. It is these enterprises that manifest all the features commonly associated with informal-sector activities: small size of operations, reliance on family labor and local resources, low capital endowments, labor-intensive technology, limited barriers to entry, a high degree of competition, an unskilled work force, and acquisition of skills outside the formal educational system. Microenterprises as they are defined here, as well as other businesses that might be labeled informal under some definitions, also fall within that sector of economic activity that is not registered with government agencies, is uncounted or undercounted by official statistics, does not comply with regulations governing labor practices, taxes, and licensing, and has a nonunionized work force (Sethuraman 1976).

Informality and Women's Work

Informality is an attractive concept for referring to microenterprises, and to a significant segment of women's work, largely because of the five characteristics that this work often shares.

Internal Organization.   The so-called informal-sector activities are informal in terms of the internal organizational structure of the unit of production or occupation in question. In other words, the hierarchy of work and roles within the workplace are more flexible and informal. An extreme case of this informality is that of the own account or self-employed worker who combines the roles of worker, manager, and owner in a single individual.

Relations with the Outside World.   Informal-sector occupations tend to be informal in terms of their relationships with the world that surrounds them—for instance, their relations with suppliers, clients, and the state. These relations are less defined or more fluid than those in which formal or modern businesses participate; that is, they lack formal contracts, the hours of operation are flexible, and contacts are irregular. This informality, in part, explains why the sector is also known as the "unprotected" or "unorganized" sector, particularly with respect to labor. Because their relations with the outside world are hard to pin down, informal-sector businesses have a character of "invisibility" and often go uncounted by official statistics, particularly by economic censuses.

Branch of Activity.   Here informality is defined by the fact that combinations of different activities exist in a single unit of production, commerce, or services, and by the simultaneity of activities as well as frequent change in activities, particularly on a seasonal basis. Not only do informal-sector businesses often include retail outlets for their own manufactured products, but they may also sell products that are purchased elsewhere. In such cases, it is difficult to classify the business according to the standard industrial classification that separates manufacturing and commerce activities. At times, individuals who consider themselves to be artisans, for example, may actually earn a larger proportion of income from the sale of products that have not been produced in their shops.

Process of Production.   In the informal sector the product cycle tends toward discontinuity, variability, and flexibility due, in part, to the rudimentary level of technology used by informal-sector businesses, and their low level of capitalization. Because informal-sector business operators have little access to working capital, they are often forced to stop production when they run out of the necessary raw materials. They are unable to accumulate an inventory or, in the case of a service business, to purchase the necessary implements that would enable them to undertake different types of jobs. Or the business operator might purchase a new type of tool or implement just to undertake one particular job and this piece of equipment is subsequently underutilized by the business. In other words, the limited nature of the technology being used not only hampers the ability of business to produce continuously but also limits the operator's time horizon for planning for investment and operations.

Lack of Separation of Consumption and Production.   Economic analysis treats consumption and production as different spheres; when policies and programs are developed to improve the production and income side of the economic equation, the consumption side is generally ignored except as a source of demand for additional products. However, it becomes extremely difficult to apply this separation to micro-scale economic activities, where business expenditures, income, assets, and labor are inextricably linked to those of the household. As Tokman (1978) points out, part of what allows informal-sector businesses to stay alive is their reliance on personal assets, such as living quarters, vehicles, and even furniture. For women in the informal sector, an added dimension is the simultaneous use of time for domestic and business purposes; nowhere is this clearer than in the case of child care.

Conceptualizing the Informal Sector: Where Do Women Fit In?

The five types of informality, when applied to women's work, may draw us into an identification of women's work with informal sector work. And, be-

cause so many authors have highlighted the importance of women's participation in what they call the informal sector, the identification of women's
work with informal sector work is an even greater temptation. But what do
these observers really mean when they say that women are an important part
of the informal sector? And does the term "informal sector" imply anything
about women's work in an analytical sense?

In order to answer these questions let us look at the theoretical under-
pinnings, and not merely the descriptive aspects, of the definition of informal sector. Venessa Cartaya's succinct categorization of the definitions of informal sector provides an illuminating background for the discussion of
women's work in the sector (Cartaya 1987). According to Cartaya there are
four distinct approaches to the analysis of the informal sector. These are the
approach based on a theory of excess labor supply often identified with
PREALC; a neomarxist approach; the "black market" or underground economy approach; and the neoliberal approach. Each of these has different implications for analyzing women's work and developing policies and programs to assist women.

Excess Labor Supply

The structuralist approach based on excess labor supply is identified with
the Latin American branch of the International Labour Organization, the
Programa Regional de Empleo para América Latina y el Caribe (PREALC). In
this book, it is exemplified by the type of analysis contained in Chapter 3 by
Mezzera. The argument holds that the bulk of those employed in the informal sector are working in this sector because of lack of employment opportunities in the modern formal sector. The lack of employment opportunities
is due to structural imperfections in the capital market which lead to the formation of oligopolies and limit competition in many markets, while at the
same time maintaining high prices for the commodities consumed by the
higher income groups. This situation limits the demand for labor on the part
of the modern firms producing for the high-income sectors. As a result,
many who seek employment in that sector are unable to find it and must
therefore create their own jobs in the informal sector, jobs that often pay
very low wages. Deriving from an analysis of structural imperfections in the
capital market and the segmentation of labor markets, this approach provides an attractive framework for analyzing women's work, as it is often as-
serted that women form part of a disadvantaged sector of the labor force
which is excluded from more desirable employment in the formal sector.

Neomarxist Approach

The approach that Cartaya has labeled "neomarxist" emphasizes the exploitation of informal-sector workers by the capitalist producers of the formal
sector. It is based on the argument that the exploitation of laborers and
operators of informal-sector businesses helps first, to reduce the costs of
raw materials and inputs for formal-sector production, and second, to keep

formal-sector labor costs lower by providing wage goods to formal-sector workers at a lower cost than the formal sector itself could generate (Moser 1978; Mies 1986).

This analysis is somewhat analogous to the marxist conception of domestic labor or housework as playing a part in the low-cost reproduction of the labor force, which benefits producers in the formal sector. According to this view, female unpaid labor in the household provides commodities that are consumed by the workers in the formal sector at a very low cost and, therefore, allows formal-sector employers or the capitalist class in general to pay lower wages to their workers. Because women's work in the informal sector is often described as an extension of household or domestic work, the linkage between the household and informal sector analyses is clear. Functionally, women's unpaid work in the household and women's work in the informal sector, although performed for an income, serve the same purpose of reducing labor costs or raw material costs for capital.

The Underground Economy

The analysis of internationalization of capital or changes in international competition that has been carried out since the 1970s has heavily influenced this approach. According to this view, the underground economy is the result of pressures of increased competition on an international scale which have led to the development of a new type of manufacturing based on subcontracting and piecework (Boyer 1986; Sassen-Koob 1984). Such a system allows employers to have greater flexibility in the hiring and firing of workers, in changing the tasks that workers perform, and in changing the styles and components of their products. Employers are therefore able to respond more rapidly to the quick pace of changing tastes and patterns of consumption on an international scale and, as a result, to compete better in international markets and in the domestic market in cases where international goods are also in competition with domestic products. In the last few years, a number of studies have been undertaken in developing and developed countries alike, which point out the importance of female labor in these types of subcontracting or outworking arrangements (see, for example, Beneria and Roldàn 1987). It follows that women are major participants in the informal sector if the sector is constituted by these types of businesses and these types of work arrangements.

Neoliberal Approach

This perspective, often identified with Hernando de Soto of Peru (1986) and other conservative analysts, defines the informal sector in terms of the absence of legal documentation or requirements on the part of the firms that compose the sector. In other words, the formal sector is that sector where firms comply with legal regulations including licensing, minimum wage regulations, and social security payments, and the informal sector is that group of firms that does not observe these legal conventions. In the case of women who operate informal-sector businesses, legal restrictions take on an added dimension. As Lycette and White note in Chapter 2 of this volume, women's access to credit and other inputs that would be beneficial to the expansion of their economic activities is limited by legal regulations that require them to obtain their husbands' signatures when applying for loans, and constrain their independent control of property and their inheritance rights. Protective legislation that limits women's opportunities for wage employment by restricting the hours that they can work and providing them with extra benefits that male workers do not receive, also serves to exclude them from formal-sector employment, and may lead women to create their employment in the informal sector.

None of these approaches completely captures the intuitive understanding of the informal sector, but each one of these definitions contributes an element that is useful in helping identify the sector.

Perhaps the broadest definition is offered by the excess labor supply framework used by PREALC. A major difficulty with this definition is its strong implications for women, as it involves the question of how to categorize domestic service. Domestic service is partly a manifestation of the inability of women to find employment in other more lucrative occupations and their consignment to less productive, poorly paid jobs. Because many of those who are employed in domestic service would want to work in the formal sector if such work were available, a large portion of them should be considered as part of an excess labor supply, following the definition of PREALC. As pointed out by Mezzera in Chapter 3, the inclusion of domestic service makes the informal sector in Latin America appear heavily dominated by women because women often account for up to 80 to 90 percent of those employed in domestic service. Because domestic service workers are a large and relatively homogeneous group whose characteristics and needs are completely different from the other large group that makes up the sector—the small economic units also known as microenterprises—their inclusion within the informal sector would lead to a specific focus of policy and project recommendations that are perhaps not applicable to the whole sector. Analysts from PREALC like Mezzera have suggested that the informal sector be considered only in terms of units of economic activity and not with respect to individuals, thereby excluding domestic service from what they call the informal sector. It remains unclear, however, whether individuals should be excluded from the informal sector in conceptual terms.

Characteristics of Women Microentrepreneurs

The terms "microenterprise" and "microbusiness" have often been used interchangeably with "informal sector," as they are by many of the authors in this collection. While recognizing the importance for women of other activities that might be included in the informal sector (particularly domestic service), this volume focuses on economic units in the sector, the microenterprises. However, in order to address gender-related questions, it is necessary not just to look at the enterprises as such, but also to study their owners/operators, both male and female. In addition, most of the individual contributions in this volume are framed within the broad context of the informal sector.

The notion of informal sector is useful first, in the sense that the concept of informality captures certain qualities that are not reflected by a size-based definition alone, and that determine the peculiarities of the economic activities that should be addressed by policy and programming. Second, whereas the original approach to the informal sector centered on the poorest workers and the self-employed seeking out a living, the latest surge of interest in the sector has a danger of abandoning this poverty focus, zeroing in on potentially dynamic microenterprises (Liedholm and Mead 1987; deSoto 1986). The term "microentrepreneur" itself, used here to refer to the owner/operator of a microbusiness, evokes the Schumpeterian vision of the dynamic entrepreneur, a vision not applicable to a large portion of the business owner/operators in the microenterprise sector (Sanyal 1986). Abandonment of the poverty focus in programming for the informal sector would translate, among other things, into diminishing the possibility of incorporating initiatives for women.

Even within the microenterprise subset of the informal sector, heterogeneity is the rule. Different groups within the sector suggest different types of interventions, and these have implications for women. It is helpful to use two types of classifications in dividing the informal microenterprise sector. The first refers to the industrial classification of those enterprises among industry or manufacturing, services, and commerce. It is also important with regard to the size distribution of microenterprises. Whereas a service or commerce business with more than five employees might already be considered beyond the microlevel, a manufacturing operation with up to ten employees could still be considered a microenterprise. Even with such limitations, the microenterprise sector probably still accounts for over 90 percent of the establishments in the developing countries (Liedholm and Mead 1987).

The second type of classification of microbusinesses refers to different characteristics of firms as they relate to the economy as a whole. Three major groups can be identified under this heading. First, there are the various forms of what has elsewhere been referred to as "casual work" (Bromley and Gerry 1979), including temporary or seasonal activities (or activities that are carried out while their operators are in search of other more stable employment). It would also include precarious survival activities, such as carrying heavy loads and street vending at no fixed locale. (See Escobar, Chapter 4, for a discussion of the distinction between street vendors and others.)

The second group contains microbusinesses that are independent and more or less stable, such as small stores or small manufacturing operations. These may be businesses that compete, by providing other types of style, quality, or prices, or do not compete with formal-sector businesses. A subgroup of this category is the traditional artisanry, which can be considered a holdover from an earlier stage of development but still exists even in the developed countries, although it does not play as important a role for the economy as a whole.

The last type is that of subcontracting; many of the microenterprises in this group constitute a form of disguised wage employment, rather than independent businesses. Generally, these firms have one or a very few clients who purchase all of their production. They often produce only certain components of a product which are then sold to a formal-sector firm or a larger firm for assembly. Although women are concentrated in this and the first group, it is to the second group ("independent" businesses) that most small and microenterprise programs target their efforts.

With these divisions in mind, we can make certain generalizations about women's participation in the microenterprise sector without too much fear of exaggeration.

- Women are an important proportion of microenterprise owners/ operators in Latin America. An average of one-third of the microentrepreneurs and their workers in Latin America are women, although in a number of countries this proportion is much higher (see also PREALC 1981). In Honduras, for example, women comprise 39 percent of self-employed and wage and salary workers, and in rural areas 60 percent of the small and microenterprises are owned by women (Liedholm and Mead 1987). In Chapter 2 Lycette and White provide additional information to support this claim.

- Women are concentrated in certain activities. Women microentrepreneurs are particularly visible in commerce, personal services, certain branches of manufacture-garment making, and food production, although there are intra- and intercountry variations. For example, in Ecuador, women in the Andean city of Quito represent over 70 percent of those employed in commercial microenterprise activities, but in coastal Guayaquil, Ecuador, 70 percent of those in commerce are men (Farrell 1985). Escobar, in Chapter 4 of this volume, deals explicitly with the characteristics, problems, and prospects of the heavily female-dominated commerce activity in the city of La Paz.

- Women's microbusinesses are concentrated among the smallest and least remunerative activites. Although a large proportion of both women and men microenterpreneurs operate one-person businesses, the concentration within the one-person firms is greater for women.

- Many of women's microenterprises are an extension of their domestic roles, and this is evident in the importance that garment making, food production, and the sale of processed foods and perishable items has for women.

- Women's microenterprise activities are often organized within their homes, in theory providing them the opportunity to combine in the same space their domestic and market responsibilities. It is unclear, however, whether women choose these activities in order to be able to combine their household and market roles more effectively, or whether they are consigned to these less remunerative activities by virtue of the lack of employment elsewhere.

These characteristics of women's microenterprise activities have implications for the design of development policy, programs, and projects that should incorporate this important segment of the microenterprise sector.

POLICY, PROGRAMS, AND PROJECTS

The chapters in this volume have a decidedly programmatic orientation; they are concerned with the practical application of knowledge concerning women and microenterprise in Latin America. The focus is also a pragmatic one—to take existing projects, programs, and policies and look at them alongside the features of women's business ownership in the region, in order to determine how the existing interventions can be made more responsive to the needs of women. Yet even with the use of this backdoor approach, it is often difficult to integrate women into the preexisting framework when projects are designed around segments of the microenterprise sector where women are not involved. Some of the larger, mainstream projects, such as those of the Banco Industrial del Perú (see Chapters 12 and 13), are scaled-down versions of assistance programs for medium- and large-scale businesses, which fail to take account of the features of "informality" of women's businesses and the organic linkage between household and business that is characteristic of both male- and female-owned microenterprises. The remaining pages of this chapter briefly review the types of interventions directed to microenterprise in the public and private sectors.

Public Sector

This volume gives considerably more attention to programs and projects than it does to policy. Generally speaking, the policy side has been given less attention until recently, and there is scant experience with different policies in microenterprise that lend themselves to assessment. However, policy interventions *are* central and the policies that will support the micro-enterprise sector are those that are oriented to the smallest economic activities and do not unduly harm certain sectors of activity, such as commerce. This precept is particularly true for women's businesses, because they are concentrated in particular activities and are among the smallest. For example, in Chapter 2 Lycette and White point out the potential positive impact that deregulation of the financial sector, as well as administrative reform in the banking system, can have on women and men microentrepreneurs.

Macroeconomic and regulatory policies should be designed to complement direct interventions that are being developed in a number of Latin American countries to favor the growth of microenterprises. In addition, some development experts argue that support for microenterprises will have a positive impact on macroeconomic goals, such as increased economic growth and reduced reliance on imports (Kilby and D'Zmura 1985; de Soto 1986).

Manpower training and education policy are also important areas that can have a positive impact on the microenterprise sector. Formal institutions should be encouraged to develop curricula that are relevant to the needs of the self-employed, as this will be one of the few employment options for many graduates and school-leavers. In Latin America, vocational training institutions are already beginning to recognize this trend in the design of short courses to upgrade business and technical skills (see McKean, Chapter 6).

In addition, we must remember that at this particular time, Latin American governments are severely restricted at the policy level in terms of their options for increased expenditure and services. The current climate is one of austerity policies and decreases in social expenditures. Thus, there is a restriction in the amount of funds available for the development of human resources and public services, two areas that will have a major negative impact on women's employment opportunities in the medium to longer term.

In order to be able to improve the situation of women and their families, policies designed to assist the microenterprise sector should be oriented around a dual strategy:

- to strengthen and assist those microenterprises that have the possibility to expand, and thereby create new jobs that can be filled by both women and men; and
- to ensure the provision of assistance to those activities that require help in order to improve the income levels and the standard of living of their operators, even when such activities seem to provide little possibility for expansion.

If there is focus only on the first strategy, women will tend to be excluded in greater numbers than men. Although we hope that the expansion of successful microenterprises will provide additional employment for women, past experience shows that a large proportion of women entering the labor force will do so as operators of their own independent activities. The proposition that support for larger microenterprises will create new employment opportunities for the self-employed they displace, neglects the fact that it is the smallness of the microscale activities that ensures their survival. In addition, employment creation per se is not the main obstacle for many in the informal sector; their goal is increasing the productivity and incomes of those who have managed to create their own employment (Weeks 1977; Kahnert 1987). Neglect of these very small activities will have negative distributional consequences and negative consequences for other development goals as well, including improvement of the health and welfare of the family as a whole.

Many of the government interventions that can be used to assist the microenterprise sector will have to be focused at the local level, including the level of municipal government. For example, police harassment of small and microvendors is a major constraint to the stabilization of their operations and to increases in productivity on the part of the owners/operators. Therefore, the tolerance of local governments for such activities or programs to assist vendors in obtaining fixed locations for their work will perhaps be more important than, for instance, the effect of exchange controls on the operation of these businesses.

A major area of government activity that is being developed in Latin America is direct assistance to small and microenterprises. Although it is too soon to reach a definitive conclusion about women's participation in these government-sponsored interventions, it appears that many of these experiences have not been very successful in including women. In the case of Colombia, which Lycette and White and McKean discuss in this volume (Chapters 2 and 6), the government has been instrumental in assisting private foundations to obtain access to resources for loans to microenterprises and in facilitating their organization in an umbrella network that increases their efficiency. Peru has recently developed a massive program in Lima which is now providing loans to over 40,000 microenterprises, the majority of them operated by women. However, earlier experiences fostered by the Peruvian government (see Arias, Chapter 12) were not as successful in reaching women. In Guatemala the government is in the process of designing new microenterprise assistance programs for the municipal area of Guatemala City which will take account of both the Colombian and Peruvian experiences. At this time, however, it is still too soon to judge the progress of these activities.

Legal reform is an important area in which the government can remove restrictions to the expansion of microenterprise. In the case of women, the government may also undertake reforms in the civil code, banking laws, and labor laws to ensure that women's economic participation is expanded.

Private Sector

Contrary to the experience of many government credit projects, certain pri-vate-sector organizations have an excellent track record in incorporating women into programs designed to assist microenterprises. As noted by Lycette and White in Chapter 2, the participation of women in these projects ranges from 20 to 80 percent of total beneficiaries. Their participation tends to be significantly higher in projects organized around the solidarity group mechanism (see Otero, Chapter 5, and Reichmann, Chapter 8). The reasons for this orientation are twofold: first, the cost of lending to very small busi-nesses is reduced by the bundling together of loans in a group which allows projects to include more women whose demand for credit is concentrated in small loans; second, some argue that the solidarity group also provides a support mechanism that encourages women to participate in a credit activity with which they have less familiarity than men.

In grappling with the issue of whether assistance to women business owners is better provided through women-specific or integrated projects, some institutions have opted for the former. Buvinic (1986) has cautioned against having traditional women's organizations take on economic projects with which they are unfamiliar, because of the tendency for economic goals of these projects to be overwhelmed by the welfare orientation of the institu-tion, dooming the projects to failure. However, several successful cases of women-specific microenterprise programs, run by new women's organiza-tions that have broken out of the traditional mold, are still operating and expanding in Latin America. A prime example is MUDE Dominicana, dis-cussed in Chapter 9. Others, such as Women's World Banking (discussed in Chapters 10 and 11), have extended their services to both men and women in recognition of the link between households and microenterprise.

Despite the achievements of many of the private sector projects, organi-zations hoping to provide assistance to women microentrepreneurs should take into account a number of problems. First, although training and techni-cal assistance are often seen as necessary components of these projects, such activities can be more burdensome to women in terms of the time con-straints of their responsibilities both at home and in market work. Often projects seek to provide additional training to women, in particular oriented around their household roles. Others devote considerable attention to non-formal education activities designed to raise women's awareness of the so-cial barriers they face as women, an activity recommended by Placencia in Chapter 7, or to strengthen their leadership ability (a common approach of Overseas Education Fund programs, discussed briefly by McKean in Chapter 6). Another problem has been encountered by projects that seek to create new enterprises from their very start, particularly with women who had not previously participated in income-earning work (see McKean, Chapter 6, and Placencia, Chapter 7). This type of activity has proved to be very costly and the success rate has not been high.

One of the most serious drawbacks of private-sector projects is their scale of operations. They tend to be very small scale, helping at most a few hundred or perhaps a thousand businesses, when the potential demand for credit and assistance in the microenterprise sector goes far beyond the capability of these organizations. They are often limited by organizational or managerial weakness and lack the necessary funds to expand and to serve a greater number of microenterprises. Therefore, although these organizations are reaching women in greater proportions than are government projects, they reach a small total number of women. In order to overcome this problem, an attempt should be made to incorporate some of the successful mechanisms these organizations have developed into larger-scale public- or private-sector interventions.

A recent tendency to try to exclude commerce activities from the pool of eligibles for microenterprise projects, in the belief that these activities have less potential for creating new jobs, will have a negative effect on women's participation even in private voluntary organizations (PVO) projects (see Reichmann, Chapter 8). This restriction is misguided for two reasons. First, many commerce businesses are operated by individuals who are engaged in small-scale manufacturing or service activities simultaneously with their commerce activity. This duality is especially true of women, who can be seen producing handicrafts and other items while they are attending their street or market stalls. In addition, microvendors often change their activities seasonally, and this flexibility is a strength of their overall business strategy which allows them to seek out those activities that are more remunerative according to seasonal changes and changes in the market. Also, the belief that commerce activities cannot create new employment may be overstated. The study by Berger, Buvinić, and Jaramillo (see Chapter 14) shows that commerce businesses do create new jobs, although on a lesser scale than manufacturing and service activities. In addition, commerce businesses may provide a steppingstone to more lucrative activities for their operators. Therefore, the rigid identification of the commerce sector with low job-creation potential is misguided and should be avoided if women's participation is considered an important element in a microenterprise program. Finally, the goal of increased productivity and income is equally as important as the goal of employment creation (Kahnert 1987).

A final concern, raised by McKean in Chapter 6, is the excessive emphasis on individualistic solutions that is embodied in PVO approaches. PVO projects identify the key constraints of microenterprise as individual access to credit and lack of skills on the part of the individual microentrepreneur. However, this approach overlooks the obstacle to microenterprise expansion both by government economic and other policies and by structural barriers that hamper the microenterprise sector as a whole. For example, we noted earlier in the case of the street vendors the constraint that is placed on them by police harassment. The solution to this constraint cannot be found in individual training or credit activities. Therefore, the organizing of micro-entrepreneurs to lobby on their own behalf becomes important, as does a possible brokering role that private organizations could play for individual microentrepreneurs in providing them services that, by themselves, they could not afford to acquire (examples include marketing, assistance with legal problems, and lobbying).

NOTE

1. The International Seminar, "La Mujer y su Acceso al Crédito en América Latina: Sugerencias para Programas de Desarrollo," was organized by the International Center for Research on Women (ICRW), the Instituto Latinoamericano de Investigaciones Sociales (ILDIS), and the Comité Interinstitucional de Desarrollo Microempresarial (CODEM), and was held 11–12 September, 1986, in Quito, Ecuador.

2

Improving Women's Access to Credit in Latin America and the Caribbean: *Policy and Project Recommendations*

MARGARET LYCETTE and KAREN WHITE

I nternational donor agencies and the governments of many developing countries, after recognizing in the early to mid-1970s that the results of growth and output-oriented development policies had been rather disappointing, have been devoting increased attention to expanding employment and earnings opportunities rather than attempting rapid industrialization of the developing countries. One major focus of the development community now includes programs of assistance to small-scale rural enterprises, the subsistence agriculture sector, and the urban informal sector.

The tools with which development and government agencies are working to implement these programs include tax incentives; realignment of industrial, financial, and foreign exchange policies; and the development of infrastructures conducive to the growth of small enterprises and more efficient small farming techniques. One of the most important developments, however, has been the increased amount of resources devoted to the provision of credit. Credit is now the largest component of the World Bank's agricultural lending program; the Inter-American Development Bank (IDB) has developed an entire program of credit assistance to small enterprises and the Agency for International Development (AID) supports numerous rural- and urban-based credit projects worldwide. In addition, many governments of developing countries have given credit programs the lead role in rural and industrial development.

This thrust toward the development of credit programs is for the most part focused on improving the growth and profitability of small enterprises, which are frequently hindered by the lack of small amounts of capital, and on encouraging the small farmer's adoption of technology through access to capital. Of course, critical bottlenecks in marketing and transportation, or input supplies, must be overcome in order to ensure that injections of capital will be effective in promoting these objectives. Nevertheless, the availability of credit seems to be the binding constraint in most developing countries.

Studies show that small and microenterprises have little access to capital through formal channels (Liedholm and Mead 1987). For example, credit and capital were found to be the greatest perceived needs of small business owners in Haiti (Chuta and Liedholm 1979). It is widely agreed that credit is a necessary, if not sufficient, condition for achieving increases in productivity and income.

In the past, development agencies and governments of developing countries have attempted to meet the credit needs of small farmers and entrepreneurs in rural and urban areas through the establishment of special lending institutions such as multisectoral development banks, agricultural banks, and credit cooperatives. Most development banks, however, now have highly centralized bureaucratic structures resulting in high administrative costs and an inability to adjust programs to local conditions. Thus, although their original purpose was often to benefit small business owners, artisans, and subsistence farmers, they primarily lend to large industrialists and farmers. Unfortunately, existing evidence indicates that credit cooperatives also tend to be inaccessible to the small borrower. Larger borrowers tend to dominate boards of directors and exercise a great deal of control over the approval or promotion of credit applications because of their higher level of education and broader commercial experience. Small borrowers, on the other hand, often cannot even read the required credit applications and may attend few of the cooperatives' meetings.

Commercial banks and financial institutions have developed more efficient disbursement techniques than other formal-sector channels for lending in developing countries. They are generally less prone to political pressure and abuse than are government agencies and keep adequate records and obtain better repayment performance by borrowers than do government banks. Unfortunately, commercial banks tend to be inflexible with regard to repayment schedules and to concentrate on short-term lending and large loans that are not designed to reach the small borrower. In addition, less than 20 percent of the total number of borrowers from commercial institutions tend to receive about 80 percent of the agricultural credit they disburse. Limited access and a high degree of portfolio concentration also characterize commercial, industrial, and housing finance.

In recent years, in recognition of the inability of the formal sector financial institutions to effectively service the small borrower, the illiterate, and the politically powerless, the development community has begun to experiment with innovative, small loan programs that do not rely upon large institutions for implementation. It has been through experience with these small-scale programs that the development establishment has recognized the link between women and credit. Time after time, project evaluations have shown that a majority of borrowers in these programs have been women, even though the programs have not been restricted to, or been specifically aimed at, providing women with credit. In a World Bank–financed urban development project in El Salvador, for example, 85 percent of the beneficiaries of a credit component for small enterprises turned out to be women (Blayney 1979).

The extremely high demand by women for credit in these community-based programs provides at least indirect evidence that women's access to credit in the formal financial system is restricted. Because the vast majority of development funds still flow through the formal system, the ramifications of this restriction may be enormous, given the major role that women play in providing for the economic well-being of their families.

This chapter will discuss the importance of credit for women, the degree to which women's access to credit has been limited and why, and their strategies for coping with this limitation, in order to derive development policy and project recommendations for improving women's access to credit.

FINANCING WOMEN: WHY IS IT SO IMPORTANT?

In the past three decades, women in Latin America and the Caribbean have entered the labor force in unprecedented numbers. But in many developing countries paid employment opportunities for women have been limited to marginal jobs that tend to provide low wages, few fringe benefits, poor working conditions, and little chance of advancement. As a result, increasing numbers of women have turned to self-generated employment in the informal sector. In urban areas, women take up occupations such as street vending and personal and domestic service. In rural areas, women process and market produce or use local raw materials in handicraft production. Earnings and mobility are low in these informal-sector activities, but for most poor women access to this sector is easy compared to the problems they face in obtaining formal-sector employment. In much of the Third World, the informal sector rivals formal employment as a source of jobs for both men and women.

The Need for Credit

The major problem for the operators of informal-sector businesses is lack of capital. In a 1984 study of microentrepreneurs in Peru, the majority of the women interviewed stated that lack of working capital was one of their major problems (see Chapter 13 of this volume). Without sufficient working capital, the typical small entrepreneur has only enough cash to buy raw materials and stock for one or two days. When the inventory is depleted, production or sales drop and the business is often forced to shut down while the owner makes a trip to purchase materials. This production/sales discontinuity is inefficient and results in low productivity.

Moreover, lacking sufficient capital, informal-sector entrepreneurs are seldom able to take advantage of quantity discounts on raw materials and, in order to obtain enough cash to meet their daily living expenses, must sell their output immediately, whether or not prices in the market are high enough to make their businesses profitable. Finally, because of a lack of capital, only a small proportion of informal-sector businesses are able to extend credit to customers—an arrangement that would allow them to expand their businesses to service the needs of persons who are paid weekly or biweekly and would be mutually beneficial for businesses and consumers.

Thus, access to credit is one of the keys to an improved standard of living for the large proportion of women in developing countries who operate in the informal sector. Surveys consistently show that the majority of men and women in the informal sector recognize the vital importance of credit and almost always feel that government and international development programs should focus on providing capital to micro- and small-scale businesses (Farbman 1981).

In rural areas, particularly in the Andean region and in the Caribbean, where a high proportion of women are widowed, single, or de facto heads of household, male migration to urban areas in search of employment has resulted in increasing numbers of women who not only are farmers, but also manage their farms alone. For them, too, credit is vital both to obtain immediate needs such as seeds, fertilizer, and farm labor services, and also to adopt technology that can improve productivity over the long term. In St. Lucia, for example, a survey of farm women's needs showed that credit assistance was the agricultural service most desired (Knudson and Yates 1981). Women also need credit for consumption purposes between harvests or for stabilization of cash flow during seasonal downturns in business.

Finally, as the incidence of woman-headed households in urban areas increases and the cost of urban land continues to rise, more and more women will need to finance housing costs. An International Center for Research on Women (ICRW) survey of women heads of household applying to a major housing project in Quito, Ecuador, indicated that for the great majority of these women (70 percent) savings will cover less than 6 percent of the cost of the project's least expensive housing (Blayney and Lycette 1983). Even if these women were to liquidate all but their most necessary assets, the majority would need to finance 90 percent of the cost of housing. Similarly, a study in Jamaica found that more than 75 percent of all working women applying for mortgage loans under the standard criteria being applied by financial institutions would be disqualified on the basis of income (Blackwood 1986).

Yet, in spite of their clear need for access to credit, women are apparently severely limited in the extent to which financial institutions and programs service their needs.

WOMEN'S LIMITED ACCESS TO CREDIT

Lack of Data

Little direct evidence of women's limited access to credit exists, mostly because of the lack of sex-disaggregated data. Even when sex-disaggregated data are available by borrower, however, they may not accurately reflect the actual beneficiary of the loan. Women occasionally take out loans in their own names for family-run businesses or for businesses run by male relatives (see Chapter 13 of this volume), particularly in credit projects directed specifically at women. Similarly, men may borrow money for businesses run by their female relatives. In Jamaica, for example, a large number of loans extended to men were in fact managed by female relatives (Pezzullo 1983). These practices make it difficult to accurately assess women's access to credit and repayment rates by sex.

The lack of data in and of itself, however, appears to reflect the relatively minor degree to which women participate in, or are afforded the services of, formal financial institutions. Several studies report that bankers do not maintain records of financial transactions according to sex because women are such an insignificant proportion of borrowers and depositors that such recordkeeping is rendered worthless. The data that are available, mostly in the form of small-survey results, seem to confirm this notion.

Urban Women

Women small-business owners in urban areas face problems with regard to credit that men do not. For instance, a study of the Urban Small Enterprise Development Fund (UEF) of the Banco Industrial del Perú (BIP) found that only 16 percent of the Fund loans went to women (see Chapter 13 of this volume). Beneficiaries of the UEF must have legal business status or be in the process of obtaining such status, must reside in the *pueblos jóvenes* of cities in the program, and must provide collateral. Statistical comparison of data for men and women clients showed that the low proportion of women in the UEF is due not to the fact that more women are rejected for loans, but rather to the fact that few women apply.

Interviews with women borrowers and nonborrowers revealed that women experienced several obstacles to obtaining credit through the UEF: the demand for collateral, excessive paperwork requirements, the large average loan size and the difficulty of obtaining BIP approval of credit for businesses in the commerce and service sectors.

The data also showed that women borrowers receive smaller loans more frequently than do men, while men tend to receive large loans. These differences can be explained by the fact that women predominate in low-income activities such as services, commerce, and garment-making, whereas men predominate in the higher-income area of manufacturing. Women's smaller loans do not, therefore, stem from a bank preference for loaning to men. It was impossible to determine, however, whether or not discrimination against women in the preselection process could have discouraged them from filing formal applications for loans.

Rural Women

Women in rural areas are particularly disadvantaged in their access to credit, in part because the majority of credit goes to urban areas. In addition, however, rural women face problems that rural men do not, despite the critical role these women play in agriculture. In Guyana, for instance, 44 percent of the women in a rural sample survey were heads of household and farmers, and in a St. Lucia study, 25 percent of the farm operators were women. Yet women farmers in St. Lucia received only 1 percent of the total loans disbursed by the Agricultural and Industrial Bank (Knudson and Yates 1981). In Peru, the Banco Industrial del Perú extended 6,000 loans to small entrepreneurs in the high jungle and sierra departments between 1975 and 1982; less than 20 percent went to women (Arias 1985).

In rural Mexico, women farmers often have much difficulty in getting the state to provide them with the credit and technical assistance to which they are legally entitled (Arizpe and Botey 1987). This not only prevents them from improving the productivity of their land and generating more income, but frequently gives a woman's male relatives a pretext for taking over her land.

There is good evidence that women desire and are willing to pay for credit; moreover, there is mounting evidence that women's repayment records are as good as those of men. Some observers, such as bank officials involved in the Rural Enterprise Fund in Peru, claim that women are more responsible than men about repayment (Arias 1985). Because banks attempt to maximize the returns to their shareholders, women should represent a large pool of potential customers from whose business the banks would stand to profit. Why then do banks and other formal-sector financial institutions have such low proportions of female clients?

In some instances, women's limited participation in financial institutions is due to out-and-out discrimination. The cultural ideal that the woman is supported by her husband and bears responsibility only for maintaining the home environment may be so strong that bankers refuse to face the reality of women's economic roles and do not see them as being involved in productive activities, or as being responsible individuals in regard to financial obligations. It is difficult to imagine, however, that such strong biases would continue to exist in the face of potentially profitable business with a group that constitutes over half the population in most countries.

Two sets of economic factors—supply factors and demand factors—seem to provide better explanations of women's limited participation in credit programs. Supply factors involve the willingness of banks to lend to women who are small and/or inexperienced borrowers. They are closely linked to the perceptions of the financial institutions about the small borrower in general. Demand factors, on the other hand, relate to the willingness and ability of women to apply for and accept credit from formal financial institutions and are strongly associated with the characteristics of women borrowers.

Supply Factors

Because of their position in the economy, most women in developing countries require and can handle only *small* amounts of credit. Thus, as small borrowers, women are faced with the reluctance of financial institutions to lend in small amounts.

Unit Costs of Lending

The unit costs of making small loans are greater than the unit costs of making large loans, especially because in most developing countries there are severe deficits of trained personnel to administer credit. Financial institutions seek to minimize administrative costs by making large loans as often as possible.

Repayment Rates

Financial institutions usually have little or no control over technological developments, market prices, and timeliness of input supply, all of which are key factors in ensuring the success of small enterprises and, thus, high repayment rates on small loans. Although small borrowers tend to have higher loan repayment rates than large borrowers when they have access to an appropriate package of credit, technology, and technical assistance, actual repayment rates on small loans are frequently much below the potential, increasing the unit costs of recovering credit from small borrowers. Financial institutions therefore equate small loans with risky, costly loans.

Regulating Policies

Finally, the governments of most developing countries have kept interest rates fixed for long periods of time while in real terms these rates have often been negative, erratic, and unpredictable. These interest rate policies have actually contributed to, rather than reduced, the restrictions on access to credit that women and small borrowers in general face because they bring about lower interest rates by forcing financial institutions to bear the opportunity costs of providing cheap credit. This "cheap credit paradox" has developed in many countries where well-intended or politically motivated regulations have been imposed to hold interest rates below their free-market level. At below-market rates of interest, demand for credit exceeds the amount of financing that lenders are willing, and find profitable, to supply. Lenders must therefore ration the amount of credit they are willing to supply among borrowers who wish to borrow much more than the amount available. When this non–price rationing takes place, it is almost inevitable that the smaller borrower, the borrower lacking influence, and the female borrower are unable to gain access to credit. Loans are made, instead, to the lenders' wealthier and more influential clients.

It is important to note here that the financial regulation typically imposed in developing countries differs from a policy of credit subsidy. When credit is subsidized, lower interest rates are made available to borrowers while financial institutions are reimbursed by the government for the costs of lending at the lower rates. Financial institutions thus have less incentive to restrict the amount of credit supplied and excess demand for funds does not arise. Most governments, however, cannot afford to provide the total amount of subsidy required to provide all the credit that is demanded at the subsidized rate. Under this circumstance, demand for credit again exceeds supply, and rationing—with all its ensuing inequities—occurs.

Research has shown that most cheap credit, whether regulated or subsidized, is concentrated in relatively few large loans (von Pischke and Adams 1980; Gonzàlez-Vega 1981). Recent studies in Colombia (Vogel and Larsen 1984), Bolivia (Ladman 1984), and Costa Rica (Vogel 1984) suggest that subsidized interest rates and accompanying rationing devices tend to concentrate subsidized credit in large loans to large farmers.

In fact, the lower the real rate of interest, the more heavily concentrated will be the loans in the hands of relatively few borrowers. Formal lenders may make a number of small loans to the poor and multiple large loans to the wealthy, resulting in a modest average size of loan and a large number of loans. But this average obscures the fact that only a few people receive most of the benefits of cheap credit, and that, ironically, those who receive cheap credit are typically those who are least in need of low interest rates. Lenders who ration credit in this manner are merely behaving rationally in a situation of excess demand for below-market-rate loans that encourages them to allocate their funds to their most profitable and powerful customers.

Low interest rates also have a very regressive effect on income and asset ownership. Low interest rates on loans force financial institutions to pay even lower rates, usually negative in real terms, on savings deposits. These low rates hurt small savers who cannot assemble enough savings to buy nonfinancial assets, such as land or cattle, or financial assets that require substantial initial investments in order to obtain better rates of return. The small saver is forced to accept a "tax" on financial savings. In imperfect capital markets, wealth and access to credit are not independent. For bankers, wealth is an important determinant in non–price rationing. Thus, low-interest loans not only fail to reach small, low-income borrowers but actually make it less likely that the small borrower will ever amass enough wealth to have access to credit.

Demand Factors

A number of factors inhibit women's demand for credit from formal financial institutions. They include transactions costs, collateral requirements, cumbersome application procedures, and cultural constraints.

Transactions Costs

Interest payments make up only a part of the costs of credit. Additional costs include payment for paperwork, travel costs to visit the lender, and the opportunity costs of time taken to negotiate and repay loans. For women, who are often new and small borrowers, these loan transactions costs may be several times as great as the amount of interest charged. To the extent that the lender, because of low interest rates and the resulting low-interest receipts, is less willing and able to provide high quality, dependable, flexible financial services, these transactions costs will be increased. Thus, the total cost of borrowing from formal financial institutions becomes substantially higher than indicated by the interest rate charged and perhaps looms out of reach of the borrower.

In addition, the hours of operation of credit institutions may be inappropriate for most women borrowers who are responsible for cooking, cleaning, and child care, in addition to their work outside the home. Time allocation studies of low-income women have shown that even when women participate in the labor market, the time they devote to household chores does not diminish; rather, it is their leisure time that declines (King and Evenson 1983). Thus, because the opportunity cost of time spent making applications for loans may be higher for poor women, they may be discouraged from seeking credit.

Collateral Requirements

Women are less likely than men to be able to meet collateral requirements of borrowing because these often necessitate land or other property ownership. Unfortunately, in many Latin American countries such as Brazil, Bolivia, and Peru, married women are still denied the right to hold property in their own names, making women's independent access to credit impossible. Even when women have rights of inheritance to land, they often lose it to male relatives as a result of ignorance of their legal rights (Yudelman 1987). When businesses are accepted as collateral, women may not be considered good credit risks because they are engaged predominantly in small-scale informal enterprises and do not have the documentation of formally registered businesses. Where regular salaries are required as collateral, women again fare badly because they predominate in precisely those sectors of the economy where regular salaries are the exception.

In addition, land titling projects often designate the individual considered to be the household head (usually a man) as the land owner, a status that provides access to credit, subsidized farm inputs, and extension services. In the case of divorce, separation, consensual union, or widowhood, the wife may have no claim to the land. Similarly, if the wife becomes the farm manager as a result of male out-migration, she is not eligible for credit programs, because the land is not in her name (Palmer 1985).

Application Procedures

Elaborate application procedures may be required of potential borrowers, particularly when interest rates that financial institutions may charge on loans are regulated. Often these procedures are one of a number of rationing mechanisms used by banks that must decide how to distribute their "sweet" (that is, low-cost) credit in the face of excess demand. Under these circumstances, women's demand for credit is inhibited because of their higher illiteracy rates and overall lower educational attainment relative to men. Many poor women are incapable of completing application forms that require more than rudimentary reading and writing skills. In addition, rural women in the Andean countries, Guatemala, and Haiti may know only indigenous languages and rarely know how to write.

Although school enrollment and literacy among girls have increased greatly in the Latin American region, literacy rates are still low among older women, precisely the age group that tends to engage in informal-sector activities. In Guatemala and Honduras, for example, literacy rates for women thirty-five years and older are 30 and 37 percent, respectively. Only in Chile and Argentina do the rates for this age group exceed 80 percent (Chaney 1984). In rural areas, too, literacy rates are lower among women. A 1985 study of the rural population in the Dominican Republic, for instance, showed that only slightly over half of the women knew how to read or write (Mones and Grant 1987). Large disparities in literacy rates between rural and urban women are common throughout Latin America.

Another factor that can restrict women's access to credit is the requirement that spouses co-sign applications for loans. In practice, this requirement is often translated to mean that married women must obtain the cosignature of their spouses to qualify for a loan, whereas married men do not. In Peru, for instance, married women must have their husbands countersign their loan application forms to be eligible for credit. They also need their husband's consent to establish a business (Arias 1985).

Social/Cultural Constraints

In addition to the factors discussed above, women often face social and cultural constraints that further restrict their demand for credit. For example, it may be considered inappropriate for a woman to travel alone long distances between her home in a rural area and the banks in town, or to offer the occasionally necessary bribe to a male official in charge of credit applications. Moreover, women may be intimidated from entering formal credit institutions through lack of familiarity. For instance, market women in Managua refused to use a loan office that had opened in the Central Market because they found the office too formal and its procedures too strange and impersonal (Bruce 1980). In Lima, men tended to approach the offices of a micro-enterprise credit project alone, whereas women tended to go with friends (Reichmann 1984b).

Even more important, women are often excluded from local male-oriented organizations, such as agricultural cooperatives or social clubs, through which information regarding sources of credit and application procedures can be obtained. Without access to these channels for distribution of information about credit, women cannot take advantage of many sources of loans.

Many agrarian reform programs only benefit the permanent agricultural wage workers employed on the estates and exclude the seasonal labor force from cooperative membership, the channel through which credit is obtained. A study in northern Peru, for example, found that, although women make up 40 percent of the temporary labor force on cotton plantations, only 2 percent belong to cooperatives (Fernàndez 1982).

In addition, with the exception of Cuba and Nicaragua, land reform programs in Latin America have thus far designated only household heads as beneficiaries of agrarian reform. Thus, only women who are widows or single mothers with no adult male present in the household can be potential beneficiaries. In Bolivia and Honduras, the law explicitly provides for the inclusion of woman-headed households in agrarian reform programs. However, these laws are not always carried out in practice (Deere 1987). In Honduras, the 1962 agrarian reform law gave widows and single woman household heads the right to own land (though not single women without dependents). In practice, however, input into decision-making and access to agricultural credit depended on membership in the male-dominated collective organizations to which women rarely belonged (Youssef and LeBel 1981).

Only in Nicaragua and Cuba has the incorporation of rural women into the agrarian reform process been an explicit state policy goal. But even when women participate fully in the productive activities of the cooperative, they often play a subordinate role to men in cooperative decision-making and seldom hold positions of leadership (Deere 1987).

WOMEN'S STRATEGIES FOR OBTAINING CREDIT:
THE INFORMAL SECTOR

Given the many constraints, how have women, who are so active in agriculture, trade, and informal-sector businesses, met their needs for credit?

Caught between the inadequacy of formal financial institutions as a source of credit and their increasing need for capital, women have turned to informal sources to bridge the gap. Particularly in low-income groups, women rely on relatives, moneylenders, pawnbrokers, other intermediaries, and a variety of indigenous savings associations to provide them with the credit they so urgently need to maintain and improve their standard of living and that of their families.

For example, family members and friends were second only to personal savings as the most important sources of start-up capital for women who owned small-scale enterprises in thirty-six different Haitian localities. Friends and relatives were also found to be a crucial source of funds as the businesses developed. The combined funds provided by family, friends, and personal savings enabled 90 percent of the entrepreneurs to buy equipment for their businesses (Haggblade, Defay, and Pitman 1979).

Borrowing from moneylenders and pawnbrokers is also prevalent among women and has been documented in Mexico (Chinas 1973), Nicaragua (Bruce 1980), and Peru (Reichmann 1984b), among other countries. In fact, women in the Dominican Republic reported that the credit source they use most often is the *prestamista,* or informal moneylender (Reichmann 1984a).

Finally, women's informal savings and loan associations are common throughout Latin America and the Caribbean. In the *pueblos jóvenes* of Perú, for instance, women often rely on the *junta* or *pandero,* a revolving savings/credit association, to meet their credit needs (Reichmann 1984b). These associations consist of a group of persons who agree to make regular contributions to a fund, which becomes the property of each contributor in rotation. These organizations perform an important intermediary role in mobilizing capital and are often a very effective way for women to meet their credit needs collectively by providing mechanisms both to save and to borrow.

What are the characteristics of these informal sources of finance that make them so appealing and accessible to women? They appear to be:

- low transactions costs due to proximity of borrower and lender;

- immediacy of loan disbursement;

- willingness to extend small loans;

- flexible repayment requirements due to the familiarity of the lender with the borrower's situation;

- minimal and flexible collateral requirements (moneylenders, for example, often accept jewelry as collateral).

Relatives, Friends, and Neighbors

Relatives only rarely turn down requests for small loans, because a loan to a family member is in one sense a loan to the entire family. Relatives well know each other's needs for financial assistance or capacity to lend, and when a loan is made the guarantee that funds will be returned is implicit. Repayment is not required until the borrower is in a position to return the loan, and interest is not often explicitly charged. Because relatives are usually nearby, loans can easily be arranged and, perhaps most important, made immediately available.

Borrowing from women neighbors has several advantages. Neighbors can readily understand the dynamics of household food supplies and cash problems. Wives can lend to other wives when the lender is a little better off than the borrower. Borrowers can repay the loan in a variety of ways. They can offer to tend their neighbors' children, work in their fields, or extend small loans when their own situation improves. In fact, reciprocity is common to borrowing among neighbors—there is a tendency for borrowers to become lenders and for lenders, in turn, to become borrowers. Again, loans are easy to arrange in small amounts and can be made available to the borrower immediately.

Moneylenders and Pawnbrokers

Like relatives and neighbors, moneylenders are familiar to the borrower, as they are usually local traders, merchants, or landowners. They make loans available with little or no collateral requirements and are flexible with regard to payment. Unfortunately, they often charge very high interest rates—either because the costs of providing small-scale, flexible financing are high or because they are in the position of being able to extract monopoly profits. In Latin America, it is common for local moneylenders to charge interest rates from 10 to 20 percent per month to 20 percent per day (Ashe 1984). However, because small borrowers are not deterred from turning to the moneylender for financing, the immediate and flexible financial services they provide are apparently high valued.

Pawnbrokers are attractive in that they allow women to put up jewelry, ornaments, or gold as collateral. In instances when women own few cattle or plots of land, or lack control over productive outputs, these personal items constitute their only form of collateral. Like moneylenders, pawnbrokers provide small loans in a timely and flexible fashion.

Shopkeepers, Wholesalers, and Intermediaries

These sources of credit are particularly important both for assisting women in meeting basic family needs and for maintaining women's daily participation in the marketplace. Shopkeepers may extend credit to well-known, consistent buyers for food and other household requirements by maintaining a record of the purchases and allowing the bill to remain unpaid for some time. Interest is usually not explicitly charged; rather, it is implicitly charged through higher prices for goods. Wholesalers, too, allow clients to leave bills unpaid until the purchased goods are sold at retail. Middlemen will advance women credit to buy raw materials and expect, in return, to buy women's products at lower than usual prices.

Rotating Savings Associations

Rotating savings and credit associations (ROSCAs), or contribution clubs, are attractive to women because of their ease of formation and entry and their flexibility in access. Members can often take their turn at borrowing before they have paid their full share of contribution. Many clubs also charge members a "safe money" fee in addition to their regular contribution. In this way the club can extend separate loans to members who are faced with an unexpected need for cash. Interest rates for these special loans are low relative to the local moneylender's rates, and repayment is flexible.

Drawbacks of the Informal System

There are several drawbacks to informal borrowing systems. Perhaps most important is the limited amount of credit available through these systems. Relatives and neighbors can lend only as much as their personal savings allow; the capital available from moneylenders and shopkeepers is also limited, particularly as these lenders maintain no savings facilities for their communities that could be used to maintain credit availability. Even the availability of small amounts of credit is highly inconsistent in informal systems and, especially in rotating savings schemes, may depend on the continued participation of other members.

Additionally, borrowing through informal systems often means doing business with a lender who maintains a virtual monopoly on credit resources. In this case, borrowers may be exploited and caught in a vicious cycle of indebtedness. There is evidence, however, that borrowers will often continue to rely on moneylenders for high-interest loans even when they are provided with the alternative of low-cost, government-sponsored loans. In these instances, the advantages of immediate disbursement of funds by the moneylender and the low transactions costs of the loan obviously outweigh the disadvantage of high interest rates. The limitations and uncertainties of informal systems undoubtedly inhibit the long-term planning and investment decisions that are necessary for borrowers to achieve significant improvements in productivity. Nonetheless, although informal credit systems do not always provide sources and mechanisms necessary for the provision of credit to women, they do show that women use credit and suggest what features would be desirable and workable in a formal program intended to meet women's credit needs.

PROGRAMS AND PROJECTS

Since the 1970s, the number of projects designed to reach the urban and rural poor has increased significantly as planners realized that existing credit projects had failed to reach the poorest of the poor. In Perú, for example, small enterprise lending represented only 3.4 percent of the total number of loans extended by the state-owned Banco Industrial del Perú in 1974, but by 1981 that figure had increased to 50 percent. Even private-sector banks, such as the Banco del Pacifico in Ecuador, have established special loan programs for artisans and other small borrowers (Salmen 1983). In addition, an increasing number of microenterprise projects run by private voluntary organizations work in conjunction with private banks. This new emphasis on minimizing restrictions that the poor face in gaining access to credit has increased the chances that poor women are reached. In most countries in the Latin American region, women—particularly those who support their own households—are overrepresented in the poorest low-income groups (CEPAL 1985). Credit projects that identify the poorest of the poor as the target group should therefore reach women.

In recent years, private voluntary organizations have implemented a multitude of credit projects for microentrepreneurs. Some, like Mujeres en Desarrollo Dominicana (MUDE), have specifically targeted women as beneficiaries and have little or no participation of men. Although women receive all of the project's resources, women-specific projects tend to be underfunded. Mainstream or "integrated" projects receive much greater resources; however, these may not reach many women unless particular attention is paid to women's issues. The ADEMI (Association for the Development of Microenterprises, Inc.) project in Santo Domingo, for instance, did not specifically target women as beneficiaries. However, many of the project's features, such as elimination of collateral requirements and small loan size, proved to be conducive to women's participation. Table 2.1 shows the advantages and disadvantages of different types of projects.

Project Features

Many microenterprise credit projects have incorporated features that affect the project's ability to reach the poor, including women. One such feature, the solidarity group, relies on a group credit mechanism to take the place of

TABLE 2.1

Advantages and Disadvantages of Three Types of Women's Projects

Type of Project	Advantages	Disadvantages
Women in Development (WID)—specific	Women receive all the project's resources and benefits. Beneficiaries may acquire leadership skills and greater self-confidence in a sex-segregated environment. Skills training in nontraditional areas may be much easier without male competition.	These projects tend to be small scale and under-funded. Implementing agencies often lack technical expertise in raising productivity or income. WID-specific income-generation projects rarely take marketability of goods or services into account and thus fail to generate income. Women beneficiaries may be required to contribute their time and labor with no compensation. Women may become further marginalized or isolated from mainstream development.
Women's Component in a Larger Project	The project as a whole enjoys more resources and higher priority than WID-specific projects, which can benefit the WID component. Women are ensured of receiving at least a part of the project's resources. Women can "catch up" to men through WID components.	The WID component usually receives far less funding and priority than do the other components. These components have tended to respond to women's social roles rather than their economic roles; for this reason, domestic activities may be emphasized to the exclusion of any others. Awareness of the importance of gender in the project's other components may be missing.
Integrated Project	Women can take full advantage of the resources and high priority that integrated projects receive. If women form a large proportion of the pool of eligibles, their participation will probably be high, even without detailed attention given to WID issues.	Unless information on women's activities and time use is introduced at the design stage, these projects may inadvertently exclude women through choices of promotion mechanism, location and timing of project resources, etc. If women form only a small proportion of the pool of eligibles, they may not be included in the project. Women competing with men for scarce project resources may lose out because of their lack of experience in integrated group settings and their relatively low status in the family and community.

Source: White et al. (1986).

collateral requirements. Solidarity groups consist of a small number of microentrepreneurs—usually acquainted with each other or engaged in the same business—who take out a loan as a group. Each member is responsible for paying back the loan; group pressure usually assures repayment. A review of microenterprise credit projects in Latin America and the Caribbean found that at least thirteen institutions use the solidarity group approach. Some combine the approach with a line of credit available to individual microentrepreneurs (Otero 1986).

Another mechanism for eliminating traditional collateral requirements is the use of progressively increasing loans. The microentrepreneur usually receives a very small loan to begin with; part of the incentive to repay the loan is the promise of a bigger loan next time. In this way, each borrower establishes an individual line of credit. As the entrepreneur pays back increasingly larger loans, his or her line of credit increases. The assumption is that eventually the borrower "graduates" to a bank or other formal financial institution.

Yet another mechanism is the provision of technical assistance. Microenterprise credit projects offer technical assistance to borrowers and potential borrowers in varying degrees. Some programs require potential borrowers to take courses in accounting and management before they can qualify for loans. Others offer one-on-one assistance to clients in filling out loan application forms and opening savings accounts in local banks, or refer their clients to local organizations offering small business courses. Provision of technical assistance is particularly valuable for women, who may have more trouble then men in filling out application forms and are less likely to have bookkeeping and management skills.

Recent Microenterprise Credit Projects

During the late 1970s a number of Latin American private voluntary organizations began experimenting with programs specifically targeted to businesses with fewer than five employees. One of the earliest such programs was FEDECCREDITO in El Salvador. Also important in pioneering this approach were UNO (Northeast Union of Assistance to Small Businesses) in Brazil and the Fundación Carvajal in Colombia. Later, many of the National Development Foundations (NDFs) in Latin America adopted the microenterprise model. It has also spread through the efforts of ACCION International/AITEC, which documented the experiences of the NDF programs and provided technical assistance through the PISCES (Program for Investment in the Small Capital Enterprise Sector) Program. Although project planners did not conceive of the projects as a specific means to reach women entrepreneurs, various project features ensured their participation. During the second phase of the PISCES program, project administrators paid more attention to women's issues and collected project data disaggregated by sex.

TABLE 2.2
Features of Recent Microenterprise Credit Projects

Program	Average Loan Size	Collateral/Guarantee	Technical Assistance	No. of Beneficiaries	Other	Percent Women
UNO, Brazil	US$2,113 as of 12/82.	Brazil's highly developed check system for consumer credit; UNO doesn't refinance delinquent loans.	Business extension courses.	3,798 as of 12/82.	Lends mainly for working capital to established firms.	15%
CORSOCIAL (Corporación para el Desarrollo Social) formerly CORFABRICATO (Corporación Fabricato para el Desarrollo Social), Colombia	US$1,534 as of 9/83.	Must complete the three basic courses successfully and pass credit regulations (IDB) such as number of years operating and net worth.	Has three courses: bookkeeping, cost analysis, and investment projects. Additionally provides seminars. T.A. through SENA.	1,895 as of 9/83.	—	35%, the majority of whom are in the garment and processing industries.
Fundación Carvajal DESAP (Desarrollo para Pequeñas Empresas), Colombia	US$1,545 as of 1983.	Credit regulations on loan contract; must attend three basic courses.	Training required prior to credit. 13 courses of 12 hours each.	3,642 trained, 1,578 loans disbursed, 1980–86.	Courses and administrative open to all microenterprises, not just for borrowers.	23% of micro-entrepreneurs who received credit as of 1983.
ADEMI, Dominican Republic	Microentrepreneurs: US$486 per person; solidarity groups: US$1,160 per group as of 1986.	Progressively increasing loan amounts; quick loan approval.	T.A. on an informal one-to-one basis for all beneficiaries.	Microentre-preneurs: 1,313; solidarity groups: 260 members in 1986.	Beneficiaries must open bank accounts and savings accounts.	19% microentre-preneurs and 40% of solidarity group members as of 12/86.

Program	Average loan size	Lending mechanism	Technical assistance	Number of beneficiaries	Special features	% Women
PRODEME, Dominican Republic	Microentrepreneurs: US$1,783; solidarity groups: US$236 in 1983.	Solidarity group mechanism.	One-on-one management assistance to microentrepreneurs. T.A. in group work collective action for solidarity groups.	Microentrepreneurs: 247; solidarity groups: 373, 7/81–6/84.	Loan disbursal process handled through purchase orders rather than to loan recipients.	12.7% of solidarity group members as of 1983.
Banco del Pacífico Artisan Credit Program, Ecuador	US$300 in 1986.	Cosigners – guarantors	36% of the clients took 3- to 5-day courses.	4,210 as of 9/86.	—	26% of beneficiaries.
PRODEM, Ecuador	Microentrepreneurs US$175; solidarity groups: US$207, as of 3/86.	Solidarity group mechanism; personal guarantors and progressively larger loans for microentrepreneurs.	Short courses and some individual T.A.	Microentrepreneurs 647; solidarity groups: 2,281 as of 3/86.	$50,000 credit fund earmarked for women within the program.	65% of solidarity group members; 35% of microentrepreneurs.
FEDECCREDITO, El Salvador	US$140 for first loans.	Solidarity group mechanism.	No formal one-to-one technical or management assistance.	2,640 as of 12/78.	—	86% of beneficiaries as of 7/79.
Haitian Development Foundation, Haiti	Men average US$9,615; women US$9,750, 1980–82.	—	Yes	248, 1980–82.	—	16% of beneficiaries.
FUNADEH (Fundación Nacional de Desarrollo Hondureño), Honduras	14,450 in 1985.	Applications reviewed by credit committee.	20 hours of group training and individual T.A.	—	Lends to both individuals and associations or cooperatives.	25% of beneficiaries as of 3/85.
National Development Foundation, Jamaica	US$2,948 as of 1/83.	—	Yes	63 as of 1/83.	Long disbursement period, heavy paperwork.	33% of beneficiaries.

TABLE 2.2 continued

Program	Average Loan Size	Collateral/Guarantee	Technical Assistance	No. of Beneficiaries	Other	Percent Women
FUNDE, Nicaragua	US$10,000 for the first loan to the co-op.	Co-op mechanism. Individual loans require cosigner.	Two types of T.A., one to managers and directors of coops. Another for members.	From 1972–82 there were 71 co-ops.	Vigorous promotion campaign to reach more women.	16 of 71 co-ops are all women; 50% a majority of women.
ADIM, Perú	—	Solidarity group mechanism.	Some group members must attend business management courses.	1,522 as of 9/86.	Also offers complementary services for health or legal problems.	93% of beneficiaries as of 9/86.
IDESI (Institute for the Development of the Informal Sector), Perú	US$1,375, as of 8/87.	Solidarity group mechanism; businesses in manufacturing must have some credit history.	—	44,650 producers and 95,920 vendors as of 8/87.	—	57.1% of all borrowers. 27% of all producers and 72% of all vendors, 8/87.
Progreso Perú	Microentrepreneurs US$1,186 per loan; solidarity groups: US$938 per group.	Since 1986 has used primarily solidarity group mechanism; progressively increasing loans.	Full-scale training program with services of outside trainers paid for by clients.	Approximately 338 members in individual loan component; 4,723 solidarity groups, as of 12/86.	Also extends loans for housing construction and repair.	54% of solidarity group members as of 12/86.
Rural Enterprise Development Project Perú	2,717,413 soles 1980–82.	Collateral required in the form of machinery, real estate, or a cosigner.	Some informal T.A.; courses in marketing, management and production held in provincial capitals.	4,698 as of 9/86.	—	14% of beneficiaries, 1980–82.
Urban Small Enterprise Fund, Perú	US$2,362 in 1984.	Collateral in the form of property, equipment, or a cosigner.	—	603 as of 1/84.	—	16% of beneficiaries as of 1/84.

Source: Tendler 1983; IDB 1984; Reichmann 1984a; Reichmann 1984b; ACCION/AITEC 1986; FEDPRODEM 1986; Farbman 1981; Otero 1985; Valencia Vera 1986; Pinilla 1987; Buvinić, Berger, and Gross 1984; Blayney 1979; Berger, Buvinić, and Jaramilllo, Chapter 14 of this volume.

Table 2.2 lists some of the recent microenterprise credit projects in the Latin American/Caribbean region, their features, and the percentage of female beneficiaries.

Current Trends in Microenterprise Credit Projects

In Latin America, Colombia is perhaps the most advanced country in terms of institutionalizing efforts to assist microenterprises. First, Colombia has two umbrella organizations that represent the many solidarity group programs there and the microenterprise programs that target slightly larger businesses. Second, in 1984, the government instituted a national plan— called CONPES—for the development of microenterprises. Recently, CONPES received from the Inter-American Development Bank a multimillion dollar loan that it channels to intermediaries. It also helps coordinate government and private programs for microentrepreneurs and training programs under the national training system, SENA. In addition, CONPES helps to monitor and evaluate microenterprise programs with a standardized format (IDB 1984).

There are signs that the trend toward institutionalization may be spreading to other Latin American countries. In 1985, Ecuador initiated a program similar to the Colombian one in the hopes of replicating its model. In Ecuador, however, the program also channels money to government and private banks for microenterprise credit. To the extent that these programs retain an emphasis on credit for microenterprise, rather than drifting upward to small enterprise, the trend toward institutionalization is a promising one for women microentrepreneurs in Latin America.

The International Labor Organization (ILO) and its Latin American affiliate, PREALC (Programa Regional del Empleo para América Latina y el Caribe), have recently moved from an emphasis on researching and documenting the informal sector to advising governments on policies that will help promote the development of its microbusinesses. The ILO has even begun to design on-the-ground credit programs such as the one run by the Fundación Guayaquil. (See Chapter 7 in this volume.)

Another promising development is the practice of collecting sex-disaggregated data on women in microenterprise projects, which, until the mid-1980s, was very rare. The Asociación de Programas de Grupos Solidarios, a Latin American association of solidarity groups, is a rich source of such data, as women tend to predominate in solidarity groups. Both CONPES and the PVOs associated with ACCION International/AITEC also collect some sex-specific data in their programs.

IMPROVING WOMEN'S ACCESS:
SUGGESTIONS FOR POLICY AND PROJECTS

Given what we know about factors that limit women's access to formal sources of credit and the features of informal systems that are conducive to women's borrowing, what recommendations can we make for improving women's access to credit? A two-pronged approach is required. Because the formal financial sector will most likely continue to be the major source of credit in developing countries, policy-level changes will be vital for improving financial resources available to women. It is chiefly through policy changes that an impact will be made on the direction in which financial institutions develop.

Changes at the level of credit projects, or components of projects, will also be important. Credit projects will have an impact on women's control over financial resources not only directly, through the number of beneficiaries actually reached, but also indirectly, through demonstration of women's demand for, and productive utilization of, credit when projects are designed to meet their needs. The effects of such demonstrations will ultimately feed back into the structure of the financial sector.

Policy Recommendations

At the policy level, careful reform of interest rate policies, the development of intermediary credit institutions and programs, and legal reforms are likely to improve women's chances of obtaining financing.

Reform of Financial Markets
Transactions costs, collateral requirements, application procedures, location of the lender, distribution channels, and, perhaps most important, the degree of incentive for the lender to make small loans determine whether or not loans will be made to women. Almost all of these factors are related to the price of credit, that is, the interest rate charged on a loan. For example, transactions costs and collateral requirements, as well as application procedures, are all tools by which the lender can control the risks, and thus the costs of lending, relative to the expected returns available through the interest rate. If the interest rate is regulated and held below its market level, lenders must compensate for lower expected returns through reliance on lower risks and costs. The result is high transactions costs for the borrower and difficult and time-consuming application procedures. Informal lenders whose expected returns are not regulated can afford to impose low collateral requirements and transactions costs because the unregulated rate of interest they charge compensates them for taking higher risks.

The location of a lender also depends on the interest that can be earned by lending. An urban-based bank cannot afford to decentralize its operations unless the returns to lending are high enough to cover the loss of economies of scale associated with carrying out all lending operations at one location—the higher salaries that must often be paid to attract staff to rural locations, and communications costs.

Finally, regulation of the interest rate that can be charged on loans negatively affects the lender's willingness to make small loans and provides incentives for the lender to allocate credit to larger borrowers and more powerful customers.

Do these factors mean that deregulation of interest rates will improve Third World women's access to formal sources of credit? Theoretically, yes, as deregulation would allow market-clearing interest rates to prevail, thus eliminating excess demand and obviating the need for non-price rationing mechanisms that are disadvantageous to women and small borrowers. In reality, however, movement from regulated to market rates of interest would undoubtedly cause confusion, political problems, and adjustment problems. In addition, if there are barriers to entry into financial markets, such as a lengthy and costly process of obtaining a banking charter or other credentials for operation, or if a nation's financial institutions are controlled by a small number of firms that may collude to maintain high interest levels, deregulation of interest rates will not have the intended effect.

Specifically, the fact that governments up to now have regulated interest rates in an attempt to encourage greater use of credit implies that credit is perceived as a social good—a good that not only benefits the individual purchaser but also has spillover or externality benefits for society as a whole. In the case of a social good, the free-market price will not induce the socially optimal quality of the good to be exchanged and the subsidy of the good is required. Thus, if governments wish to induce a higher level of credit use by women and other low-income groups, they should target appropriate interest rate subsidies to these groups—by ensuring that borrowers pay optimal rates of interest that are lower than market rates, while reimbursing financial institutions for the costs of lending at the low rates. Even in this case, however, excess demand with all the ensuing inequities of rationing may arise if governments cannot afford the total amount of subsidy required to provide the optimal level of credit at the optimal price. They must then employ a "second best" solution—that is, subsidize interest rates to the point where no excess demand exists *and* the total amount of subsidy required falls within the governments' budgets.

In many cases, given severely limited budgets for subsidy, this second-best interest rate may not be far below the free-market rate. Nevertheless, even in this instance, there are clear efficiency and equity arguments for resisting the temptation to provide more heavily subsidized loans in smaller numbers. Experience in World Bank and USAID housing and small business programs has shown that too high a level of subsidy on fewer loans will, as with regulation of interest rates, inevitably deny small borrowers, inexperienced borrowers, and female borrowers access to the subsidized credit (Bhat and Roe 1979; Kane 1981). Typically, those denied access will be driven to borrow from informal sources of credit, if available, and will ultimately pay rates of interest that are often higher than the original market rate that the subsidy program was intended to lower.

Development of Intermediary Institutions and Programs

Reform of interest rate policies and provision of appropriate subsidies may be necessary conditions for improving women's access to credit, but they are unlikely to be sufficient. Ideally, financial reform should be accompanied, or even preceded, by the development of intermediary credit institutions and programs intended to "graduate" women and other inexperienced borrowers into formal-sector borrowing. Attaining this interim goal will require a commitment at the policy level to improving the financial services available to women. Governments might, for example, assist private voluntary organizations with the start-up costs of developing revolving loan funds for low-income borrowers, establish national financial extension services, and support similar privately organized services capable of encouraging more women to apply for formal credit and helping them with application procedures and negotiations. In addition, governments might provide guarantees for loans made without collateral; support research on credit needs and practices that will have implications for developing more effective intermediary programs; and, perhaps most important, work toward educating the public—particularly those in the financial sector—on women's need for and ability to handle credit, their very high repayment rates, and their commitment to fulfill debt obligations even when loans are made without collateral.

At issue is whether or not such programs must be developed specifically for women in order to be effective. There is some concern that women may be at a disadvantage relative to men in the competition for credit even in programs designed to reach small and inexperienced borrowers. Women-specific programs, on the other hand, may implicitly remove women from the mainstream of development efforts and are often welfare-oriented, reinforcing traditional misconceptions of women's economic roles. Moreover, women-specific programs may be perceived as catering to special interests and thus may be politically unacceptable. In the final analysis, the advantages and disadvantages of women-specific versus mixed-sex programs must be determined empirically on a case-by-case basis.

Legal Reforms

Although they are not strictly related to financial policy, legal reforms must be noted as critical to improving women's access to credit. In many countries, women are still required to obtain the permission to borrow, as well as a financial guarantee, from their husbands or fathers in order to qualify for loans. These requirements not only add to the transactions costs of borrowing, but represent major obstacles for the large and growing numbers of women who are widowed, divorced, or single heads of household, or whose husbands have migrated in search of employment. Clearly the repeal of any such legal requirements should be included in the agenda of goals for policy reform.

Project Recommendations

At the project level, the integration of several useful characteristics of informal borrowing systems into project design is of paramount importance. Projects intended to service the financial needs of women must be tailored to the characteristics of the majority of women borrowers. That is, credit projects must be designed to deliver loans in small amounts, transactions costs of borrowing must be manageable, repayment schedules must be appropriate, and collateral requirements must be minimal. How can these characteristics be achieved?

Certainly, interest rates must reflect the actual cost of credit disbursement, taking into account the amount of subsidy appropriate and available in the project. Achievement of this goal will allow project viability and replicability to be maintained while the following features are incorporated into the project design:

- Several repayment options, allowing a choice of repaying the loan in frequent small payments or fewer larger payments, depending on the expected income stream of the borrower. Although flexible repayment schemes may be administratively costly, they tend to dramatically reduce the rate of default on loans.

- Reduced collateral requirements through heavier reliance on repayment capacity of the borrower or a broadening of the concept of collateral to encompass security for a loan through group lending or guarantees by members of the borrowers' community. Group lending will also help reduce project unit costs of lending. When physical collateral is required, it should not be restricted to formal titles to land and business registrations but should include jewelry and other resources available to women.

- Use of information and credit distribution channels to which women have access. Large banks, agricultural cooperatives, and extension services have not been successful in distributing either information about credit or actual credit funds to the vast majority of women who need credit. Thus, credit projects should make information and funds available at the marketplace, through religious groups, small savings associations, and grassroots organizations that tend to be more aware of and responsive to the economic roles of women.

There are an impressive and growing number of success stories associated with the introduction of these considerations into development projects which should provide the incentive for project planners to more thoroughly explore innovations in the delivery of credit. Some of these, such as MUDE, Progreso, ADEMI, and PRODEM, are discussed in this volume.

THE CHALLENGE AHEAD

The reorientation of credit projects and policies recommended here cannot be undertaken by governments of developing countries and international development agencies without a great deal of political will. Such changes would not only threaten to encroach upon the vested interests of politically privileged groups but might also meet with resistance from those who are genuinely concerned with the plight of poor women but not fully aware of the implications of financial regulation. Increasing interest rates on loans, for example, might appear at first glance to be contraindicated, although more detailed investigation would justify such action. Development planners have been making progress in encouraging lending at appropriate and sustainable rates of interest, and there has been a major research focus in recent years on the structure of rural financial markets and programs of agricultural credit for the small farmer. The challenge ahead for the development community now entails focusing on women in their roles as entrepreneurs, merchants, farmers, and major sources of economic support for families, in order to promote recognition of the potential contribution of women to the development process and of the importance of access to credit in allowing women to fulfill that potential.

3

Excess Labor Supply and the Urban Informal Sector: *An Analytical Framework*

JAIME MEZZERA

DEFINING THE INFORMAL SECTOR

S tudy of the informal sector began in the early 1970s with the work of Hart (1970) and the research program of the International Labour Office (ILO 1972; PREALC 1975). Since that time the term has become popularized and extended beyond its original conceptual framework. It has even come to be used in ways that identify the informal sector with beggars and vagrants, thieves and smugglers, peddlers and prostitutes. As in all cases in which a single term means different things to different people, it is necessary to establish a specific definition. The conception of the informal sector put forward in the work of the Regional Employment Program for Latin America and the Caribbean (PREALC), and in this chapter, is based on two precepts: first, that of surplus labor supply; and second, that of a lack of productive resources to complement labor—especially capital. Based on an analysis of these two factors, this chapter presents a conceptual framework for understanding the urban informal sector in developing countries.

What the Informal Sector Is Not

We can best begin to define the urban informal sector (UIS) by eliminating some of the misconceptions that were part of the original definition set forth more than ten years ago.

The Underground Economy

One initial interpretation associated the informal sector with the so-called underground economy. The underground economy is an illegal economy that is generated for illegal purposes; it is associated with the evasion of tax payments and other state regulations. Noting that informal sector businesses do not pay taxes, some observers deduce that the UIS is the same thing as the underground economy. But it is well known that, especially in developing countries, formal sector firms evade taxes as well. Moreover, the loss of fiscal revenues as a result of that avoidance of tax payments on the part of the formal sector is probably much greater than that occurring when informal-sector actors, who do not have high incomes, do not pay taxes. Still more important, those who work in the UIS set up informal firms not to avoid paying taxes, but simply to survive. The concept of the underground economy is thus not useful, because it does not distinguish between formal and informal sector actors.

This conception has led some to suggest that the informal sector results from administrative regulations that make it difficult to establish firms (de Soto 1986). What follows immediately is that eliminating the regulations will give rise to thousands of modern capitalist enterprises—the woodworker who works with two pliers, three screwdrivers, and a hammer will be transformed into a capitalist entrepreneur just because regulations hindering establishment of modern firms are abolished. Of course, administrative restrictions are a deterrent. But eliminating the administrative restrictions will not make the informal sector disappear; much less will it be transformed into a modern capitalist sector without access to productive resources to complement labor.[1]

The Result of Mistaken Economic Policies
One of the most common interpretations of the informal sector, which emerged in academic circles in the developed countries, is the theory that it results from distortions in the labor market brought about by "mistaken" government actions such as imposing minimum wages, or the "misguided" actions of trade unions, which raise wages above their equilibrium level, thereby generating a surplus labor supply. If either of these is the reason for the existence of an informal sector, the resulting policy recommendation is that the phenomenon of the informal sector will disappear if the government eliminates minimum wages, or if it somehow destroys the power of the trade unions. This has happened in several Latin American countries in the 1970s and 1980s. But it did not lead to a reduction of the surplus labor supply, and the informal sector certainly did not disappear.

Street Vendors
There is a tendency to associate the informal sector with street vendors—the most visible manifestation of the sector. Although street vendors are in effect part of the informal sector, they certainly do not account for all of it; indeed, they are probably the group that would benefit least from opportunities for growth brought about by development of the sector.

A *Set of Occupational Groups*

A fourth commonly held point of view identifies the informal sector with the early quantification of the sector—made by PREALC—as all self-employed workers, unremunerated workers, and domestic servants. Much of PREALC's work assumes this set of occupational categories as an approximation of the labor force in the informal sector. But from the beginning it was seen as an economic sector, which by definition is not a set of people but a set of enterprises or productive units. Thus, the informal sector is a set of economic units that includes at one extreme self-employed workers, and at the other, microenterprises. It is difficult to measure the labor force of these units, except by surveys of informal-sector establishments. And given the difficulty of such a measurement, PREALC has sometimes used, as an approximation of the informal-sector labor force, this set of occupational categories.

Dualist Approach

A fifth interpretation, also quite common, identifies the UIS by reference to a dualist model of the formal and informal sectors. This model was established in the 1950s and early 1960s when economists discovered that the economic structure of the developing countries was not completely homogeneous. In works such as those of Lewis (1954) and Ranis and Fei (1961), models were set forth with one sector that operates in conditions of simple reproduction, in which a modern structure is exogenously inserted. That modern structure has no economic relationship to the traditional structure: it neither buys from nor sells to it. An example is a foreign mining or agricultural enclave that is established in an underdeveloped country, buys all its inputs from its parent company abroad, and also sells all its output there. Although the enterprise hires workers from the traditional sector, it has practically no economic connection to the traditional sector, except through the labor market.

As PREALC speaks of two sectors—modern and informal, or formal and informal—there has been a tendency to think that they support an updated version of dualism. But this is not the case, precisely because it always stresses that there are a great many economic relationships between the two sectors (Tokman 1978). The sectors buy from and sell to one another in the same way that the center and peripheral countries of the world buy and sell; the informal sector "exports" to and "imports" from the modern sector.

What the Informal Sector Is

The UIS discussed here is a heterogeneous set of productive activities that share the common feature of employing a number of people who would be unable to find employment in the modern sector and must generate their own employment with relatively little access to the factors of production that complement the labor supply. The clearest expression of their very limited access to these productive factors is the low capital/labor ratio and, as a result, low labor incomes in the UIS.

Informal economic activities in the developing countries can be classified in two groups: those that compete with the modern stratum of the urban economy, and those that do not. Both groups share the situation of being subordinated to, and indeed exploited by, the modern sector (Tokman 1978). The competitive informal units do not have access to technical advances and capital because of the concentration of economic resources in the hands of a few and the scarcity of capital. To survive in the market—a goal that implies selling at prices that are competitive with those of the modern, formal sector—they are forced to reduce the returns to labor (Mezzera 1981) and even to other assets of their own (Tokman 1978).

The other informal-sector firms, those that do not compete directly with the formal sector, insert themselves into "interstices" or "niches" of economic activity that, for a variety of reasons, are not occupied by modern firms. In general, these activities are not very attractive as potential generators of oligopolistic rents, and therefore the informal-sector workers employed in such activities are those who have been excluded from the profitable activities in which the modern capitalist sector is concentrated. In addition, because this process of insertion into "niches" is dynamic, the constant expansion and transformation of the modern sector continuously destroy and recreate them (PREALC 1975; Robinson 1977; Souza 1979).

Workers who carry out these activities in the urban informal sector can also be divided into two groups. First, the successful informal entrepreneurs who run viable informal sector firms that in some cases have a positive capacity, even if very small, to accumulate. Evidence has suggested that in many cases these microentrepreneurs entered the informal sector after a period as wage workers in the modern economy which made possible the accumulation of physical and human capital. Accumulation of physical capital can take the form of financial savings or purchase of equipment; human capital includes the acquisition or upgrading of productive techniques and knowledge of the basic skills needed to survive as an entrepreneur.[2] In such cases, informal entrepreneurs often leave their wage-earning jobs to take on new roles that make use of their entrepreneurial ability and their capital. In this triple role of entrepreneur-capitalist-worker that characterizes self-employed workers and owners of microenterprises, they generally earn total incomes greater than those obtained by wage-earners in the modern sector who have the same characteristics. Nonetheless, it is likely that compensation to labor alone is less than they could make as wage-earners.[3]

Given their income level, these microentrepreneurs do not constitute a "reserve army" for possible expansion of employment in the formal sector. Their status suggests an apparent inconsistency with the notion that the informal sector is an expression of excess labor supply. However, this view is macroeconomic, in the sense that not enough employment is offered in the modern sector to absorb all the urban labor force. This view is consistent with the observation that some specific members of the informal sector are not part of excess labor (in the micro sense that they have chosen to work in the informal sector). The excess labor supply should thus be understood as a number of workers who have been excluded from modern employment, and not as a specific group of people who have remained outside the modern sector.

In countries such as those of Latin America, the members of the UIS account for most of the urban excess labor supply, a term we use to refer to the difference between total urban labor supply and modern, or formal, urban employment.[4] The excess supply is forced to choose among three possibilities: to take up, as most do, low-income informal occupations; to remain unemployed, "standing in line" to enter the formal sector; or to withdraw from the labor force, and thus become part of what is called "hidden unemployment" (Llona and Mezzera 1985; McDonald and Solow 1985).

Labor market segmentation, as understood here, does not result from the characteristics of labor supplied; there is only one supply of labor, and individuals can move from one sector to another. Under this model, labor market segmentation arises from the conditions of the demand of labor. Part of this demand comes from the oligopolistic firms of the modern sector, which establish and maintain barriers to competition and then share some of the profits resulting from such barriers with their workers. The other part comes from informal productive units whose logic makes survival of its members a greater priority than accumulation.

Five questions arise from this perspective. First, why is there a surplus? Second, why is that surplus large and permanent? Third, why has the informal sector emerged as the main manifestation of that surplus? Fourth, what does the segmentation of labor incomes mean? And fifth, how do the surplus labor force and the informal sector evolve during the business cycle? This chapter endeavors to set forth coherent answers to these five questions.

The chapter is organized into four sections. The first presents statistics describing the urban informal sector, providing an empirical profile. The second describes formal and informal firms in terms of the operational features that have the greatest impact on the labor market and proposes a theoretical framework that analyzes the informal sector as the result of the oligopolistic structure of the goods and capital markets in the Latin American countries. This framework is based on differential access to capital. The third section shows that given segmented capital markets, technological change generates an excess labor supply that is unable to find employment in the modern or formal sector; as a result, the differential introduction of technological progress makes inevitable the existence of a group of workers with extremely low labor incomes, indeed even lower than the prevailing ones before technological change was introduced. The last section analyzes the performance of both sectors throughout the business cycle and describes the way in which the labor market adjusts itself in the face of increases and declines in the modern sector's demand for labor.

PROFILE OF THE URBAN INFORMAL SECTOR

Estimates of Employment in the Urban Informal Sector

Correctly calculating the size of the urban informal sector requires, in theory, that a mixed survey be carried out. This term refers to a household survey in which all potential heads of informal-sector firms (that is, self-employed workers and owners of small firms) are asked to report on the location of the establishments they operate. In a second phase, the mixed survey becomes a research project on those informal establishments, making it possible, among other things, to measure the volume of informal sector employment.

Because that method is costly, it has been used only in a limited number of cases. The best indirect estimates use data from household-based research, that is, censuses and surveys. This source in turn necessitates the use of proxy variables to estimate which workers are informal. The most common proxies are occupational category and size of establishment. In other words, the size and makeup of informal employment are approximated assuming that most informal workers are self-employed, family workers, and owners and wage-earners of small firms.

Long-Term Trends

In PREALC's first empirical estimates in the early 1970s, the volume of informal-sector employment was estimated in proportions that ranged from 40 to 50 percent of the urban labor force (PREALC 1981). There is evidence, albeit not conclusive, suggesting that from 1950 to 1980 the weight of the informal sector in the EAP held quite constant, as illustrated in Table 3.1. In those thirty years both the formal and informal sectors grew dramatically. The main effect during that period was the conversion of the employment prob-

TABLE 3.1

Latin America: Composition of the Nonagricultural Economically Active Population (EAP), 1950–80

	1950	1960	1970	1980
Formal	69.3%	71.3%	70.4%	71.3%
Informal	20.0	19.5	20.1	20.3
Domestic service	10.7	9.2	9.5	8.4
Total	100.0	100.0	100.0	100.0

Source: PREALC, based on national censuses.

lem into an essentially urban phenomenon as a result of rural to urban migration. In effect, in thirty years urban employment has shifted from accounting for two of every five Latin American workers, to two of every three, as shown in Table 3.2.

Table 3.2 illustrates the growing importance of the nonagricultural sector as a source of employment over the last 30 years, reflecting Latin America's rapid urbanization. These figures roughly parallel trends in urban (nonagricultural) and rural (largely nonagricultural) employment.

Within urban areas, the modern sector has been able to maintain its share of total employment generated in the cities, despite its relatively small initial size and tendencies toward overcapitalization. As a result, the relative proportions of the two main urban sectors remain constant, with only a

TABLE 3.2

Latin America: Percentages of the Agricultural and Nonagricultural Economically Active Population (EAP), 1950–80

	1950	1960	1970	1980
Agricultural EAP	54.7%	43.5%	42.0%	32.1%
Nonagricultural EAP	44.1	54.3	57.1	67.1
EAP in mining	1.2	2.2	0.9	0.8
Total EAP	100.0	100.0	100.0	100.0

Source: PREALC, based on national censuses of the following countries: Argentina, Bolivia, Brazil, Chile, Colombia, Costa Rica, Ecuador, El Salvador, Guatemala, Mexico, Panama, Peru, Uruguay, and Venezuela.

slight decrease of domestic employment as a share of total urban employment, as seen in Table 3.1.

If we consider that the informal sector and domestic service are two distinct manifestations of the excess urban labor supply, then we observe that the proportion of this surplus within urban employment remained almost constant for thirty consecutive years, varying from almost 31 percent in 1950 to just under 29 percent in 1980. Finally, within the traditional or informal sector, the volume of urban informal employment, which in 1950 was one-fourth of its rural counterpart, increased proportionately to three-fifths by 1980 (Table 3.3).

Observations on Women in the Informal Sector

No systematic data exist on the participation of women in the informal sector in Latin America as a whole. Table 3.4 presents an example, providing data on the percentage of informal sector jobs held by women in the city of San Salvador. These data in turn are related to the discussion of whether domestic service is part of the informal sector.

TABLE 3.3
Composition of the Traditional Sectors

	1950	1960	1970	1980
Traditional rural sector	70.7%	60.9%	61.4%	49.7%
Urban informal sector	19.1	26.6	26.2	35.7
Domestic service	10.2	12.5	12.3	14.6
Total	100.0	100.0	100.0	100.0

Source: PREALC, based on national censuses.

Domestic Service

PREALC's first studies included domestic service within the informal sector, in part because an all-encompassing concept was sought, that is, one that would cover all workers with problems in the labor market. It has since become quite common to include domestic services within the informal sector. However, PREALC's current approach is to use the concept of excess labor supply to cover all those who have problems in the labor market, and to limit the use of informal sector to a specific segment.

For two reasons PREALC analysts have concluded that domestic service should not be included in the informal sector. The first is theoretical: the informal sector is a set of productive units, not of people, and an individual who works in domestic service is not a productive unit, but a wage-earner who generally depends on income from the modern sector. The second reason is empirical: including domestic service in the informal sector introduces an enormous conceptual bias of the informal sector in favor of the personal characteristics of this particular group, which is quite large and homogeneous. The vast majority are women, particularly unskilled young women who are migrants and wage-earners with low incomes and long working hours. The result is that the informal sector becomes identified with unskilled women who are migrants and wage-earners who have no relationship to microenterprises.

The figures in Table 3.4 show that including domestic service in the informal sector gives rise to a great preponderance of women. But, when the nondomestic informal sector alone is considered, 30 percent of men and 32 percent of women are classified as informal-sector workers. Thus the percentages of men and of women employed in the nondomestic informal sector are almost identical, at least in the case of San Salvador. However, in other countries women's participation in the informal sector is proportionally greater (see, for example, Escobar, in this volume).

Informal Sector Women and Human Capital

The second point is put forth mainly as an issue for reflection, and has been raised in PREALC as a topic for future research. It is the differential validity of

TABLE 3.4
San Salvador: Employment by Sex and Labor Market Sector, 1974

	Men	Women	Total
Informal sector (includes domestic service)	29%	63%	46%
Nondomestic	28	31	30
Domestic	1	32	16
Modern sector	70	36	54
Government	18	13	15
Private	52	23	39
Total	100	100	100

Source: PREALC, *Sector Informal: Funcionamiento y Políticas.*

the human capital theory among different sectors and sexes. Human capital theory posits, in essence, that labor incomes depend on the qualifications a particular individual has, especially those related to education. But disaggregating the informal and formal sectors reveals that the association between qualifications and income is much greater in the formal sector than in the informal sector. This finding reflects in part the fact that incomes in the informal sector tend to be a composite of returns to labor, returns to capital, and compensation for entrepreneurial risk. In both sectors, but particularly in the informal sector, the return to qualifications is much less for women than for men. This is an interesting research subject that should be further examined.

Composition of the Labor Force

Finally, if we adhere to the definition set forth here, most women in the informal sector are microvendors. This finding leads to the recommendation that credit and training policies for women in the informal sector should probably differ from those geared to men, who are concentrated in production of goods and services.

AN ANALYTICAL FRAMEWORK FOR
UNDERSTANDING THE INFORMAL SECTOR

Segmentation of the Goods and Capital Markets

This section offers an analytical framework for explaining the origins and persistence of the informal sector in Latin America as an expression of excess labor supply. To show the existence of a structural excess labor supply, it is not necessary to resort to arguments about labor market distortions. Unequal capital endowments and imperfections in the capital and goods markets are the main factors that give rise to disequilibrium in the labor market, which is manifested in the existence of an informal sector.

The Oligopolistic Modern Sector

The Latin American economies have a modern, formal sector, which is dominant, and an informal sector, which is subordinate to the modern one. To understand the informal sector, we must understand the dominant sector, that is, modern firms. The modern sector of the Latin American urban economies is a set of firms that produce goods and services in oligopolistic markets—in other words, they operate in markets that are controlled by a small number of firms (an oligopoly) or even one firm (a monopoly). These firms maintain control through ownership of a major portion of the assets in the line of production of a particular good or service. In practice, just a few firms hold 70 to 90 percent of the productive assets in each branch of industry (in terms of the four-digit international classification). Even though there may be twenty or thirty other firms that produce the same product in a country, in terms of the sums of capital invested, a limited number maintain oligopolistic control.

Two characteristics of the modern sector, capital intensity and oligopoly, are inseparable. Making a massive investment in a capital-intensive industry necessitates a long horizon for planning the investment. In other words, a firm must know that for many years there will be a flow of profits that will make it possible to recover its investment and, at the end of the process, to produce a net profit. Simply by virtue of being highly capital-intensive, and the investments being massive, a firm cannot afford to respond to existing prices, as postulated in the neoclassical economic model of perfect competition, but rather it must set prices that assure recovery of the investment. The main factor that determines whether firms survive, grow, or fail to grow, is therefore the degree of success they have in establishing and maintaining oligopolistic barriers and returns.

Modern firms need to manage their markets to maintain these returns. This goal requires, in turn, two strategies that have a major impact on the demand for labor. First, the firm chooses the most modern technology it can finance, because such technologies not only imply lower costs, but also create an image more in line with the style in demand by the highest-income sectors.[5] A firm that acts in this manner will be in a position to offer the "best" product at relatively low cost. And, because it is an oligopolistic firm, it can set its sale prices to generate a cash flow that will allow it to continue self-financing planned expansion (Kenyon 1978).

The second way of maintaining domination of the goods market is to have sufficient idle capacity to be able, if necessary, to inundate the market and win a price war against any potential rival. Thus, the most capital-intensive activities are also the most attractive ones for investors in the modern sector. The mere size of the initial investment establishes, in countries with a chronic capital shortage, a very effective barrier preventing competition from potential rivals that might wish to enter the market but cannot afford to do so.

To eliminate uncertainty regarding the availability of investment funds—at appropriate terms and interest rates—for financing future expansion, a firm not only needs to guarantee a price that generates profits; it also must ensure that there is an adequate flow for future investment. These firms avoid turning to the capital market, which does not assure them that availability of credit at adequate terms and interest rates, relying instead on price-setting, which is done to guarantee internal financing for the firm. Modern firms only turn to the capital market to meet their short-term capital needs, that is, for working capital; rarely do they approach it for expansion. This pattern is confirmed by surveys that ask firms where they obtain funds for expansion. The answer is virtually always the firm's internal cash flow, which accounts for 80 to 90 percent of total investment. It can also be demonstrated by studying the structure of the terms of bank loans. In the Latin American countries—with some exceptions in housing—banks generally do not lend for terms greater than twelve months.

Furthermore, families that own capital have an interest in maintaining control over their investments, even if in theory there are alternative uses of the funds that promise greater returns (Ramos 1980). This tendency to reinvest in themselves may imply expansion of the productive capacity of the same firm that generated the funds, or it may be directed to other firms—mainly in other markets that the group is in a position to invade—that belong to the same owners.[6]

Forced to bring the very large scale of their investments into line with their personal desire to control them, owners of formal firms tend to choose those productive, administrative, and managerial methods that enable them to simplify, mechanize, and automate their operations so as to minimize use of their scarce resource (managerial capacity) at the cost of maximizing use of capital, which is abundantly available to them (Ramos 1980).

These strategies, adopted by the oligopolistic firms, cause demand for labor to be much less than assumed by conventional models of competitive markets. These strategies are the main explanation for the existence and permanence of a large urban excess labor supply that must choose between informal employment, unemployment, and withdrawal from economic activity.

How the Excess Labor Supply Is Generated

The existence of labor market dualism has recently come to be accepted by orthodox neoclassical economics, in part because of the work of Harberger (1971), who made the distinction between a protected sector and an unprotected one. According to this perspective, government intervention for social reasons related to income distribution results in the establishment of a minimum wage and other laws that distort the equilibrium wage/profit ratio. Unemployment results because firms adjust the marginal productivity of labor to a new higher wage rate by using more capital-intensive production techniques. Nonetheless, enforcing labor laws is costly, and thus they affect only the large firms, which constitute the protected sector; they are the firms that are most visible to the government and trade unions. On the other hand, reducing employment in the protected sector provides the necessary labor supply for small firms that have to pay only the reserve price of labor. Thus, two distinct wage levels are observed for employed workers, along with an unemployment level below what it would be if minimum wage regulation were costless.

The remedy for labor market segmentation that emerges from this approach is the elimination of wage-regulating laws. This "solution," however, is a mistaken one, because it assumes a partial equilibrium situation in which only one distortion exists—the wage floor. But in Latin America there is a general disequilibrium in which imbalances in other markets (above all, in the capital market) have implications for the labor market.

Effects of Technological Progress

The introduction of new technologies that are more efficient in their use of labor is one of the factors contributing to the general disequilibrium. When a new and more efficient technology is introduced, all the firms that can do so adopt that new technology. Nonetheless, if the capital market is imperfect in the very simple sense that the financial system lends only to large firms, then only those firms can effectively implement the new technology. The small firms will not have access to the credit they need and, in theory, will be forced to cease producing because they will be unable to compete.[7]

If this process is generalized to several branches of industry simultaneously, the workers who were in the small firms will not find work elsewhere. Perfect markets and perfect technological flexibility would lead to the conventional result of a decline in wages, promoting adjustment in the capital/labor ratio and the reestablishment of full employment at lower wages. Yet in practice the technologies cannot be altered once they are installed, and the larger firms prefer to buy good relations with their personnel by paying high wages. Therefore, full employment will not be reestablished, and workers in small firms will have to accept a lower income to avoid unemployment (Mezzera 1981).

Segmentation of Labor Incomes

In politically normal situations, modern-sector firms have an interest in sharing their oligopolistic rents with their organized workers. This practice yields firm political benefits, benefits of passive labor unions within the firm, and productivity benefits resulting from the operation of internal labor markets (Doeringer and Piore 1971). Of these benefits, one of the most important is that paying wages above the minimum that the market would tolerate ensures the immediate availability of a "line" of applicants for any job that the firm decides to offer. This guarantees the firm a choice of skilled workers, without large personnel selection and training costs. Also, the cost of maintaining wages above their minimum possible level is not very great, because the share of labor costs in total production costs rarely rises above 15 percent in the modern sectors of Latin American industry.[8]

Thus, the behavior of the modern firms leads to labor market segmentation between a large number of workers who benefit from sharing in the oligopolistic rents of the firms, and others who are excluded from these benefits and forced to survive as they can in informal activities with low returns.[9] In order to survive, the small firms have to reduce their incomes below what they had been before technological progress arrived, and they end up producing with a capital/labor ratio lower than the one they started out with.

No doubt the introduction of technological progress in an initial situation that is heavily imbalanced is detrimental to workers in small firms. This result does not depend on any intervention in the labor market, whether from the government or trade unions. Nevertheless, the effect of the concentration of wealth and the endogenous imperfections of other markets—in this case, the capital market—is such that the appearance of an informal sector of very small firms that use obsolete techniques of production and are in competition with the modern firms becomes inevitable. To survive, these firms are forced to reduce the labor incomes of workers employed in their sector. As Tokman (1978) points out, turning to unpaid family workers who simply participate in the average productivity of the family microenteprise is one solution. Another is the use of durable consumer goods, such as the family car, or parts of the home, in the microentrepreneurial production process.

Adjustment of the Labor Market

The analysis of the effect on the labor market starts from a situation of excess labor supply. Because people, especially heads of households (both men and women) cannot remain unemployed for long, one of the only options is to become self-employed in the informal sector. Thus, the informal sector ends up being the main expression of the excess labor supply. It is a set of economic units deprived of access to capital, in which people work because of the urgency of earning an income.

Demand for Labor

The formal sector's demand for labor comes from a relatively small number of large firms with very capital-intensive technologies. The adoption of such technologies is sometimes motivated by protectionist measures against imports, and by government credit schemes that offer very low or negative interest rates for intensive capitalization. However, these are probably second-order causes of the low demand for labor in the modern sector, on two accounts. First, it is an empirically established fact that many modern production techniques save on all factors of production and are thus superior to the old ones at any factor/price ratio; therefore, correcting "erroneous" prices would have little impact on choice of technology. Second, firms have powerful incentives to reinvest in themselves using modern, capital-intensive technologies in order to maintain their oligopolistic position in the goods markets.

In addition, because these firms are oligopolistic, they face a relatively inelastic demand curve in the goods market. In the short term they can be considered to be restricted by sales in the sense that their effective demand for labor is constrained by insufficient demand for the goods they produce.[10] Thus, in the short term, demand for labor is a given—that is, it does not vary with the price of labor.

The Supply of Labor

The supply of labor, in contrast, is not segmented; but it is composed of individuals with a variety of characteristics who are ranked in ascending order of "quality" and a descending urgency to obtain labor incomes (Llona and Mezzera 1985). The term "quality" is used here in a sense similar to the more general conceptions of human capital theory, that is, those that include experience and other variables as part of human capital, together with formal education.[11] Quality naturally has as its most important component formal qualifications, but it includes more than these. For example, a study by PREALC (1975) measured seven characteristics linked to what we call here labor quality. All were found to influence significantly the determination of the wage-earners' incomes.[12]

The quality variable, defined within the limits of a noncompetitive group, results from the interaction of several characteristics. Some can be changed by the worker and are relatively easy to verify. The best example of these is formal educational attainment. Others also depend on the worker's actions, but are not as easy for the firm to check, such as the specific contents of work experience. Finally, aspects such as natural intelligence and intensity of dedication to one's work cannot be satisfactorily measured *a priori*. Firms rank workers according to these qualities on a continuum with discrete gradations. Workers are also situated on the supply curve in accordance with their own assessment of the wage that corresponds to their quality in the market in question. The choice between remaining unemployed— "standing in line," waiting to find relatively high-income wage-work in the modern sector—or joining the informal sector depends on the urgency with which the worker must earn an income; the difference between the expected wage in the modern sector and expected income in the informal sector; and the possibility of finding wage labor in the formal sector (Todaro 1969; Harris and Todaro 1970). The worker aims to maximize his or her income, within the obvious restrictions of information and processing of that information, by choosing the activity that affords the highest expected income.[13] Those who opt for an informal occupation are, presumably, those for whom earning an income is the most urgent. Although unemployment is voluntary in this approach, belonging to the excess labor supply is not voluntary. Thus, the arguments regarding the nonvoluntary nature of unemployment are applicable to what in this broader scheme we call the nonvoluntary nature of exclusion from formal-sector employment.

Total income of the informal sector depends, no doubt, on the income generated in the modern, formal sector. Empirical research has shown that the capital goods used by informal firms come from the formal sector, even though in most cases they are secondhand or have been adapted for uses other than those for which they were originally intended. Likewise, many of the inputs of the informal sector, for both industrial and commercial firms, come from the formal sector. Therefore, just as a peripheral country needs to export to the center countries in order to purchase from them the capital goods and inputs it needs, so the informal sector as a whole needs to sell to income-earners—firms or workers—from the formal sector to be able to "import" those goods from it. This reasoning led Tokman (1978), for example, to calculate a sort of "balance of trade" between the two sectors.

Within this framework we can say that the total output of the urban informal sector is linked to changes in the formal sector's output. The total income of the UIS is shared by a variable number of informal workers. Their number is some proportion of the urban excess labor supply; but this proportion is not fixed, because it will depend on the variables mentioned above. What is important is that total output does not vary with the number of workers who share it.[14]

Average income in the informal sector cannot be less than the reserve price of labor. The formal-sector wage, in a strict sense, does not exist as an identifiable figure. Between the reserve price for labor in the formal sector and the value of labor productivity in the sector's firms there is room for negotiation between firms and workers, the latter seeking to appropriate a share of the oligopolistic rents generated by the firms.

The Informal Sector and the Economic Adjustment Process

The adjustment process of the segmented labor market begins when the formal sector sets its employment level and negotiates the distribution of wages. At this point workers who are excluded from the formal sector choose between being unemployed and entering the informal sector, on the basis of the criteria set forth above. All the individual decisions taken together simultaneously set the size of informal employment and unemployment, along with the average income level in the informal sector. The dynamics of these relationships throughout the business cycle depend on the evolution of employment and wages in the formal sector.

This section examines the impact of macroeconomic factors on the informal sector, and the concrete effects of the current crisis in Latin America. Let us suppose that wages increase in the formal sector,[15] and that this increase, given the rigidity of the formal sector's demand for labor in the short term, does not induce changes in the employment level in the sector. Some of those who previously opted for employment in the informal sector will tend to seek a formal-sector job whose "premium" is now greater. As a result, on the one hand there will be an increase in the average income of the informal sector, and on the other hand both wages and unemployment will increase.

If we remove the assumption that total income in the informal sector remains constant, and introduce the classical assumption that wage-earners in the formal sector have a greater marginal propensity to consume in the formal sector than do capitalists, increasing wages without changes in the modern-sector employment level will imply an increase in total consumption, part of which will increase the possibilities of generating income in the informal sector.[16] This change implies an increase in the total demand for informal-sector goods and services. So long as no changes are observed in informal-sector employment, there will be an increase in the average income of informal-sector workers, which will make informal-sector employment rise, reducing the number of unemployed. That reduction may partially offset, exactly offset, or more than offset the increase in the unemployment rate that we initially referred to. This mechanism explains why, in the face of changes in the formal-sector wage level, open unemployment may change in an unpredictable direction. Therefore, open unemployment is an extremely ineffective indicator of the labor market in the short term.

This short-term labor market dynamic brings about changes in the cyclical excess labor supply we referred to in the introduction of this chapter. Let us assume that, in the face of growing external restrictions, both unemployment and wages are reduced in the formal sector. Now, the informal sector needs to sell a part of its output to actors in the formal sector, whether they be firms or workers. Yet, it seems reasonable to assume that the vast majority of such sales are to formal-sector wage-earners, because the very characteristics of informal-sector production make it unable to meet the requirements of punctual deliveries, quality control, and others that are typical of production—and the demand for inputs—in modern firms. Therefore, the fall in the mass of wages paid by the formal sector should have a repercussion in the form of decline in total informal-sector income.

Thus, the restrictions on formal employment and wages have generated a fall both in average informal-sector income and in its employment level, which leads to an increase in the unemployment rate. The gross excess labor supply also increases.

In the first four or five years of the 1980s there was a tremendous decline in formal-sector employment in Latin America. If the informal sector is the alternative to unemployment, the drop in modern formal-sector employment must be generating an increase in informal-sector employment. In this sense, the informal sector is the cushion that absorbs a part of the workers displaced from the formal sector; it thus explains why open unemployment rates in Latin America have increased only 2 percent, when output has fallen much more, on average 12 percent.

In Table 3.5, the calculations indicate that from 1981 to 1985 employment in the informal sector increased by approximately one-third, and that the sector's average income fell by approximately one-fourth. The informal sector generates income opportunities that are divided among all who want to join the informal sector, or who were left without work. Therefore, if there is no increase in total informal-sector income, the movement of formal-sector workers to the informal sector causes a fall in the average income of the UIS, which is also reflected in these tables.

TABLE 3.5
Employment and Income in the Informal Sector

	Indexes of Employment in the UIS (for 1985; 1981 base = 100)	Indexes of Average Income per Employed Worker in the UIS (for 1985; 1981 base = 100)
Argentina	131.2	71.9
Brazil	139.3	79.2
Chile	110.7	82.9
Costa Rica	160.4	63.1
Peru	123.9	75.9
Venezuela	135.6	67.9
Average	133.5	73.5

Source: Calculations based on data from the individual countries.

SUMMARY AND CONCLUSIONS

The urban informal sector as discussed in this chapter consists of a heterogeneous set of productive activities. Yet these activities are related by their common situation of employing people who would otherwise be unable to find employment in the modern sector, including a large number of the self-employed, and by having a low capital/labor ratio. These informal economic activities can be classified in two groups: those that compete with firms in the modern sector of the urban economy; and those that insert themselves in "niches" of economic activity not occupied by the modern sector.

Workers in the urban informal sector can also be divided into two groups: the successful informal entrepreneurs who run viable informal sector firms, and workers who are a part of the excess urban labor supply by virtue of their exclusion from formal employment. Those who make up the excess labor supply must choose among three possibilities: to take up low-income informal occupations, to remain unemployed, or to withdraw from the labor force (as part of hidden unemployment). The informal sector is not merely the expression of excess labor supply, but also includes workers who choose not to work in the modern sector. Women make up a significant proportion of those working in the informal sector, in both of these groups.

Demand for Labor

New technologies that are more efficient in their use of labor are quickly adopted by those formal-sector firms financially capable of doing so, cutting out smaller firms (which have extremely limited access to capital) from the competition and creating barriers to entry into the market. The benefits reaped by the oligopolistic, modern firms in the formal sector are shared with their workers in the form of above-market wage rates. This practice has two consequences. The first is the creation of a constant supply of labor for formal-sector firms, because the demand for labor by formal-sector firms is relatively inelastic in relation to the price of labor (it is more dependent on the demand for the firm's output). The second consequence is the necessary acceptance of lower incomes by smaller firm workers whose only other option is unemployment. Thus, the demand for labor, not labor supply, is the cause of labor market segmentation between those workers who share in the oligopolistic rents and those who are excluded from these benefits and generally turn to informal sector activities to survive.

Labor Supply

The supply of labor, on the other hand, is not segmented but is composed of individuals with distinct characteristics. The quality of human capital (for example, education) is certainly important in determining the wage rate of a particular worker, yet there are other factors of consideration. The decision of each individual worker to wait for a better paying job in the modern sector, or to become self-employed in the informal sector, is determined on a case-by-case basis, and his or her final area of employment is dependent on factors such as the urgency of income needs, the difference between expected income from the two sectors, and the probability of finding a job in the modern sector. Overall, it is the imbalance of wealth and the imperfections of the capital market, including unwillingness to lend to small firms, that have inevitably led to the creation of an informal sector of small firms using obsolete production techniques and receiving reduced labor incomes.

Formal and Informal Sectors in Relation to the Business Cycle

Because most firms in the informal sector rely on capital and/or goods from the formal sector, there is an obvious economic relationship between the two sectors. In periods of recession, the contraction of the demand for labor by formal-sector firms decreases demand for informal-sector products that were formerly consumed by formal-sector workers. Contraction of demand for labor by modern firms also decreases the earnings of workers in the informal sector as the proportion of the labor force that must find employment in the sector, and therefore the number of people who will share in the limited income produced there, expands. Because of the current economic crisis in Latin America, between 1981 and 1985 employment in the informal sector increased by approximately one-third, while the average income of those employed in the sector fell by about one-fourth.

NOTES

1. See also Rossini and Thomas' critique (1987) of the Soto's (1986) tenuous statistical basis.

2. This aspect tends to be particularly crucial in the case of migrant workers.

3. There would be no reason for this phenomenon to exist, from the standpoint of capital, if capital markets were "perfect" in a conventional sense; if they were, the optimum strategy for the worker who has accumulated capital would be to continue working for a wage and to participate as an investor in the capital market. The impact of the main imperfections of capital markets in developing countries on segmented labor markets is discussed later in this chapter.

4. The gross excess labor supply has two components: a structural one, which is the surplus that would exist even if the modern sector were working at full installed capacity; and a cyclical one, which is made up of, in addition to the structural component, all who at a given moment do not find work in the modern sector for reasons relating to deficient aggregate demand. In principle, we refer mainly to the structural surplus, leaving consideration of the cyclical component to another section.

5. Pinto (1965) says that the Latin American markets constitute "an economy of the masses—without masses," referring to the fact income distribution is such that only a small percentage of families has access to industrial consumer goods (not food products). This income distribution results in small markets in which the norm is the constant introduction of new varieties, hence the importance of style and fashion.

6. All this implies that, in order for the firms' running excesses to turn to the capital market to offer their excesses there, that market would have to offer them a significant premium above those funds' opportunity cost, which is composed of the marginal yield they would have if reinvested in the family businesses, whether it be the original firm or others belonging to them. In practice, on the other hand, the nominal interest rate is rarely greater than inflation.

7. Assuming that before innovation all the firms had a common oligopolistic margin, the same result is achieved, since the larger firms' total resources for investment will enable them to adopt the new technology, whereas the small ones will be unable to do so.

8. We shall return to this point below.

9. Here we must recall Anibal Pinto's emphasis (1965, 1970) on the linkages between structural heterogeneity—whose expression in the labor market we call segmentation here—and concentration of the benefits of technological progress.

10. Clower (1965), in particular, explains with full neoclassical rigor the reasons why full employment can come about only by chance: because there are no endogenous trends in the system toward achieving equilibrium with full employment of all the factors.

11. To cite Llona and Mezzera (1985, p. 75): "We admit that defining 'quality' is very difficult, perhaps as difficult as defining human capital in the context of that theory; we hope that the reader is as patient with the notion of the 'quality' of labor as he tends to be when it comes to measuring human capital."

12. Four personal characteristics were measured—age, sex, education, and work experience—along with three related to the form of insertion in the labor market: hours worked, branch of economic activity, and size of the firm in which one is employed.

13. Naturally, this idea can be made more sophisticated, as in the Harris-Todaro approach, introducing at least the concepts of noneconomic well-being (for example, the desire not to work for a wage), of nonmonetary income (whose most obvious application is to peasants' incomes, although this can also occur in urban areas), and of career perspectives and discounting from future income. These approaches are not followed explicitly in the text because they do not affect the essence of the argument.

14. This formulation is made in the spirit of the "income-sharing" models that describe the behavior of peasants in the traditional rural sector; adaptation of that spirit to the informal sector is valid because it deals with the *modus operandi* of the two traditional sectors (one rural, the other urban) in which the rules of maximization of the modern capitalist sector are not applicable.

15. There is no "single" modern-sector wage but rather a distribution of them, because the differentials among wage levels in the modern sectors are relatively rigid.

16. Discarding, naturally, the unreal possibility that the informal goods and services are "Giffen goods," that is, those that have negative income elasticity.

4

Small-Scale Commerce in the City of La Paz, Bolivia

SILVIA ESCOBAR

COMMERCE IN THE URBAN LABOR MARKET IN BOLIVIA

Beginning in the 1970s, commerce began to account for an ever-increasing share of total employment in Bolivian cities, especially in the city of La Paz. The annual growth rate of employment in commerce rose from an average 1.3 percent for 1950–70 to 4.7 percent for 1970–5, and averaged 12.0 percent between 1976 and 1983. The combined impact of the economic crisis that began to manifest itself in the late 1980s and the general recession—especially contraction of the industrial sector—has led to a progressive increase in excess labor supply and a strong concomitant expansion of tertiary-sector activities, especially in small-scale commerce of consumer goods. Because of the relative ease of access to these activities, both in terms of financial and technical considerations, thousands of women and men have found in commerce a source of personal or family income, enabling them to meet their basic consumer needs.

With the worsening of the economic crisis of the 1980s, more and more women have been turning to economic activity. In La Paz, the percentage of women who are economically active has increased from 28 percent to 44 percent, as a result primarily of the rise in self-generated employment in commerce; the same growth pattern has occurred to a lesser degree in personal services and cottage industries. The significant increase in employment in commerce in La Paz and other Bolivian cities clearly reflects the greater participation of women in the sector. As Table 4.1 illustrates, by 1983 practically one of every two women employed in La Paz (45 percent) worked in commerce (INE 1976, 1983).

TABLE 4.1
La Paz: Commerce as a Percentage of Total Employment, by Sex, 1976–83

Sex	1976	1983
Men	10.7	14.4
Women	28.4	45.0
Total	16.3	27.4

Source: National Population and Housing Census, INE, 1976; Permanent Household Survey, INE, 1983.

Because of the inability of the Latin American economies, and in particular the Bolivian economy, to generate employment with high levels of investment, a large part of urban economic activity and employment is concentrated in the informal sector. In this context, commerce is of particular importance, its activities structured basically around very small economic units, with small capital endowments, minimal formalization of organizational structure, and limited importance of wages as a form of remuneration. As Table 4.2 illustrates, in La Paz some 90 percent of those employed in commerce work in the UIS; 76 percent work in family economic units where work is organized around a single independent worker or a self-employed worker who, in some cases, is supported by other members of his or her family group. The remaining 13 percent of vendors make up a semi-entrepreneurial segment as owner-operators or wage workers.

Research carried out by the Centro de Estudios para el Desarrollo Laboral y Agrario (CEDLA) in the city of La Paz focused on family businesses within the UIS, making it possible to assess in approximate terms the main characteristics of the economic units and self-employed vendors. Because of its economic and organizational characteristics, this segment, which encompasses 76 percent of all persons employed in commerce, is an adequate approximation of microcommerce.

In contrast to other commercial strata, one of the distinguishing features of microcommerce is the great ease of access for new entrants, both because of financial reasons and because of the limited organizational qualifications needed. A large number of the economic units can be established with very little working capital. There are no major problems in terms of location: this can be established in the owner's home, in markets, or in the streets. Given the small scale of their transactions, microvendors do not need to be highly qualified. The appearance and progressive growth of the number of self-employed microvendors respond, above all, to a survival strategy adopted by an important part of the population of active age as an alternative to inactivity or open unemployment. They opt to generate their own jobs, taking advantage of market opportunities to sell some products,

TABLE 4.2

La Paz: Total Employment and Employment in Commerce by Sectors of the Labor Market, 1980–83 (in percent)

	1980		1983	
Sectors	Total Employment	Commercial Employment	Total Employment	Commercial Employment
Formal	*43.1*	*15.2*	*37.2*	*11.2*
Public	22.0	0.1	19.5	0.6
Private	21.0	15.1	17.8	10.6
Informal	*51.5*	*84.8*	*57.2*	*88.8*
Semi-entrepreneurial	15.8	10.6	19.5	12.8
Family	35.7	74.2	37.7	76.0
Domestic Service	5.4	—	5.4	—
Total	100.0	100.0	100.0	100.0

Source: Urban Migration and Employment Survey (EUME, 1980); ILO/FUNAP, Ministry of Labor and Labor Development, 1980; Permanent Household Survey (EPH), INE, 1983.

since neither the state nor the modern firms provide them the means for their survival.

This chapter gives a detailed picture of informal commerce in the capital city of Bolivia, La Paz. It draws on data gathered by CEDLA in research carried out in 1983 on self-employed workers in La Paz (Casanovas 1985). The method used to compile the data is that of a mixed survey of household establishments of self-employed workers, that is, households with at least one independent worker, whether head of the household or not. The sample size was 450 units.

Based on the results of the research project, this chapter analyzes the characteristics of microcommerce from the double standpoint of employment and establishments, differentiating between units run by women and those run by men. It also outlines some policy recommendations, with a view to improving the incomes and living conditions of the women and men employed in the informal sector.

Microvendors: Numbers and Characteristics

From 1976 to 1983 the number of self-employed microvendors in La Paz increased by 70 percent, and the number of female microvendors increased by 83 percent (see Table 4.3). Typically, more women than men work as microvendors. In 1983, of 41,615 microvendors in the city of La Paz, 71 percent were women. The following are some of the main reasons why women are involved to a greater degree than men in small-scale commerce:

- Self-employed commercial activities do not demand, in most cases, a stable schedule or a fixed location.

- Such work can be done in the home itself. Therefore, working as a microvendor does not have to conflict with the traditional female role of homemaker and childrearer. Even in cases where the activity demands being outside the home, working as a microvendor permits a certain flexibility in the work day and may involve taking the children to the place of work.

- The low levels of schooling and qualifications generally found among poor urban women limit their incorporation into other sectors of the labor market in which these attributes (among others) play an important role.

- The lack of capital and of access to credit and training are obstacles to diversification to other types of nonwage work within the UIS. Therefore, employment opportunities for urban women tend to be limited to commerce and domestic service, which constitute an extension of domestic work into the market. In this context, only the most qualified women have access to public services and the private entrepreneurial sector.

Female microvendors tend to be somewhat older than other women in the work force. According to EHCTP and INE surveys (1983), the average age of a microvendor is 38, five years older than that of the female economically active population in general. This difference can be explained by at least two factors. First, the self-employed, especially women, tend to join the sector at an older age, once they have gained a certain familiarity with the market and have generated—through personal or family savings—a small sum of start-up capital. And second, this age structure reflects the minimal occupational mobility of microvendors, who have worked in the sector an average of more than ten years; the structure is especially true of those who have a fixed place of work and have consolidated their operations. Because of the institutional requirements for access to fixed stalls, and also because of the inability of the existing infrastructure to make room for new entrants to the sector, most young and new vendors work as street vendors.

TABLE 4.3
La Paz: Microvendors by Sex, 1976–83

Sex	1976	Percentage	1983	Percentage	Percentage Increase
Men	8,280	33.8	12,054	29.0	45.6
Women	16,185	66.2	29,561	71.0	82.6
Total	24,465	100.0	41,615	100.0	70.1

Source: Survey of Households of Self-Employed Workers, EHTCP, 1983.

Forty-three percent of microvendors are heads of households, including 80 percent of the men and 32 percent of the women. The percentage of female microvendors who are heads of households is similar to that of the female economically active population (EAP) as a whole, but higher than the percentage for all women. This finding indicates that most of the working women in La Paz belong to the "secondary" labor force (not heads of households), seeking employment to complement the family income. At the same time, a significant number of women microvendors—almost a third—are heads of households.

Most of the women recently incorporated into small-scale commerce are from households headed by another independent worker whose income, because of the impact of the crisis, is not enough to cover household living expenses. Nonetheless, the fact that one of every three women microvendors and 80 percent of the men are heads of households is a clear expression of the importance of incomes from small-scale commerce in reproducing the labor force of families in this sector.

As is the case with the EAP as a whole and with self-employed workers (SEW), the proportion of migrants in microcommerce is slightly above that of persons originally from La Paz (EHTCP 1983). In all of these cases, approximately 53 percent of the employed population, as of 1983, was accounted for by migrants, an indication that members of the surplus labor force who seek self-employment, in commerce and other activities, are not only migrants, but also members of the broad sectors of the local La Paz population excluded from job opportunities in the modern sector.

The most significant difference between migrants working in commerce and those in the rest of the EAP is their place of origin. Seventy percent of migrants working in commerce come from rural areas, which contrasts with 57 percent of the EAP as a whole. This feature, together with the older average age of the men and women of the sector, contributes to a lower educational profile among microvendors. They have, on average, 2.5 years less schooling than the average for the EAP. Similarly, there is an important difference within the sector, with women having, on average, less schooling than men: 18 percent of women, as compared to 6 percent of men, had no education in the formal school system. Women microvendors have an average of only 4 years of education.

Occupational Changes and Length of Time in Occupation

An examination of the previous work experience of microvendors, going back to their first job in the city of La Paz, indicates that 60 percent (in similar proportions for men and women) began their employment experience in commerce: 50 percent entered as self-employed workers, and 10 percent as wage-earners or as unpaid family workers. Twenty-nine percent originally worked in services, most of these being women whose first job was domestic service. A large percentage of migrant women—who initially joined the work force in domestic service—had no choice but to leave their jobs and seek other ways of contributing to the family income when they established their households. These women generally become involved in those small-scale commerce activities in which requirements for capital, experience, and qualifications are relatively low. Thirty percent of the female microvendors have had such an occupational history.

Finally, only 11 percent of the current microvendors originally worked in industry as wage workers. In those cases in which there has been mobility, whether among sectors of the economy or occupational categories, the most important cause has been related to the precarious status of the first job in terms of working conditions and income. This cause was identified primarily by women who worked in domestic service, the servile connotations and low incomes of which are apparent; and by those microvendors who previously worked in artisan activities where the regulations of the general labor code were not adhered to. Both groups of vendors account for the largest share of those who had changed occupations since initiating their working life (see Table 4.4).

Microvendors, particularly those who have been able to obtain a fixed location or stall on sidewalks and in markets, work in this capacity for an average of ten years. The absence of employment opportunities and the limited availability of capital, resources, qualifications, and experience, all on the supply side, contribute to a certain stability of the vendors in their occupation. Even in the marginal stratum of commerce, vendors remain in the

TABLE 4.4
**Main Economic Sectors and Occupational Categories
of Microvendors (First Job)**

Breakdown	Percentage
Commerce	*59.8*
Self-employed	49.2
White collar worker	6.1
Unremunerated family worker	3.0
Worker	1.5
Services	*28.8*
Domestic worker	21.2
White collar worker	3.8
Self-employed	2.3
Blue collar worker	1.5
Industry	*11.3*
Blue collar worker	8.3
Self-employed	3.0
Total	100.0

Source: Survey of Households of Self-Employed Workers, EHTCP, 1983.

occupation over long periods of time, to avoid open unemployment. In some cases, when faced with declining demand, they may be forced to take a different course and reduce the scale of their sales, as long as their available capital enables them to do so; others dedicate themselves to commerce based on the divisibility of certain products, selling very small quantities, such as individual cigarettes. Finally, when the situation is more critical and decapitalization is almost total, they may opt to subordinate themselves completely to middlemen, becoming semi-wage workers of their suppliers. All these strategies explain in some way the job stability of small-scale vendors; these same strategies, with some variations in form, are analogous to the struggle waged by independent workers to continue working as such, often at the cost of greater underemployment or overexploitation.

Economic Characteristics and Operations

Internal Composition and Economic Function

Microcommerce is mainly oriented toward the sale of products that make up the basket of basic household consumption goods. As Table 4.5 illustrates, 62 percent of the vendors sell food products (household staples and agricultural products); the sale of other articles for use and consumption, and processed foods, accounts in each case for only 12 percent of employment. The breakdown of microvendors by sex shows that women specialize in the sale of basic wage goods, while men are more involved in the sale of nonessential consumer goods.

Given the number of people employed in petty commerce and the fact that it takes place throughout the city, such activities play a key role in the distribution of commodities in La Paz; and above all, they play a central role in the reproduction of the labor force by generating income for microvendors. Furthermore, petty commerce plays a functional role, complementary to formal sector production and commerce because it constitutes a vast

TABLE 4.5
La Paz: Microvendors by Goods Sold, and by Sex, 1983

Goods Sold	Total	Percent	Men (29%)	Percent	Women (71%)	Percent
Household staples	14,924	35.9	4,018	33.3	10,906	36.9
Agricultural products	10,906	26.2	2,870	23.9	8,036	27.2
Clothes	5,740	13.8	861	7.1	4,879	16.5
Processed foods	4,879	11.7	287	2.4	4,592	15.5
Other products	5,166	12.4	4,018	33.3	1,148	3.9
Total	41,615	100.0	12,054	100.0	29,561	100.0

Source: Survey of Households of Self-Employed Workers, EHTCP, 1983.
  Note: Includes only self-employed workers. In 1983 there were just over 8,000 people, mostly women, employed in commerce as nonremunerated family members.

intermediary network that enables formal distributors to avoid expenditures on infrastructure, transportation, labor, and other costs required for the circulation of commodities. Likewise, by allowing for rapid circulation of products it indirectly favors the faster turnover of capital and thus increases formal-sector profits and accumulation.

Organization of Small-Scale Commerce

Location and Structure. Commerce is one of the most flexible economic activities in terms of the infrastructure required for start-up. Eighty-eight percent of small-scale vendors in La Paz operate in the streets, in stalls, or as street vendors, or establish themselves in their homes. In this way they can deal with their lack of capital, which, because of its limited size, can be used only for their operations. Few vendors, among them the most stable and those with the highest levels of capitalization, have a locale outside the home used exclusively for their business (see Table 4.6).

TABLE 4.6
**La Paz: Microvendors by Location and Type of Locale,
1983 (in percent)**

Location and Type of Locale	Total	Men	Women
Established locale in the home	29.5	37.6	26.2
Established locale outside the home	12.5	12.0	12.8
Stall in street or market	38.0	12.0	48.4
Street vendor (no fixed locale)	20.0	38.4	12.6
Total	100.0	100.0	100.0

Source: Survey of Households of Self-Employed Workers, EHTCP, 1983.

In La Paz, sidewalk and market stalls are the most common type of workplace among female vendors. Almost 50 percent of women vendors operate under these circumstances. Obtaining a fixed location often results from spontaneous occupation of the public streets or municipal properties that later become markets or stalls through municipal ordinances that permit the operations in exchange for an annual fee (municipal permit) plus payment of a daily sum (*sentaje*) that legitimizes use of the space for sales in the eyes of the municipality. A few years ago, women in La Paz held almost all the market stalls used for selling agricultural products and household staples; today there is a ratio of four female vendors for every male vendor operating such stalls.

Parallel to the distinction in the types of goods they sell, it is more common for men to work as street vendors and in locales established in their homes; but 26 percent of female vendors also work from their homes. This form of microcommerce is more common among older vendors, independent of the length of time they have been working as vendors (retirees and older people cannot compete with other members of the work force for the few jobs generated in other forms of microcommerce); or in sectors of the economy in which wage employment predominates. In La Paz there is one neighborhood store for every seventeen households, counting only those stores that are operated exclusively by family members.

In contrast, street vendors who are found primarily in areas of heavy transit, that is, around markets and downtown areas of the city where it is possible for products to circulate more rapidly, tend to be the younger vendors. Because most male vendors are heads of households, they attempt to shelter themselves from excessive competition by establishing mobile stands.

The rapid growth in the number of vendors in recent years has not been accompanied by government expansion of the physical infrastructure, which might make possible the gradual absorption of vendors precariously installed along the city streets. New vendors, in growing numbers, work the busiest streets and thoroughfares in the early morning and at night, because of repression from the municipal government during normal working hours. In practice, possession of a stall "legalizes" commercial activity and provides greater security and stability; thus, despite the precarious state of the stalls, women vendors value them and wage a never-ending struggle to obtain them. This lack of change is not the case with male vendors, who, with some exceptions, tend to view commercial activity simply as short-term employment and therefore are less likely to enter the competition for physical space for their work. Eighty-seven percent work in the same type of locale as when they first entered microcommerce. This lack of change reflects their minimal capacity to generate profits or, in any event, to channel them into upgrading their installations.

Availability of Capital. The marginal character of most economic units in this sector of commerce is evident in their reduced levels of capital investment. Two-thirds of microvendors have investments less than or equal to US$100 ($B100-$B50,000). Nevertheless, there is an important differentiation to be made in investment levels, which reflects the internal heterogeneity among self-employed vendors. Fourteen percent have capital ranging from US$200 to US$2,000 (see Table 4.7).

Available data do not permit an analysis of differences in investment by sex. Nonetheless, if we bear in mind that two of every three microvendors are female, the distribution shown in Table 4.7 should reflect to a significant degree the capital endowment of women.

Vendors of agricultural products and processed foods tend to be concentrated in the lowest investment brackets, whereas a larger percentage of vendors (mostly men) of "other products"—clothes, and to a lesser extent groceries—have relatively larger capital endowments.

Female vendors are concentrated in the categories with smaller capital investment, such as the sale of agricultural products, processed foods, and

TABLE 4.7

La Paz: Microvendors by Capital Invested and Goods Sold, 1983 (in percent)

Capital Invested (in $B)[a]	Total	Groceries	Agricultural Production	Clothes	Processed Foods	Others
100–10,000	27.1	26.0	37.8	5.0	58.8	11.1
10,001–20,000	9.5	4.0	10.8	15.0	5.9	16.6
20,001–50,000	29.2	36.0	29.8	30.0	23.5	11.2
50,001–100,000	20.0	18.0	16.2	35.0	5.9	27.8
100,001–1,000,000	12.1	14.0	5.4	15.0	5.9	22.8
1,000,000 or more	2.1	2.0	—	—	—	11.1
Percentage of Women[b]	100.0	36.9	27.2	16.5	15.5	3.9
Total	100.0	100.0	100.0	100.0	100.0	100.0

Source: Survey of Households of Self-Employed Workers, EHTCP, 1983.

a $B500.00 = US$1.00.

b Women as percentage of total employment for each category.

groceries. The close link among capital invested, rate of return, and income casts some doubt on whether these activities constitute a viable occupational alternative for women. In conditions of accelerating growth in the number of female vendors and a general economic decline, competition among new entrants to the sector and the lack of growth in demand for their products lead to a progressive reduction of profit margins, which causes extreme underutilization of this segment of the labor force.

Organization of Work. As is generally the case with other small-scale economic activities in La Paz, in commerce participation of other members of the family group is somewhat limited. One of every five microvendors has the active support of a family member in some phase of the work (supply, service to customers, or other areas). Participation of other family members is more common when the activity operates out of the home and thus facilitates part-time help. However, the fact that most of the establishments are one-person operations is more closely related to the limited scale of operations, which does not require more intensive use of labor.

Supply, Marketing, and Markets

The products sold by retail vendors tend to be domestically produced. Imported products, mostly luxury goods, spare parts, and tools, are usually marketed by economic units in the semi-entrepreneurial sectors. Contrary to the image of the microvendor, only 20 percent concentrate on sales of foreign products, most of which are smuggled into the country (clothes, toiletries, cosmetics, liquor, cigarettes, and so forth).

Microvendors in La Paz acquire the products they sell mainly through wholesale middlemen and, to a lesser extent, from other small-scale merchants. Direct purchasing links with the industrial sector are quite weak and there are few direct purchases from peasant farmers.

The forms of supply are closely linked to the total working capital with which the microvendors operate, which forces them to buy from middlemen in small quantities—on a daily or weekly basis—at generally higher prices. This practice obviously diminishes their profit margins.

Since 1983, because of staggering inflation it has become practically impossible for microvendors to obtain credit from suppliers. Thus, they must generally make purchases in cash, and in small volume; these limitations explain in part their weak relationship with the industrial sector at that time. At present, there are no signs of a change in supply channels, but recent research has indicated a certain change in forms of payment; that is, suppliers have become more flexible in selling on credit, though in small quantities and for a very short time.

Among the main supply problems that microvendors pointed out were high prices, scarcity of certain items, and long distances to suppliers, all of which had a clear impact of reducing the total volume of purchases and increasing their frequency and cost.

Seventy-six percent of the buyers of products sold by microvendors are the end-users, who are primarily from the urban and rural poor and the middle-class. Approximately 90 percent of the vendors report that their customers come from these social strata. Fourteen percent, in addition to selling to the general public, sell to other merchants, primarily street vendors.

Noted Problems.   Problems such as competition from other vendors, declining demand, and falling profit margins indicate that the sector's ability to absorb new members is offset by a diminishing level of activity and income for all employed therein. According to some authors, in the case of the UIS commerce more than other activities involves growing absorption with persistent underemployment.

Access to Credit and Sources of Financing

Microvendors, like all self-employed workers and other small proprietors in the UIS, have extremely limited access to credit. Capital resources have traditionally been channeled to the various activities of the modern sector, and within these to speculative activities. Table 4.8 illustrates the difficulties UIS economic units, particularly vendors, face in providing the required individual guarantees and collateral and in paying the high interest rates prevailing in a system not designed to attend specifically to their credit needs.

In the last year of operations, only eight of every one hundred self-employed workers surveyed received credit, whether in cash or in kind. In 80 percent of the cases this credit came from informal sources (suppliers and friends or relatives). Among microvendors this percentage is slightly higher, given that they are able to obtain credit in the form of products. Nevertheless, their access is still quite limited: only thirteen of every one hundred vendors obtained some credit in the last year of operations; nine of these thirteen obtained this credit in the form of commodities. Both monetary credit and advances of products came primarily from informal channels,

TABLE 4.8
**La Paz: Access to and Sources of Credit, Microvendors, 1983
(in the last year of operations)**

Access to Credit	Total	Private Banks	Suppliers	Money-lenders	Friends/ Relatives	Government Institutions
Microvendors	13.1					
	100.0	5.2	58.0	10.5	26.3	—
In cash	4.2					
	100.0	15.5	33.3	35.0	16.2	—
In products	8.9					
	100.0	—	69.2	—	30.8	—
Total SEW	8.1					
	100.0	6.7	48.5	13.5	29.0	2.3

Source: Survey of Households of Self-Employed Workers, EHTCP, 1983.

whether from suppliers, moneylenders, or friends and relatives. No vendor reported having obtained any institutional credit. These findings reflect the complete absence of lines of credit—with some exceptions among productive activities—for the tertiary sector of the UIS.

The few vendors who have recourse to informal credit are subject to conditions such as the following: credit is extended for brief periods, ranging from one week to three months; amounts loaned are quite small; and for loans from moneylenders, interest rates are high.

For those who did obtain credit, the breakdown by size of loans clearly shows that the vendors receive tiny loans, ranging from an equivalent of US$10 to US$20. In 1983, almost half had obtained a loan no larger than US$20 (see Table 4.9).

TABLE 4.9
La Paz: Amount of Credit Obtained by Microvendors, 1983

Amount of Credit (in $B)^a	Percent
Up to 5,000	36.8
5,001–10,000	10.5
10,001–30,000	31.6
30,001–100,000	5.3
100,000 or more	15.8

Source: Survey of Households of Self-Employed Workers, EHTCP, 1983.
^{a} $B500.00 = US$1.00.

The vendors interviewed indicated that one of the main obstacles to obtaining credit, which is directly related to the absence of credit sources, is their lack of information regarding possible sources of development credit; they also noted that the guarantees required and high interest rates are further obstacles to obtaining institutional credit.

Structure and Level of Incomes

Data on income are pertinent to this analysis, despite the well-known problems of reliability of such data owing to factors such as inaccuracy of income and the close connection between sales and family consumption in this sector. However, we should note that the income levels declared by microvendors in 1983 were very much affected by the economic conditions prevailing at that time. Also, undersupply of products for meeting basic needs introduced a distortion in the population's consumption levels, thereby temporarily increasing demand to ensure the availability of these products during the most severe shortages. The very scarcity of certain basic products enabled microvendors to turn over their capital more rapidly, and even to speculate on a small scale. Both phenomena, which are closely intercon-

TABLE 4.10

La Paz: Average Income of Microvendors, by Capital Invested, 1983

Capital Invested (in $B)[a]	Average Income per Week	Percentage of Microvendors
100–10,000	2,373	27.1
10,001–20,000	3,475	9.5
20,001–50,000	4,561	29.2
50,001–100,000	10,871	20.0
100,001–1,000,000	6,206	12.1
1,000,000 or more	26,833	2.1
Total	5,738	100.0

Source: Survey of Households of Self-Employed Workers, EHTCP, 1983.
  [a] $B500.00 = US$1.00.

nected, help explain the relatively higher incomes of microvendors in 1983 as compared to other self-employed workers (see Table 4.10).

While self-employed workers in La Paz had an average weekly income of $B5,363 in 1983 (equivalent to 1.3 times the minimum wage income), vendors received $B5,738 on average. Vendors of nonessential products ("other products"), agricultural products, and clothing received average incomes that were substantially higher than the average for all vendors, and than the average for independent workers.

One noteworthy aspect is the difference between men's and women's incomes. The average income of female vendors was only 62 percent of the average for their male counterparts. Given the close relationship between investment and income, this difference can be attributed largely to the lower capital endowment of women's businesses as compared to those of men, for even within the same category of commerce there is a tendency for women vendors to earn less profit.

Expressing the weekly income in terms of the minimum wage clearly shows that, despite the fact that their average income is above the legal mini-

TABLE 4.11

La Paz: Income of Microvendors in Terms of the Minimum Wage Income (MWI) by Sex, 1983 (in percent)

Income Equivalent	Total	Men	Women
Less than 0.5 MWI	27.4	7.1	36.3
0.5 to 1 MWI	34.6	28.6	37.3
1 MWI	9.4	11.9	8.3
1 to 2 MWI	17.0	33.0	9.8
Over 2 MWI	11.5	19.4	8.3
Total	100.0	100.0	100.0

Source: Survey of Households of Self-Employed Workers, EHTCP, 1983.

mum wage, the majority of microvendors, and particularly women, earn very low incomes. As Table 4.11 illustrates, 71 percent of all vendors—47.6 percent of the men and 82 percent of the women—had an income in 1983 of less than they would have had working at the minimum wage. If we take into account the transitory "bonanza" in incomes for some, it is clear that jobs in commerce, especially for women, are of a marginal character.

Beginning in 1983, the number of vendors increased considerably. After 1985, growth in the number of vendors intensified, particularly among street vendors and market vendors. This growth, along with declining wages and plummeting demand, tended to worsen the economic situation of microvendors who had previously consolidated their operations.

Microvendor Organizations

Microvendors, especially those who work in markets and stalls, have their own union-type organizations, which are affiliated with a central organization: the Federación de Gremiales y Comerciantes Minoristas. This Federation also encompasses larger-scale merchants who, given their volume of capital and operations, cannot be considered part of the UIS. As is the case for all organizations that have an economically differentiated membership, the best organized and most powerful unions within the Federation are those made up of the merchants with more capital. Although the microvendors' demands are brought before the central organization, its leaders do not always bring them to the national or local authorities.

For almost thirty years women market vendors in La Paz have had an organizational system parallel to the trade organization through which they establish a direct relationship with the municipal government to resolve the day-to-day problems regarding municipal permits, general services, and problems of placing new vendors accepted by the trade organization, or hindering their placement, as the case may be. They annually elect a representative called the *Maestra Mayor,* who deals directly with vendors and passes on their demands to the municipal government.

Notwithstanding the existence of such organizations, only 40 percent of the small-scale vendors, mostly those placed in markets, indicate that they have any knowledge of them. As a result, affiliation and active participation in such organizations are limited. Only 24 percent of the vendors—21.5 percent of the men, and 25 percent of the women—state that they are affiliated with a union or *maestradillo,* and even this affiliation does not necessarily mean that they actively participate in the organization. It is precisely the minimal degree of participation in these associations that explains why only a small percentage of microvendors, even when they are actually members, consider themselves to be affiliated.

The constant internal conflicts affecting the existing organizations (ranging from problems of representation to political and union problems), together with the extreme dispersion of the vendors, make it impossible to mobilize and incorporate vendors further into these organizations. These factors also hinder organic, solid, efficient, and representative development of the organizations. Such hindrance is reflected in a serious inability to undertake collective actions aimed at promoting and defending the organizations' interests.

CONCLUSIONS AND RECOMMENDATIONS

In recent years microcommerce has become an important source of employment and income in Bolivia's main cities. The small capital base and limited training required for entering this activity, as well as the opportunities offered by the markets, have led many women to become involved in microcommerce. The ease of entry into this stratum of commerce is accompanied by a high degree of competition that tends to bring down the incomes of all employed in the sector. This finding is especially true for street vendors, who account for a larger share of "new" vendors. In 1983, 77 percent of all vendors—48 percent of the men and 82 percent of the women—earned incomes below the minimum wage level.

Although employment positions can be generated with low capital investment, microcommerce is still far from constituting a homogeneous sector. Some of the small-scale vendors who have consolidated their operations have a physical space or fixed location for sales, have won a market share, and generate surplus to reinvest in their business, reaching higher investment levels than the average for the sector.

Others, also consolidated in the sector, are just eking out an existence. They continue to work in microcommerce to generate an income that contributes in part to covering the costs required for their reproduction. For these vendors, advancing their business generally requires extreme privation in other areas of consumption, such as housing, education, and health. Finally, a smaller group of microvendors is employed in commerce on a transitory basis, awaiting another activity, either as independent workers or as wage workers. Within these broad groups we can also make distinctions based on location, stability, availability of capital, income, and capacity to generate surplus.

Of all the problems that microvendors face, their limited working capital and lack of access to credit are perhaps the most important. Moreover, they are located in highly competitive markets, given the explosive increase in the number of vendors and the progressive fall in demand, which tends to drastically reduce their incomes. All these factors are reflected in permanent instability and insecurity of incomes, extension of the working day beyond its normal bounds, and progressive decapitalization.

In addition, vendors face the growing problem of an increase in competition and thus a decrease in possible locales, and are subject to constant repression by the municipal government. In a recessionary situation, such as the present one, the factors that affect small-scale commercial activities and the incomes earned by those employed in such activities are related more to macroeconomic factors than to limitations on the supply side. In this regard, as an effect of the widespread recession in economic activity, parallel to the entry of new individuals to employment in the sector and the decline in the population's wages and income, there has been a significant reduction in the aggregate volume of sales, which affects all segments and categories of small-scale commerce, aggravating the situation of underpayment and poverty.

In this regard, actions to promote small-scale commercial activity should be oriented to improving the incomes of those already employed rather than expanding capacity to generate additional employment, because of the saturation of the sector in terms of the number of persons employed. Nonetheless, considering the size and internal heterogeneity of the sector and of its differential perspectives for future development, a certain selectivity of the individuals for promotion and actions to be taken is indispensable.

First, the support programs should place a priority on those categories in which the main basic consumer goods are sold, and of these, those that promote circulation of domestically produced goods (household staples, agricultural products, clothes, artisan production of household durables). If these sales lines are chosen, the participants in interventions would be mainly women, and generally those vendors with less capital and those who do not have an established locale (that is, those with stalls in streets and on sidewalks, and street vendors), as they usually distribute such items.

Given the minimal experience in Bolivia with implementing specific programs to support informal-sector activities in general, and commerce in particular, it is advisable to consider implementation of small pilot projects for promotion which, within the subset identified above, would encompass in the first place, heads of households—both men and women—who have worked for a certain length of time and have acquired a certain level of experience in the sector, in order to guarantee success of the actions proposed.

A second line of action, oriented to improving the incomes of people working in the sector, is clearly to create opportunities for access to development loans, which would enable microvendors who have consolidated their operations to have a larger sum of working capital. Given microvendors' usual scale of operations, the loans required would generally be small. Therefore, it is important to design credit programs in line with the economic and sociocultural characteristics of microvendors, that is, to sidestep current institutional obstacles and complex procedures and deal with the central problem posed by the inability of these individuals to post collateral.

Programs of this nature, which can be undertaken by social promotion institutions, whether public or private, should be accompanied by programs offering training in areas related to achieving greater efficiency in all phases of the work process: supply, marketing, and organization in all forms (associations, trade unions, and federations). Training programs should also consider motivation for the establishment of associative organizations that would make it possible to use promotional actions with greater success.

Given the importance of women in small-scale commerce, there is also a need for specific actions to improve their precarious working conditions. These include construction of new markets in those areas where the largest number of sidewalk stalls are located; establishment of day-care centers near areas of work; and improvement of sanitary services in the markets. These services, which are demanded of the municipal government day after day, can be made a reality with the participation and complementary self-help efforts of the women vendors themselves.

Although such programs can contribute in part to improving the incomes and working conditions of some of the microvendors, it is only through reactivation of local and national production, and improvement of the income levels of the wage-earning labor force, that the growth of employment in commerce can be curbed, thereby making it possible for all those working in the informal sector to improve their incomes and standard of living.

5

Solidarity Group Programs:
A Working Methodology for Enhancing the Economic Activities of Women in the Informal Sector

MARÍA OTERO

C redit programs that serve microenterprises often provide assistance through "solidarity groups." This chapter explores some of the characteristics and results of microenterprise programs in Latin America which use the solidarity group mechanism, discusses how these programs affect women microentrepreneurs, and suggests areas for research and alternatives for program design and implementation.*

The first successful efforts of agencies using solidarity groups include those of PRIDECO/FEDECCREDITO in El Salvador, a combination of a community development agency and a credit union; the Working Women's Forum in India, a local private nonprofit organization; and the Grameen Bank in Bangladesh, a semi-private development bank that works with the rural poor (Farbman 1981; World Bank 1985). These pioneer efforts demonstrate that credit and other services can reach large numbers of the urban and rural poor who are engaged in small-scale economic activities even while keeping costs low, using a relatively small paraprofessional staff, and achieving high payback rates (Fraser and Tucker 1981; Chen 1983; World Bank 1985).

---

*This chapter is based on a larger document the author prepared on the solidarity group concept, its characteristics, and implications for working with the urban poor at the request of Private Agencies Collaborating Together (PACT). See María Otero, "The Solidarity Group Concept: Its Characteristics and Significance for Urban Informal Sector Activities." New York: PACT, 1986.

These programs suggest that project costs can be lowered, responsiveness increased, and beneficiary commitment to the program enhanced, if beneficiaries assume responsibility for as many aspects of the program as possible such as promotion, selection, group formation, group coordination, and loan repayment. The process of involving the beneficiary in the operation of the program strengthens the cohesion of the solidarity groups that are formed and reinforces each group's ability to operate collectively (Chen 1983; World Bank 1985). In the case of El Salvador and India, these programs led to both information exchange and, more significantly, emergence of service and advocacy organizations among program participants (Fraser and Tucker 1981; Brown 1981).

ACCION International/AITEC, a U.S.-based nonprofit organization that works in Latin America with programs of microenterprise development, studied the solidarity group experiences and adapted the methodology for use with its counterpart institutions. As a result, there are currently over fifteen institutions in nine Latin America countries which rely on solidarity groups to reach large numbers of the urban poor with credit, training, and organizing skills (Otero 1986). In the last five years these organizations have developed considerable expertise and completed valuable documentation on the solidarity group approach that has been used in the preparation of this chapter.

CHARACTERISTICS OF SOLIDARITY GROUPS

General Features

Solidarity groups generally consist of five to eight members—producers or vendors usually engaged in similar activities—who organize themselves into a group in order to participate in a program of credit and training. To form the group, microentrepreneurs turn to acquaintances they know well enough to guarantee collectively the loan made to the group through the program.

When an individual microentrepreneur approaches an institution to seek credit, she or he is urged to form a group among colleagues, and then to apply for a group loan to be divided among the members equally, or as the group decides. It may also happen that the program field workers, or "promoters," as they make their daily rounds visiting program participants, will motivate prospective borrowers to form themselves into groups. Once a self-selected group is formed, its members receive training and guidance from the promoter to help consolidate the group in a formal manner, select a coordinator, and prepare the members to operate as a group. At this stage, the group members and the promoter develop a credit application based on a simple analysis of the members' needs, and on each individual's ability to repay the loan. These loans can begin as small as US$50 per member and grow to US$300–$400 over time. The promoter explains the terms of the loan, discusses the importance of timely repayment, and helps the group understand the responsibility it is undertaking.

Each loan application undergoes an established review procedure within the organization. If the loan is approved, a check is disbursed to the group coordinator, who then divides the loan among group members. In most programs, the time that elapses between loan application and loan disbursement oscillates between five and eight working days (Otero 1986). The coordinator later collects the weekly loan payments from members and pays the institution. If the loan is repaid on time, the group can receive a subsequent loan, on the same day, for the same or a slightly higher amount. Because the group members serve as guarantors for éach other's loans, no collateral or other guarantee is required from them. It is the insistence on collateral by traditional lending institutions that often excludes many microentrepreneurs, especially women, from credit programs (Lycette 1984).

Institutions that utilize solidarity groups in their work adapt the group mechanism to reflect their own philosophy, and add to it components that have proved effective in their own development experience (Reichmann 1984c; López Castaño 1985). Mobilization of savings, provision of additional services such as health care, legal aid, literacy, home improvement programs, and emphasis on reaching subsectors of microentrepreneurs, such as microvendors or a given line of microproducers, are a few of the innovations of the approach (Coto 1985; Reichmann 1984c).

The emphasis that institutions give to the active participation of group members in the program also varies. In some programs, existing solidarity groups are responsible for promoting the program and assisting in the formation of new groups. They also contribute to the development of appropriate training materials and curricula for use along with credit extension. In the more advanced programs, such as those in Cartagena, Colombia, and in Santo Domingo, Dominican Republic, solidarity groups are considered an intermediary step to broader-level organization among program beneficiaries who, as a result of having participated in the groups, form cooperatives or other types of associations (Reichmann 1984a; Otero 1986).

The usefulness of the solidarity group approach resides in the creativity used in its design that is shared across institutions and in the fine-tuning that has been achieved in the elaboration of the three main components of solidarity group programs: credit, training, and organization of beneficiaries in groups.

Credit

The provision of credit in solidarity group programs emerges from the well-known lessons learned in earlier programs with rural and urban poor: credit, offered at reasonable rates, is a key ingredient to the sustainability and growth of microenterprises (Farbman 1981; Sebstad 1982). What solidarity group programs contribute to the "state of the art" in credit schemes is an emphasis on delivery systems blending features that benefit the borrower, as well as features that benefit the lending institution—in this case, the dozen or more private development organizations, cooperatives, community development organizations, and social service institutions that implement these programs.

Solidarity group programs combine characteristics of informal lending practices with elements used by formal lending institutions (Reichmann 1984c and 1984b). From the perspective of the borrower, credit must respond to the need for working capital, offer simple and quick application and disbursement procedures at affordable rates, and take into account the borrower's limited or nonexistent experience with formal credit operations. Because most borrowers are microvendors they operate at very low profit margins, and lack of liquidity on a day-to-day basis is one of their biggest problems (Martínez 1985). The microproducer often must wait to sell the day's production before purchasing material for the next day's operation.

From the point of view of the lending institution, however, institutional priorities do not end with responding to the beneficiaries' need for credit and training. For the institution, credit also must be managed in a way that ensures loans are used for income-producing activities, reflects as close as possible the real costs of lending, maintains close control of arrearage levels, and includes a monitoring system that gives daily information on the key factors that govern the credit portfolio.

These interrelated factors directly affect the institution's ability to sustain lending activities, to generate income from interest earned, and to cover an increasing percentage of the program's operating costs. This search for self-sufficiency in program operations constitutes one of the main institutional objectives of solidarity group programs (Gross 1984). At times, this objective may be in conflict with the major objective of providing credit in as responsive and agile a way as possible, always focusing on the beneficiaries' needs. The solidarity group mechanism presents a delivery system that emphasizes the complementarity of these two sets of priorities, while minimizing their potential conflict.

All solidarity group programs consider training an essential component of the solidarity group strategy and define its role as that of a catalyst for personal and group development. When a program combines training with other ongoing processes—credit extension and use, organization, follow-up—the training process is believed to contribute to changing attitudes, solving problems, overcoming existing limitations, and breaking down barriers (Asociación de Organizaciones de Programas de Grupos Solidarios 1985). Training is seen not as an end in itself, but as a means of achieving overall program objectives (Lynton and Pareek 1978; Honadle and Hannah 1982; Kindervatter 1983).

Training

Training is provided in a manner parallel to credit, in small groups of fifteen to twenty-five, in short sessions. Very few, if any, of these are conducted prior to disbursement of the first loan. Most programs differentiate the three or four hours of "orientation and information" given to each group prior to loan approval from the periodic, scheduled training sessions that occur throughout the life of a solidarity group. These sessions are based on needs assessment and established guidelines. However, they differ from technical assistance; the latter is one-on-one, is not scheduled, and concentrates on production issues specific to each microenterprise.

The approach to training varies from the more traditional credit programs for the poor that dedicate many hours to training prior to lending (IDB 1984; Otero and Blayney 1984). In solidarity group programs, the average number of hours of training per month is three. Because the costs of training are very high to both the trainee and the institution and more time spent in training detracts from the enterprise, experience does not indicate that, in the case of training, more is better (Otero 1986).

The training materials and curricula used in solidarity group programs vary considerably from program to program, but the content is very similar and can be divided into economic and social training modules. The former relate to enterprise production and concentrate on managing credit, buying and selling, and bookkeeping. These sessions directly address the process of credit extension and seek to fortify the borrower's ability to manage and use credit. The social units are designed to help the microentrepreneur better understand the context within which he or she operates, develop traits that will enhance his or her ability to act collectively, and increase the cohesion of the solidarity groups.

Training sessions, especially the social modules, are tied closely to the programs' objective of organizing microentrepreneurs. The subjects treated in these courses include leadership, personal needs assessment, group ownership, human relations, awareness of individual and group worth, and concepts related to cooperative or association formation. Some institutions have also found that the provision of training in areas specifically requested by the beneficiaries, though not directly related to the program's objectives, increases the beneficiaries' sense of commitment and ownership of the program. The Asociación para el Desarrollo y la Integración de la Mujer (ADIM) in Peru, for example, provides legal aid and health and family planning information to its women participants. In Honduras, field workers of Asesores para el Desarrollo (ASEPADE) dedicate some of their free hours to literacy training for solidarity group members who request it.

Organization

The third main component of the solidarity group methodology—organization—is the most difficult to achieve, and the one that the institution and the program staff control the least. The decision to organize ultimately comes from the program beneficiaries; the only thing the programs seek to accomplish is to develop beneficiary capacity in this direction, and to create an environment that promotes collective action.

The approach used by solidarity group programs suggests that organization among program beneficiaries may be one way to address the myriad of problems they face, not only in their businesses, but in their families and communities. Problems shared by most of the urban poor—such as inadequate housing, lack of access to health, sanitation, and other services, constant economic instability, and little or no leverage to pressure the government and other power structures to address their needs—cannot and should not be addressed by a credit and training program. However, solidarity group programs often contend that they can be vehicles for helping microentrepreneurs themselves seek solutions to common problems through their own initiatives (Otero 1986).

The experiences of programs in various countries show that formal organizations can emerge from solidarity group programs, and that participation in the programs can help microentrepreneurs make demands on their own behalf to local government and other institutions. Perhaps the most well-known example—the Asociación de Tricicleros in the Dominican Republic—had, in 1984, elected officers and over 200 members; it was active, among other things, in reviewing licensing and other municipal requirements that raise the operating costs for its members (Reichmann 1984c). The stall vendors or "tenderos" who participated in a solidarity group program in Cartagena, Colombia, have formed an association, drafted bylaws, elected a coordinating committee, and started outlining priority actions (Otero 1986). Others in Peru and Colombia have experimented with cooperative formation and market vendor organizations (CIDES 1985; Reichmann 1984b).

Features of Success

Existing studies and field work help identify five characteristics prevalent in all solidarity group programs that are advantageous for the institution and the beneficiary and that can be considered the basis of the programs' effectiveness (Ashe 1985; Stearns 1985; World Bank 1985; Blayney and Otero 1985). First, loan application procedures for initial loans require collection of minimal information on the business and the microentrepreneurs, and the loan passes through two to four quick steps for approval.

Along with agility in loan disbursement, the solidarity group mechanism also has the advantage of flexibility in the terms of the loan. Disbursements generally take place on one or two assigned days each week at the institution or a predetermined bank, usually no more than one week after the application has been presented. Subsequent loans are made almost immediately upon timely payment of the previous loan. Each subsequent loan can be for a slightly higher amount to be paid in short but flexible periods ranging from two to twelve weeks in most programs.

Third, interest rates are affordable, but high enough to cover program costs. All programs charge commercial rates computed weekly or monthly and, in most cases, charge an additional .05 to 1 percent fee per month for training and other services.

Fourth, the group itself, perceiving the availability of a line of credit that is affordable and quick, becomes the most important incentive for timely repayments. In most programs, the promoters also visit the groups one or two days prior to their scheduled payment.

Finally, solidarity group programs include a training curriculum of social and economic topics used with beneficiaries who receive credit. The frequency and quality of the training vary considerably and can depend on the institution's philosophy regarding the utility of training and the level of evolution of the program.

Table 5.1 summarizes these features and their advantages and disadvantages in terms of implementors and participants. When operating together, these factors serve as a combination of incentives and protections, for the beneficiary and for the institution.

A PROFILE OF BENEFICIARIES

A survey of eight solidarity group programs in Colombia shows that program beneficiaries fall in the lowest 20 percent of the income categories among the economically active population in urban areas. Almost 100 percent of these beneficiaries have a monthly income below what is needed to purchase what the government defines as a minimum consumer basket of basic goods and services; that is, few solidarity group members earn an income equivalent to the monthly legal minimum wage (ACCION/AITEC 1985). Although nearly half of the solidarity group members have completed some schooling, most are considered to be functionally illiterate. In one program, 12.1 percent of group members had never learned to read or write, yet they had developed basic mathematical skills needed to run their businesses. The average age of program participants in most programs is between thirty and forty, with women concentrated on the higher end of the age spectrum (ACCION/AITEC 1985; Reichmann 1984a and 1984b). Most participants have also been engaged in economic activities for a number of years; in one program the average experience was eleven years (Fernández 1984). In another, where sex disaggregated data are available, most women participants were in their thirties, had basic education, had an average of sixteen years of experience in business, and were heads of households supplying the bulk of the family income (Reichmann 1984a and 1984b).

Why So Many Women?

From the outset, solidarity group programs set out to reach a particular income group within the informal sector, rather than to reach men or women.

TABLE 5.1
Five Characteristics of Effective Credit Lending in Solidarity Group Programs

| Characteristics | The Implementing Institution | | The Beneficiary | |
	Advantages	Disadvantages	Advantages	Disadvantages
1. Agility in Loan Application and Review	Decreases staff time spent in these activities Lowers operating costs Results in a more responsive program Relies on decentralized decision making	Requires high level of loan liquidity	Doesn't require elaborate application procedures Makes credit quickly available Strengthens organizational skills for group formation Relies on and promotes self-help	None
2. Flexible Terms of Loan (loan amount, frequency of payments, duration of loan)	Results in a more responsive program Greater demand for credit Speeds up portfolio turn-over, generating more interest income	Is more labor intensive Is harder to monitor Has a higher overall financial ability on initial very small loans	Is adapted to each borrower's needs Is more suited to borrower's financial ability to repay. Takes into account the cycle of activity of a given business Reaches the smallest	None
3. Commercial Interest Rates	Can reflect the real costs of lending Generates interest income to cover program costs Contributes to meeting self-sufficiency targets Incurs receptivity/ greater acceptance by local business community and local sources of funds	May not be high enough to cover all operations May be perceived as too demanding of the beneficiary	Allows much lower costs of borrowing than from alternative sources (moneylenders) Paves the way to dealing with other commercial lending institutions Increases availability of credit (by avoiding de-capitalization) for subsequent loans	May be considered too high by some

4. Built-in Incentives for Repayment	Improves repayment rate Helps control fund decapitalization resulting from high rates of arrearage and default Requires less staff follow-up for repayment, and therefore lowers costs	Does not guarantee 100 percent repayment Requires careful monitoring	Ensures that credit fund doesn't dry up Makes larger loans available to the creditworthy Makes group responsible for collecting payments on time Fosters group cohesion	Whole group suffers if one member fails to pay
5. Linked to Training and Technical Assistance	Increases beneficiary's commitment to the program Strengthens trust between staff and beneficiary Expands staff capacity and ability to work with microentrepreneurs Provides mechanisms for airing beneficiary needs and problems Provides information to measure program performance and impact	Increases costs Generates little income through "fee for service" and other schemes Can lead to beneficiary dependency if not designed and conducted properly	Increases skills and ability to manage an enterprise Develops leadership and analytical skills, tools for empowerment Increases awareness of context in which microenterprise operates Helps beneficiary to strategize and gain capacity to promote his/her own interests	Takes time away directly Increases cost (transportation, fees, etc.) May not respond to his/her needs

These programs quickly found that women abound as owners of the tiniest businesses, operate as serious entrepreneurs, and are turning to credit programs in growing numbers. Overall, more than half of the beneficiaries of solidarity group programs are women; most of them are microvendors selling prepared foods, produce, or other agricultural products in streets or marketplaces (Otero 1986).

This prevalence of women among the smallest enterprises occurs in part because factors that govern economic activity in the informal sector are particularly attractive to women. It seems that the informal sector is more flexible and less constraining in time and space than other employment sources, allowing women to combine productive activities and family responsibilities. A survey of women market vendors participating in a solidarity group program in Peru revealed that a high percentage had young children whom they looked after while tending their market stalls (Reichmann

1984b). The prevalence of women in these informal businesses also reflects women's increasing economic needs. A number of studies of the last decade confirm that the incidence of woman-headed households, especially in the urban areas, is growing dramatically and that, as a result, women are assuming a greater share of income-earning responsibilities within the family (Harrison 1981; Buvinić and Youssef 1978). The current recession experienced in developing countries also has added to the pressure on poor households and has increased the importance of women's earning capacity (White et al. 1986). In addition, women face fewer barriers to entry into the informal sector, as occupations in the sector require less education, training, capital, and experience than do formal jobs (Dulansey and Austin 1985).

Within this context, many aspects of solidarity group programs and their credit delivery mechanisms are conducive to women's participation and overcome the following constraints in having access to credit that plague women more severely than men (Lycette 1984; Dulansey and Austin 1985; Pezzulo 1983):

- Women are small borrowers and can easily be excluded from participating in programs that require a minimum size of loan that is above their capacity to absorb.

- Women are less likely to meet collateral requirements, especially when collateral is in the form of land or property. Aside from the economic factors, legal codes and practices often preclude women from holding land or property.

- Women tend to have less experience in completing application forms and can be dissuaded from seeking credit if procedures are too complicated. Therefore, a self-selection process occurs even before a woman entrepreneur approaches the institution and submits a loan. In the case of beneficiaries interviewed in Lima, over 50 percent of the women reported that they first approached the program's office in the company of a friend, whereas only 8 percent of the men first went to the office with a friend (Reichmann 1984b).

- Women have the smallest firms and the transaction costs of administering small loans often discourages institutions from lending to the smallest businesses.

Women and Group Formation

The emphasis of solidarity group programs on collective responsibility through participation in a group may also contribute to the high percentage of women in these programs. One can argue that the group mechanism is particularly attractive to women because it builds on the informal associations and networks that women have formed throughout the developing world. In many cultures, village women unite to respond to adversity or crisis, or to create separate resources, alternative conditions, or autonomous influences. In their exhaustive analysis of women's informal associations, March and Taqqu (1982) suggest that although defensive women's networks to address emergencies exist in almost every society, also prominent are informal associations that actively seek to strengthen the economic position of women within their setting. These loosely formed organizations help women find work, learn a new trade, and even pool resources.

The characteristics of autonomous, informal women's associations or networks, especially those that operate rotating loan funds, are strikingly similar to those of the solidarity groups. The former are based on collective effort in which all participate and all benefit in return; they are constituted by self-selected members who form the association with a specific objective; and the group finds ways to protect itself from dissenting individuals. All three are also key characteristics of solidarity groups. Inadvertently, the group formation mechanism of solidarity groups resembles that of many informal collective activities of women throughout the developing world. This factor, in addition to the breaking of the barriers to access, may contribute significantly to women's active participation in solidarity group programs.

Groups seem to help women in their economic tasks. The recent findings of Till and Chaudhuri (1986) regarding women's cooperatives and group formation in Honduras argue for the importance of group formation as a starting point for enhancing women's economic activities. Through interviews with over fifty cooperatives, associations, and informal groups, and over 360 women in urban and rural Honduras, these authors establish a correlation between a woman's ability to manage credit and her participation in a group. Women have a better idea of credit and its ramifications, the authors found, if they belong to a supportive group. Furthermore, the greater the level of organization that is achieved, the more cognizant women appear to be of the use of credit for productive activities. Finally, their findings show that the strongest incentive for group formation among women is the group as a mechanism to address individual economic needs.

RESULTS AND IMPACTS OF SOLIDARITY GROUP PROGRAMS

Monitoring

Among the greatest challenges that solidarity group programs face is the timely and efficient monitoring of the state of their loan portfolios and the results they achieve. Among the data that must be collected regularly are: number of loans, average size of loans, total amounts lent, new versus second and subsequent loans, portfolios in arrearage, real costs of lending, number of beneficiaries reached, and number of women participants. When studied over time, this information can help bring to the surface patterns or problems in lending that can be addressed quickly, such as a decline in the number of new borrowers, or a jump in the arrearage rate.

It is in this area in particular that the technical assistance of ACCION International/AITEC has had demonstrable impact. As solidarity group programs evolved, AITEC assisted in the use of simple and quick methods for monitoring results and for studying the movement of the credit funds. Today, each institution collects monthly and cumulative information on about twenty program variables. Over time, this information has been systematized so that all solidarity group programs in Latin America collect the same data, circulate it among themselves, and use it for program analysis (Gross 1984).

Table 5.2 provides a comparative example of the monitoring techniques utilized by solidarity group programs; it uses twelve Colombian programs and seven other Latin American programs to illustrate the type of information available, as well as the summary results of each program. Programs use this data to flag problem areas. For example, one can compare the level of participation of women and investigate the reasons why it may be low in a given program. Similarly, one can obtain the relationship between outstanding loans and loans in arrearage to determine if a program should pay particular attention to this factor.

The monitoring system is also a summary of program results. It shows, at a glance, the individual and aggregate results of these programs. In Colombia, as of October 1985, these programs had reached over 3,500 beneficiaries with nearly 6,000 loans, totaling approximately US$800,000. Five of the seven other Latin American programs show that between 49 percent and 69 percent of the beneficiaries were women, while the other two show women represented 31 percent and 40 percent of beneficiaries. These programs also show arrearage rates—payments that are overdue one day or more—from less than 1 percent to 27.1 percent. High arrearage rates are unusual for solidarity group programs and, when they occur, may be partly due to policy changes that favor wholesalers and undercut the activity of the solidarity group members. The average rate of arrearage for the nineteen programs was only 12.7 percent at the end of 1986.

Finally, the programs that are at least two years old show that they cover between 54 percent and 187 percent of their operating costs from interest earned in the program, figures that do not include the cost of money, as nearly 100 percent of the programs' loan funds are grants or soft loans. In sum, a quick review of the programs' monitoring system yields considerable information regarding each program's accomplishments, as well as the overall results obtained.

Socioeconomic Impact

Determining the socioeconomic impact of solidarity group programs is essential to any assessment of their usefulness. Because these programs aim to

TABLE 5.2

**Summary Results of Nineteen Solidarity Group Programs in Seven Countries, 1986
(in US$; preliminary data)**

Country	Peru	Dominican Republic	Colombia	Ecuador		Honduras	Costa Rica	Paraguay	Total
Program	Progreso	ADEMI	12 Programs[a]	FED	FEE	ASEPADE	AVANCE	Fundación Paraguaya	19 Programs
Starting Date	November 1982	December 1985	See below	May 1984	June 1984	September 1984	April 1986	January 1986	
1. New Groups Formed	1,023	39	540	94	81	165	80	109	2,131
2. Number of Loans Disbursed	5,233	128	4,849	596	280	1,139	142	668	13,055
3. Average Size of Loan	$938	$1,600	$520	$265	$391	$363	$312	$551	$563
4. Total Amount Disbursed	$4,431,000	$155,000	$1,523,000	$139,000	$102,000	$354,000	$60,000	$432,000	$7,187,000
5. Total Amount Recovered	$3,500,000	$135,000	$1,340,000	$141,000	$75,000	$334,000	$52,000	$292,000	$5,869,000
6. Interest Earned	$150,000	$2,100	93,000	47,000	$12,000	$20,000	$1,400	$15,500	$341,000
7. Arrearage (%)	3.6%	0.8%	12.2%	21.3%	5.0%	27.1%	24.2%	3.7%	12.7%
8. Cost per US$	$.02	$.13	$.13	$.21	$.27	$.07	$.50	$.30	$.20
9. Self-Sufficiency (%)	187%	54%	68%	82%	60%	63%	4%	20%	63%
10. Total New Beneficiaries Reached	4,100	246	2,194	260	256	540	178	747	8,521
— % Women	52%	40%	59%	69%	49%	62%	31%	49%	45%

Source: ACCION/AITEC; Statistics for 1986.

[a] The twelve programs in Colombia are: CIDES, Bogot; Women's World Banking, Cali; FUNDESCOM, Cali; CDV, Cartagena; ACTUAR, Medellín; CORFAS, Bucaramanga; Cruzada Social, Manizales; Women's World Banking, Popayán; Women's World Banking, Medellín; ACTUAR, Tolima; CORFAS, Bogotá; and Women's World Banking, Puerto Tejada. The first four started in August 1983; three additional ones started in mid-1985; and the remaining five in 1986.

affect the beneficiaries' lives in financial and economic terms, as well as in less easily measured social ways, they should be examined at four levels:

- *the firm:* volume of sales; net profit; investment levels;

- *the beneficiary and the family:* changes in income, employment, savings; allocation of additional income within the household; new technical and management skills; participation in associations or groups, involvement in community activities; increased access to resources; increased access to services (health, education, housing);

- *the community or local economy:* increased organization; creation of alternative marketing channels; changes in regulations or legislation; employment generation; backward and forward linkages to productive sectors; and

- *the implementing institution:* quality/preparation of staff; management systems, revisions to organizational structure; level of impact on local environment.

There is no systematic impact evaluation of solidarity group programs that incorporates all the above areas, and no comparative impact study of existing programs. However, useful evaluative initiatives conducted either by program staff or by outside consultants give some insight into the socioeconomic impact of these programs. From those evaluations, preliminary conclusions can be drawn about the overall impact of solidarity group programs on men and women microentrepreneurs.

Existing data indicate that solidarity group programs have had an overall positive impact on the firm and may have a similar impact on the lives of the beneficiaries and their families. In terms of income changes, a recent evaluation conducted by Women's World Banking in Colombia of a sample of thirty-five assisted microentrepreneurs shows that, in an eight-month period, their business sales increased by 53 percent and their profits grew by 45 percent (see Guzmán and Castro in Chapter 11 of this volume). For its evaluation, the Acción Comunitaria Program in Peru recorded economic indicators of change on a yearly basis, including monthly sales, and level of reinvestment into firm activities on a sample of 107 participants (Fernández 1984). The results showed that overall incomes for the sample group rose, in real terms, 33.6 percent after one year and 55 percent after two years. In two programs in Colombia, results indicate an average income increase among beneficiaries of 75 percent and 35 percent respectively in the first year of operation (ACCION/AITEC 1985). The most thorough evaluation analyzes the Corporación Acción por Antioquia (ACTUAR), also in Colombia, and documents a monthly jump in sales of 7.1 percent in real terms among beneficiaries, which translates into a monthly change in income of 5.3 percent (López Castaño 1985).

In terms of employment generation, evaluations generally emphasize that solidarity group programs have more impact in helping retain existing jobs—enhancing job sustainability—and in engaging family members in more productive activities, than in actually creating additional full-time jobs. Many program participants, especially microvendors, operate at near subsistence levels, and the infusion of credit and training enables them to continue generating income through self-employment. These studies also assert that manufacturing activities, rather than retail and trading, have the greatest potential for generation of employment. The ACTUAR study cited above includes a detailed analysis of the employment generation of each type of microenterprise activity assisted by the program, thereby providing a scale of employment generation possibilities based on the type of microenterprise in question (López Castaño 1985). For example, microproducers in the area of metal processing are likely to generate more jobs than those in woodworking, and considerably more jobs than those in textile processing.

Findings and information about how these programs affect the distribution of benefits at the family level, and the impact they have on the local community, also appear to be positive but generally rely on more sketchy and anecdotal information. The Peru studies, for example, record that 95 percent of those interviewed assert that the availability of credit has enabled them to improve their living conditions, and to better address the basic needs of the family, such as health, education, and housing (Fernández 1984). The ACTUAR report identifies bottlenecks in the marketing systems and suggests that, in the case of microentrepreneurs in Medellín, assisting them to organize collective marketing systems may be as important as providing credit (López Castaño 1984). Additional indicators of social gains— capacity to organize, increased leverage, ability to make decisions, and others—are examined in general terms, but without the rigor necessary to include these among program benefits.

An important exception emerges from the preliminary findings of Blayney's (1986) review of microenterprise programs in Latin America. After field study of several solidarity group programs, he suggests that offering a poor entrepreneur the first opportunity to experience solidarity in an organization represents an important accomplishment for these programs. In the context of a solidarity group, men and women have a say, wield a vote, make decisions, experience positive outcomes, and earn a sense of "empowerment":

> Social gains are demonstrated through indicators that are personal, such as increased education, as well as collective, such as successfully petitioning the mayor to lower the license fees for street vendors . . . Leverage and access may be more tangible gains for low-income people to experience outside the family or extended network when these are experienced as a member of an "educated" group, in this case microentrepreneurs. (Blayney 1986, p. 23)

There are also examples of the complexity and difficulty of evaluating these programs, and of the importance of considering the whole spectrum of factors that determine program impact. The evaluation of a program in Cartagena, Colombia, for example, divides microentrepreneurs into three categories and records different impacts of the program on each category (Coto 1985). A survey of participants demonstrated that, although income increased among stall vendors by about 11.6 percent, it remained unchanged among microproducers and decreased by 10.7 percent among microvendors. The study highlights the increased pauperization of microvendors, despite their participation in the program, and suggests contextual factors to help explain these results, such as a drop in consumer demand due to increased competition from wholesalers or, in the case of microproducers, excessive increases in the costs of raw materials. Furthermore, the formation of an organization of stall vendors as a result of their participation in the program represents an important part of the program's impact; yet it cannot be measured as easily as the economic categories above. From this particular program experience, we can conclude that participation in the program, although not contributing to the improvement in income among the stall vendors, did make a difference in their ability to organize and in their potential for bringing about longer-term change on their own behalf.

With the exception of the Reichmann studies about programs in the Dominican Republic and Peru, work by the International Center for Research on Women (ICRW) in Ecuador, and Blumberg's evaluation of the Association for the Development of Microenterprises, Inc. (ADEMI), in Santo Domingo, there is little additional impact information that is disaggregated by sex. Nevertheless, these studies provide useful insights into the effect of the programs on women participants. For example, in the Peru program, women participants who were interviewed in depth reported an average increase in income of 25 percent since entering the program. Further disaggregation of these data shows that 28 percent of participating women suffered a drop in earnings during the time they received credit. Of the remaining 72 percent who experienced a rise in income, 40 percent reported increases of 50 percent or more. Nearly all the women who registered the highest increases in income, some more than 100 percent, were involved in nontraditional activities, such as baking soda manufacturing and stove parts and soap-dish making (Reichmann 1984b).

This finding would appear to reinforce the often-made assertion that women who are engaged in traditional activities are also engaged in the least remunerative and productive of enterprises. The finding of the ACTUAR study regarding the differentials in employment generation by type of enterprise also implies that activities in which women predominate create fewer jobs. Assisting women to diversify into nontraditional areas may be an important way of enhancing women's incomes (Buvinić 1986; Dulansey and Austin 1985).

Some preliminary data exist to demonstrate that women in solidarity group programs are good credit risks and spend additional income on meeting the family's basic needs (Blumberg 1985). As most programs do not disaggregate information such as arrearage rates, size of loans, or type of activity by sex, it is not possible to draw conclusions regarding women's performance as program participants. Solidarity group programs need to do additional work in this area, as well as to document the programs' achievements and shortcomings in reaching women. Such information not only can increase existing knowledge in this area, but also can contribute significantly to policy and programmatic changes in institutions concerned with reaching poor women, local and national governments, and donor organizations.

Barriers to Evaluation

These findings—a mere sketch of the socioeconomic impact of solidarity group programs—are presented to give a glimpse of the benefits derived from them. However, the search for impact data and for information about women's participation raises the more important concern regarding the quality and frequency of evaluations in solidarity group programs.

Unlike monitoring systems for solidarity group programs themselves, there are no established guidelines for the evaluation of the socioeconomic impact of these programs, and program organizations are only now beginning to explore this issue seriously (Ashe 1986). Partly for this reason, with one or two notable exceptions, there is little systematic evaluation at the program level, and there are no comparative baseline or impact data with which to analyze the relative socioeconomic impact of these programs.

Several factors contribute to this situation. In general, development programs fail to pay appropriate attention to evaluation and the lessons it reveals; in this sense, the solidarity group programs are no different. Second, the cost of evaluating impact is high, and it can seldom be assumed by an implementing institution that is intent on maintaining low operational costs. In the case of solidarity group programs, which aptly emphasize the need for a participatory evaluation in which the program beneficiaries and the institution's staff take an active part, the cost increases even more.

Lack of clarity regarding the audience for an evaluation also prevails. The beneficiaries, the implementing institution, the donor organization, and others interested in the program all make use of an evaluation, yet their needs and perspectives are quite diverse, and one evaluation will seldom respond to all of them. In addition, donor organizations tend to take more seriously the results of evaluations they commission directly, rather than those prepared at the request of the local institutions; yet the former may not be as useful for the implementing institutions because they are seldom translated into Spanish or systematically discussed with the program staff.

Finally, programmatic factors also affect evaluation. In most programs, for example, there is an unexploited wealth of information in the program's files; however, because of lack of time, resources, and technical expertise, this material is not systematically coded or tabulated. As a result, the possibility that evaluation material can be fed back to program activities is diminished greatly, and information rich in learning potential for the donors and the local institution remains undocumented.

CONCLUSIONS

The experience of the last five years and available data indicate that solidarity groups are an effective mechanism for increasing women's access to and control of previously unavailable services and resources. Especially in the provision of credit, poor women who are often at the mercy of a money-lender now have a viable option.

In addition, solidarity group programs, perhaps more than most development efforts, have assumed the responsibility of integrating gender issues into their planning and implementation. Programs have adapted existing procedures and requirements to accommodate women and have established gender-related targets. Currently, some programs conduct promotion through women-oriented institutions or networks, hire female promoters, seek ways to break cultural male-female barriers, and examine lending criteria to take into account the disadvantaged position of women. Some solidarity group programs have started by catering directly to women as the primary beneficiaries, arguing that they have a greater need, especially those women who head households. From this perspective, credit through solidarity group programs represents one of the most successful efforts at integrating women into development programs.

Although these solidarity group programs reflect a successful beginning, they also raise two major questions regarding women in the informal sector that need in-depth study:

1. Are credit and training sufficient inputs for women microproducers and microvendors? Consistently, we find that women operate the smallest and least productive of enterprises and that they predominate in areas of economic activity in which the aggregate economic benefit is comparatively small. Arguing from a strictly economic viewpoint, Kilby and D'Zmura (1985) suggest that retail and trading, the largest single category of microenterprise activity, generate no, or almost no, backward linkages. Some observers have argued that development projects should target the provision of credit and other resources by type of economic activity, focusing on the ones that offer the greatest economic impact. If this approach were adopted, most informal-sector women would be left behind.

Two recommendations regarding women may assist in addressing this dilemma. First, the assessment of project impact recorded in evaluations should disaggregate microenterprises by type of activity and should collect data on economic and social benefits. In this way, the targeting of specific economic activities—a decision that may merit consideration under certain circumstances (market saturation, availability of raw materials)—is not imposed solely on the basis of economic indicators such as level of sales or rate of expansion, but also involves factors such as income level, number of dependents, and alternative income sources for the family.

Second, assisting women to diversify their economic activities by entering nontraditional areas of production may be one way of enabling many of them to rise from the bottom of the informal-sector pyramid. Clearly, this suggestion requires additional research, as well as funds for skills and other necessary training. Neither solidarity group programs nor most other credit programs are equipped to respond to the question of diversification. Perhaps the issue can be addressed more thoroughly through a parallel program or institution. Regardless of the approach, we currently do not have the knowledge, especially from a gender perspective, to embark on such an effort.

2. Is gender a determinant of how effectively a solidarity group operates? Although much has been written about solidarity groups, little is known about the internal working of the groups themselves. A recent study of Women's World Banking in Cali, Colombia, suggests "indicators" of solidarity as a means of studying the solidarity group mechanism (Ashe 1986). Within this context, we must explore whether solidarity groups develop varying characteristics, administer internal operations, and evolve differently depending on whether they are all female, all male, or mixed. If gender can be isolated as a contributor to successful solidarity group programs, it may be an appropriate mechanism not only for the smallest of microenterprises, but also for those slightly larger ones that currently receive individual loans.

In conclusion, solidarity group programs provide an opportunity for reaching the urban poor, as well as for learning about the characteristics of this subsector of economic activity. As increasing numbers of urban poor in Latin America, especially women, turn to self-employment in the informal sector as a way of earning income, they will continue to demand the attention of policymakers and program planners. A glimpse of the coming decade reinforces the growing need for job creation and for improved quality of life for millions of urban poor. It may be that simple, low-cost approaches that recognize the predominance of women in this sector will present one viable alternative for developing countries.

6

Training and Technical Assistance for Small and Microbusiness: *A Review of Their Effectiveness and Implications for Women*

CRESSIDA S. MCKEAN

During the 1970s and 1980s, concern with unemployment and underemployment in the developing countries has prompted both development agencies and donors to focus on small and microenterprises in the informal sector as a relatively inexpensive source of job creation, and to promote the development of assistance programs targeted to these enterprises.[1] Several small business credit programs are currently viewed as innovative success stories in terms of their ability to increase income and employment for low-income people, while sustaining high rates of repayment and covering operating expenses out of interest revenues (Tendler 1982, p. 114; Kilby 1985; Ashe 1985; Goldmark and Rosengard 1983). However, there has been considerable controversy over the extent to which the technical assistance and training that some programs provide contributes to the development of the firms that receive it and to the income and welfare of their owners. In fact, a number of studies are pessimistic about the results of technical assistance programs for very small firms, given the programs' limited track record in developing viable enterprises and improving the incomes of poor people (Kilby 1979, p. 319; Kilby and D'Zmura 1985; Tendler 1982; Tendler 1983, pp. 101-2; Schmitz 1982).

Because of two particular trends, the debate over the relative value of technical assistance and training for small business initiatives in Latin America is of particular importance to projects that aim to reach low-income women. First, "successful" small-enterprise credit programs, managed largely by private voluntary organizations (PVOs), reach a significant number of women both in absolute terms and as a proportion of the total number of beneficiaries, especially when they encourage participation of very small (micro) businesses and commerce.[2] In Latin America, the proportion of female beneficiaries in such programs ranges from about 22 percent to 89 percent (IDB 1984; Reichmann 1984a; Reichmann 1984b; Otero 1986; ACCION/AITEC 1986; Lycette and White, Chapter 2 of this volume). The credit programs that tend to have the highest proportion of women beneficiaries are those based on solidarity group lending, in which training and technical assistance are considered integral parts of the methodology (see Otero, Chapter 5 of this volume).

Second, institutions whose primary function is to provide training and technical assistance are also beginning to develop alternative methodologies for promoting employment in the informal sector through project support for self-employment, home-based firms, associative enterprises, and microenterprises (Corvalàn Vàsquez 1985; Gonzalez Chiari 1984; Crandon 1984; Pinilla 1985; Placencia 1985). Because women are very active in the informal sector and would constitute a primary beneficiary group of such project activities, if properly designed, these initiatives merit examination. However, as we shall discover below, the record of these initiatives has not been promising, especially in regard to attempts to start up new enterprises.

As we examine the new trends and the programs associated with them, the questions that emerge are: Under what circumstances do training and technical assistance inputs have an impact on the economic performance of the enterprise, particularly on the beneficiaries' income? And, how can women managing small firms best benefit?

Buvinić (1986) cites a tendency for women's projects, particularly those that are implemented by traditional women's organizations, to "misbehave," yielding unexpected and unwanted outcomes and failing to achieve economic goals. But is it only women's projects that misbehave, in the sense that the productive objectives of the undertaking evolve into welfare actions during implementation? It may be that projects that try to take on too many technical assistance activities or those that seek to develop new enterprises from scratch also have similar problems.

This chapter contrasts three approaches to training and technical assistance for microenterprises and assesses the effectiveness of each approach and the degree to which women benefit. The first section analyzes training and technical assistance that are offered to entrepreneurs who borrow from microenterprise loan programs either as individuals or as members of solidarity groups. The second section looks at the experience of projects that use training and technical assistance to stimulate the creation of new, informal sector enterprises. The third section focuses on industry and trade-based initiatives that provide alternatives to individual, enterprise-specific training and technical assistance programs.

SCOPE OF ANALYSIS

Although there is a wide range of educational and assistance activities that indirectly impact on informal-sector businesses and their operators, this chapter focuses only on those whose explicit objective is either to supplement small business credit programs, or to promote self-employment and enterprise development. Therefore, the phrase "training and technical assistance" is used to refer to "a flow of services aimed at transferring knowledge and skills which enable the recipients to increase their usable productive capacity" (Kilby 1979, p. 31). However, even this definition encompasses a variety of services, including training in bookkeeping, cost accounting, management, and marketing, as well as leadership and cooperation; business extension and production-specific assistance; and longer term-expert technical assistance for other enterprise development services.

In practice, the objectives of small-enterprise development programs often go beyond the expansion of the productive capacity of businesses or the level of income and employment the business provides. Other complementary goals common in these programs are to aid beneficiaries in changing their attitudes about self-esteem, leadership, and cooperation, as well as about health, nutrition, and child care; to promote organization among beneficiaries which will enable them to pressure for improved access to community services, such as child care, water, electricity, and education; and to expand participation in productive activities by "pre-entrepreneurs."[3] Several evaluations and studies examining these social indicators have recognized the important contribution of this type of training and technical assistance to increased participation, solidarity, and access to social services for beneficiaries (Reichmann 1984a and 1984b; Ashe 1986; Placencia, in this volume; Otero 1986; Rahman 1986). This chapter considers these effects of small-enterprise training and assistance in only a peripheral way. Although recognizing the indirect contribution of these elements of microenterprise assistance toward the improvement of businesses, it focuses primarily on the role of technical assistance and training in affecting the economic performance of enterprises, which is principally measured by changes in income. This focus is important, as today's climate of limited development resources makes economic impact, along with project self-sufficiency, a fundamental criterion by which programs ultimately are judged.

TRAINING AND TECHNICAL ASSISTANCE
IN MICROENTERPRISE CREDIT PROGRAMS:
AN APPROPRIATE INPUT FOR RAISING INCOME?

Technical assistance and training are common components of microbusiness credit programs in Latin America. One program that stresses these elements, the Carvajal Program for the Development of Small Enterprises

(DESAP), which began in Cali, Colombia, left a legacy that has influenced the design of many credit programs for microenterprises. Developed in the 1970s, this program conceives of comprehensive training and technical assistance, consisting largely of accounting courses and management advice, as integral prerequisites and complements to credit. The Carvajal approach is to build on the practical experience of the microentrepreneur and to use training, followed by credit and business extension, to change attitudes toward business management and to provide credit to those without access (Carvajal 1985; IDB 1984). As of September 1983, thirteen different training courses were being taught to microentrepreneurs, of which four were considered mandatory in order to receive credit. The required courses focused on accounting, costs, investment projects, and personnel management (DESAP records). Individualized managerial assistance to microentrepreneurs is also required before loan authorization. Through this program component participants receive at least four visits by a DESAP staff member (one visit after each required course) to assure that administrative techniques are put into practice.

Although a number of the firms that are initially identified drop out before receiving their loans (76.6 percent of microentrepreneurs drop out between the time they are surveyed and the time they receive credit), program results have been very positive for those who remain. The arrears rate was 5.7 percent as of June 1983 (after several measures were taken to reduce the rate). Borrowers also experienced an impressive increase in income and employment. The average real monthly family income of the borrowers increased 13 percent over a period of three years and the average number of jobs per microenterprise increased from 3.8 to 5.1 over a one-year period (September 1982 to September 1983).

The Northeast Union of Assistance to Small Business (UNO), another informal-sector credit program, found training to provide fewer positive results. Tendler's study of UNO (1983) reported extension services to be fairly limited because of cost-minimizing considerations. UNO primarily focused assistance on business extension courses rather than technical assistance, which UNO differentiates as "extension involving the production process." Even though technical assistance was limited, UNO spent a considerable portion (30%) of its operating budget on training courses. UNO offers a non-mandatory two-week course consisting of four "modules": basic management, transactions with banks, basic bookkeeping, and sales promotion. Beyond the courses, UNO's extension efforts consist of visits by student staff members to clients during the period of loan application and monitoring.

The Tendler evaluation of UNO found that the courses and advice provided to clients had little impact on their businesses. Because course attendance was optional, client participation proved to be low (for example, a 1980–81 internal evaluation found that out of 35 clients interviewed for the study, only 13, or 38 percent, had attended the courses). Even worse, interviews of those who had attended the course found that most participants were unable to put to use anything they learned. The impact of recommendations to clients during visits by student staff members was found to be similarly disappointing. Because of a lack of time or because they considered the advice inappropriate, most clients didn't implement recommendations, but they put up with monitoring visits in order to receive their loans.

Tendler concluded that, although firms with no previous experience with institutional credit gained access to loans, the unit costs of lending were high, the training courses were of questionable value, and managerial extension had little impact. Moreover, the institution was unable to generate income from the credit operation, and the small firms that were benefiting were not increasing output or employment (Tendler 1983, pp. 5–8).

Over time, evaluations of microenterprise credit programs, such as UNO, and concern about cost recovery have raised questions about the impact of the training and technical assistance inputs on enterprise performance. Problems with training and extension commonly cited by beneficiaries in many programs are that the content is excessively general; the providers are inexperienced and lack specialized knowledge; and the technical assistance has minimal relevance to the practical requirements of the business (Kilby and D'Zmura 1985, pp. 118–19; Tendler 1983, p. 96; Goldmark et al. 1982, pp. 50 and 130; Farbman 1981, pp. 185; Ashe 1985). Kilby, in a review of a series of evaluations of small enterprise credit projects, came to a conclusion similar to that reached by Tendler in her study of UNO: most forms of technical assistance tried so far are not "appropriate inputs," in that they do not have the potential to reduce costs. "In all but a few situations, the recipients and the implementers reported that the results [of technical assistance] were negligible" (Kilby 1985, p. 119).

In response to these concerns, several microenterprise credit programs adopted what has come to be known as a "minimalist" approach, reducing training and enterprise-specific technical support to a bare minimum.[4] For these programs, credit itself became the primary training tool. The ADEMI program in the Dominican Republic and the Acción Comunitaria/Progreso program in Peru started out with the premise that training and business extension should be extremely simple, mostly informal advice to clients imparted in a group setting or during a routine site visit (Reichmann 1984a; Reichmann 1984b). This approach was one of several measures taken to streamline the credit delivery system, making it more responsive to the cash flow requirements of the beneficiary population. It was also designed to lower costs and thereby expand significantly the number of small firms that could receive credit. While the training and technical assistance-intensive Carvajal program reaches several hundred firms annually, some of the "minimalist" credit programs, such as those in Peru and the Dominican Republic, reach over one thousand firms yearly (ACCION 1986; IDB 1986).

Over time, some formal training and technical assistance have been reincorporated in these minimalist microenterprise credit programs, in some instances on a fee-for-service basis independent of the lending program. In the Progreso program in Peru, the demand for management advice by microenterprise borrowers, including semi-literate women, resulted in a policy decision to provide increased business extension services. Clients in this program are required to pay for monthly technical assistance visits (Reichmann 1984b, p. 30). In the Dominican Republic, ADEMI also retains a minimalist credit delivery system, but it has relied on Peace Corps volunteers and local training institutions to provide one-on-one management extension to larger businesses on a fee-for-service basis (Tippett and McKean 1987; Otero and Blaney 1984, p. 36). Continued demand by microenterprises for technical support has led to its provision on a fee-for-service basis that does not undermine the streamlining of the credit delivery process.

Another change in the approach of many microenterprise credit programs has been the adoption of a "solidarity group mechanism" as a guarantee scheme to overcome the institutional constraints and high transaction costs of lending to very tiny businesses. Members of a self-selected group guarantee each other's loans, while the program delivers credit through a financial institution in small amounts with a minimum of paperwork and technical assistance. Commerce, services, and cottage industries are eligible beneficiary sectors for these programs, whereas they are often excluded from individual microenterprise credit projects. Therefore, owners of the smallest businesses, predominately women, who were previously denied access to institutional credit, can receive loans (Ashe 1985; Otero 1986).

Managers of solidarity group credit programs in Latin America consider training to be an essential component of their strategy. Training was mandatory in eight of the ten solidarity group programs underway in 1986 in Latin America (Otero 1986, p. 11). In most solidarity group programs, participants receive an average of three hours of group training monthly in addition to promotional and follow-up firm visits. The training concentrates on entrepreneurial skills, credit management, costs and marketing, and recordkeeping, as well as on cooperation, leadership, needs assessment, human relations, and self-worth. The solidarity group programs see training as contributing to changing attitudes, solving problems, overcoming existing limitations, and breaking down barriers. Still, the training is generally not seen as an end in itself, but as a means to achieve overall program objectives (*Final Report Solidarity Group Conference 1985;* Lynton and Pareek 1978; Honadel and Hannah 1982; Kindervatter 1983 cited in Otero, this volume).

Minimalist versus Standard Training and Technical Assistance in Credit Programs: Any Difference?

As mentioned earlier, a new approach to microenterprise assistance that emerged in the 1980s seeks to reach smaller businesses in larger numbers than attained by previous efforts, by reducing training and technical assistance components, speeding up the loan review process, and granting very small loans (often US$20 or less for the first loan). One organization that has pioneered this "minimalist" approach is ACCION International/AITEC. ACCION contrasts its methodology with that of the "standard," or traditional programs, as shown in Table 6.1.

The "minimalist" approach to training and technical assistance is characterized by a small amount of training aimed at making clients viable borrowers. Usually training, when it is available, is offered on an informal basis and focuses on administrative or technical problems clients have encountered in their normal business practices. Minimalist technical assistance may be linked to microenterprise programs in which beneficiaries have received a comparatively higher level of education and thus are already more knowledgeable and have less need for technical assistance. It is also used in some solidarity group programs in which most clients have relatively few years of schooling. More important, with this approach, training and technical assistance are not required prior to borrowing, and the borrowing experience itself is set up to "train" the beneficiary in the effective use of credit.

The "standard" or "traditional" approach to technical assistance, on the other hand, is characterized by a wider variety of training courses or programs and technical assistance and is usually aimed at increasing the productivity of the firm, the number of employees, and/or the level of production,

TABLE 6.1
Characteristics of "Standard" (Traditional) and "Minimalist" (Nontraditional) Microenterprise Assistance Programs

	Standard	Minimalist
Size of beneficiary firms	Large	Small
Main emphasis	Training	Credit
Average loan size	US$800–US$3,000	Under US$100 initially; can reach US$1,000
Type of loans	Fixed investment and working capital	Working capital
Loan period	6–12 months	2 weeks to 4 months
Time between initial application and loan disbursement	1–2 months	4–7 days
Average number of credit experiences per beneficiary per year	1	4–6

Source: Stephen Gross, ACCION International/AITEC.

TABLE 6.2

Comparison of Indicators in Microenterprise Credit Programs with Standard and Minimal Technical Assistance Content in Latin America and Women's Participation (in percent)

	Increase in Income[a]	Increase in Employment[a]	Arrears Rate	Participation of Women
Credit with				
High TA Content				
Carvajal (individual)	19%	33%	6%	23%
Corfabricato (individual)	8	36	7	35
BMM/Cali (solidarity)	38	71	20	65
Minimalist Credit:				
Low TA Content				
ADEMI (individual)	52	50	21	19
ADOPEM (individual)	36	30	18	100
FED/PRODEM (solidarity)	39	15	23	33
FED/PRODEM (solidarity)	24	0	22	66
Progreso (solidarity)	43	n.a.	4	55

Source: IDB 1984; Trade and Development International 1985; Reichmann 1984a and 1984b; Tippett and McKean 1987; Otero 1986; ACCION International/AITEC 1986; Berger, Buvinić, and Jaramillo, Chapter 14.

[a]   Changes in income and employment were measured: over a one-year period (1982–83) for Carvajal and Corfabricato; over a one-year period (1984–85) for FED/PRODEM; over a one-year period (1982–83) for Progreso.

as well as raising the borrower's income. Training is usually offered in a more formal manner—through group classes, seminars, or prearranged, on-site (field) visits. Standard technical assistance may focus on anything from bookkeeping to investment strategies and some programs have even considered training in such areas as nutrition and childcare. Solidarity groups often request this more intense type of assistance because they lack access to any outside type of training and have already established groups that facilitate organized collective assistance.

When those microenterprise credit programs retaining significant training and extension services are compared with those retaining minimal technical assistance, available data do not suggest that the standard technical assistance content necessarily results in better economic performance or loan repayment (see Table 6.2). Of course, evaluation methodologies differ in many cases, but the results of this rough comparison do not indicate that credit programs with extensive training and technical assistance perform better than those with minimal technical assistance.

In regard to the participation of women, Table 6.2 also illustrates that women tend to have greater representation in the solidarity group programs, which lend to smaller borrowers. In fact, the size of loans granted and types of activities supported, rather than the amount of training or technical assistance a program offers, seem to be the primary determinants of women's participation in small and microenterprise assistance programs, as women are most active in smaller businesses and in certain sectors, particularly commerce and services (see Lycette and White, Chapter 2; Arias, Chapter 12; Reichmann, Chapter 8; and Otero, Chapter 5). In part, this concentration may reflect the relatively low educational preparation of women in the informal sector and the necessity for supplementary training to make them viable borrowers, the type of training that has been incorporated into some solidarity group programs such as BMM/Cali. Still, the rise in income and employment of beneficiaries in the solidarity group programs compares favorably with the other minimalist credit programs. We should note, however, that in the solidarity group programs that were analyzed, the base figures for the income and employment indicators were very low. Starting from such a low base figure results in higher relative increases for the solidarity group beneficiaries compared with those in individual microenterprise credit programs, who have much higher base figures for both income and employment.

Technical Assistance and Training in Solidarity Group Programs

The Solidarity Group provides a ready vehicle for training and technical assistance, as well as lending. Although lack of working capital is a primary constraint for the small firm—particularly for market vendors, who constitute a predominant beneficiary population in solidarity group programs—lack of business skills needed for expansion may also be a problem (Liedholm and Mead 1987; EPOC 1985; Cohen 1984; Otero 1986). In these programs, group-based training can help to change attitudes, solve problems and overcome obstacles, and foster the cohesion necessary to sustain group borrowing and repayment.

In minimalist credit programs, one of the primary functions of the technical support, such as firm visits, training, and ad hoc business extension, is precisely that of enabling the credit delivery mechanism to work efficiently, giving these producers access to credit. The minimalist credit model and the solidarity group mechanism have helped very low-income women, such as market vendors, gain access to credit that is responsive to the rapid turnover characteristic of commerce, with very little use of technical assistance. Making use of working capital and developing skills in credit management have increased their productive capacities and incomes, which have remained extremely modest in absolute terms (Otero 1986; Trade and Development International 1985).

In this context, the use of the solidarity group mechanism as a training tool for organizing and developing other activities supplementary to credit runs the risk of overcomplicating a relatively efficient method for providing group guarantees. A number of developments suggest that there is a risk of overloading the solidarity group lending programs. Demand for supplementary training in literacy and basic bookkeeping, as well as in nutrition and childcare, from participants in several solidarity group programs is on the rise. Also, managers of solidarity group programs in Latin America are looking to expand into complementary training services and group-based organizing (Reichmann 1984a and 1984b; Otero 1986; Guzmán and Castro, Chapter 11).

The more training seeks to accomplish, the more costly it becomes. At present, the training costs for most solidarity group programs are covered principally by grants from international funding agencies and marginally by service fees (Otero 1986, p. 21). In the case of ADEMI, the costs of training and extension implicit in their solidarity group program have been a factor leading to curtailment of this component (Tippett and McKean 1987). A primary reason for the success of similar credit programs was found to be the narrow focus of "minimalist" credit, which was not overencumbered by large amounts of training and technical assistance (Tendler 1987, p. iv).

Absorptive Capacity for Technical Assistance: A Question of Literacy, Scale, and Time

An analysis of the effect of technical assistance must take into account the responsiveness of the beneficiary, which is influenced primarily by his or her level of education, enterprise size, and time availability, as well as the expected benefits from training. The low education level of solidarity group beneficiaries, in particular, often makes literacy and basic math training a prerequisite to courses in recordkeeping (Trade and Development International 1985; Reichmann 1984a). Most microenterprises, especially very small producers and market vendors, do not have adequate background to absorb accounting courses aimed at calculating a breakeven analysis; to act on managerial extension aimed to reduce costs by improving labor productivity; or to make use of technical knowledge to increase sales by product diversification. Even the Carvajal program, which reaches primarily large microenterprises, still has had to further simplify its training and business extension services (IDB 1984).

The responsiveness of small firm owners to technical assistance and training is important in evaluating the value of extension services aimed at separating the family and the enterprise accounts. Women are often considered primary beneficiaries of such services (EPOC 1985). In microenterprises, particularly home-based activities such as prepared foods and garment production, the economy of the household is often inseparable from the economy of the enterprise. Combining the accounts gives small producers a margin of flexibility to respond to the seasonal fluctuations of the business, as well as to medical and educational demands of the family (Lipton 1980). Still, this practice is often a factor limiting expansion of the enterprise; decisions such as investment for expansion are difficult to make without knowledge of existing production costs.

Proposing a separation of accounts again raises a question of the firm owner's capacity to use the technical information provided, given the scale of the enterprise. In the case of market vendors and microproducers, basic math and literacy skills are rudimentary; capital accumulation is very restricted; and the primary objective is the survival of their economic undertaking, not mobility or expansion. The increased income of participants in solidarity programs is miniscule in absolute terms and it fluctuates daily. A family emergency can wipe out this income overnight (Trade and Development International 1985). Therefore, the risk-averse nature of such microenterprises makes it unlikely that they would make the long-term investment of both time and money that technical assistance implies.

In such a setting, revising recordkeeping may be of limited value. The time spent in keeping records has even been found to be a factor restricting, not increasing, flexible market responses, a competitive advantage characteristic of small firms (Lipton 1980; Schmitz 1982). Commonly, very small producers have limited interest in expanding their enterprise beyond its current size (Tendler 1982; Schmitz 1982). Finally, a review of solidarity group programs concluded that service fees and other revenue generated from participants do not have the capacity to cover the total operating costs of technical assistance and training currently provided (Otero 1986).

The more appropriate beneficiaries of technical assistance, which aims at reducing costs and increasing productivity and sales, are the larger microenterprises with the motivation and capacity to expand. A recent evaluation found that the Fundación Carvajal technical assistance program had enabled 53 percent of the beneficiary firms to organize an accounting system and 28 percent to reduce their costs (Universidad de San Buenaventura n.d.). An earlier evaluation of the Carvajal program by the Inter-American Development Bank found that 70 percent of the trainees had applied their accounting training to their own firm (IDB 1984, p. 33). Several factors have influenced these achievements. One, the lengthy nature of the Carvajal program, which requires successful completion of three one-week courses prior to loan approval, probably serves to "weed out" some of those less likely to succeed. A second factor is that the Carvajal program reaches predominantly the upper levels of the microenterprise sector, which would include entrepreneurs with a greater capacity to absorb such technical training and extension, given their higher education levels and more disposable income (IDB 1984). Still, the data available on the Carvajal program do not demonstrate that such technical training and extension, in and of themselves, have been a critical factor in reducing costs and improving the economic performance of the beneficiary enterprises (IDB 1986; IDB 1984; Carvajal 1985; Universidad de San Buenaventura n.d.)

Finally, time has been identified as a central limiting factor in the firm owner's ability to benefit from training and technical assistance services in several evaluations of microenterprise credit programs (Tendler 1982; Universidad de San Buenaventura n.d.; Arias 1985). In the Carvajal program, 30 percent of the entrepreneurs surveyed identified the lack of time of the advisor or themselves as a major problem (Universidad de San Buenaventura n.d.). For many women who are managing a business as well as a household, it would be difficult to find the time to attend the three weeks of required coursework. An evaluation of the small business credit program of the Industrial Bank of Peru (BIP), which studied this question directly, found that the minimal attendance of women in the training courses was attributable to their heavy household and family obligations (Arias 1985).

TRAINING AND TECHNICAL ASSISTANCE FOR THE DEVELOPMENT OF NEW ENTERPRISES IN THE INFORMAL SECTOR

Since the 1970s, both governmental and nongovernmental institutions in Latin America have begun to develop training programs for the urban informal sector, at the margin of traditional vocational training programs. The diversity of approaches and the small scale of operation of these programs are indications of their incipient character. Nonetheless, there has been a policy shift in several institutions from purely formal-sector training to assistance in the preparation for self-employment and associative enterprise development for the informal sector (Corvalàn Vàsquez 1985, p. 174; Gonzàlez Chiari 1984). The training for informal-sector enterprise promotion can be divided into two main categories: training and technical assistance oriented toward the formation of new businesses, often in the form of cooperatives or other associative enterprises, and training for existing individual microentrepreneurs. This section focuses mainly on the first type, as the second is a more recent development within mainstream training institutions, and its track record is too limited to allow for assessment.

In either of its two forms, the addition of training oriented to the informal sector through existing programs may represent an opportunity for low-income women to gain greater access to technical training. A review of women's participation in technical training institutions in Latin America found that men predominated in the formal training system offering preparation for the modern sector, whereas women predominated in short-term technical courses with a concentration in the service sector (Lembert and Nieves 1986). The result of the established formal training institutions, therefore, is the effective discrimination against women through the limitation of their access to long-term training for employment in the modern sector (with the exception of service-sector employment such as secretarial positions). An important finding of this review is that low-income women are excluded even from the short-term technical courses and have few, if any, technical training alternatives (Lembert and Nieves 1986, p. 27; De Gómez 1984, p. 107).

A number of institutions executing enterprise promotion projects have recognized that the inputs required to establish new, viable enterprises commonly go well beyond training of the participants. Skills appropriate to the trade, capital (both for the initial investment as well as for operating needs), technology, and markets are all prerequisites for enterprise development. In a training project for the informal sector in Guayaquil, Ecuador, the technical advisors found that creating new jobs by establishing associative enterprises from scratch was not a large-scale methodology for generating employment, as had been anticipated. In this case, the technical requirements of setting up a bakery and restaurant were excessively complex and costly. The time commitment was too great relative to the number of beneficiaries. In a later phase, the project directed its attention instead to providing services to established microenterprises (Placencia 1985; Carbonetto 1985, p. 360).

The experience of several women-specific enterprise development projects illustrates again the long time frame, the high costs, and the difficulties of creating economically viable group enterprises. In a project seeking to create enterprises specifically for women in Peru, organized by UNICEF and the Peruvian Ministry of Labor, the project managers came to the conclusion that group enterprise creation in the informal sector was inappropriate and unworkable and decided to concentrate on programs for the development of existing enterprises. Plans to establish a group enterprise with a US$150,000 investment were abandoned, because of the difficulties in execution and the lack of relevance to the experience of women already working in the informal sector (Pinilla 1985, p. 310).

Another women-specific enterprise development project, the Women, Enterprise and Development program executed by the Pathfinder Fund, had similar problems. Over a three-year period, Pathfinder funded women's action projects supporting the development of group-owned productive enterprises in five Latin American countries. An evaluation concluded that the semi-literate women participants benefited most from the one- to two-year training, particularly in production and management skills. They gained skills improving their employability, increased their demand for education, changed their fertility patterns, and became involved in community development activities. But after three years, only three of the five group enterprises were generating sufficient income to meet current expenses; one of these firms has since gone bankrupt (Crandon 1984, p. vii; Yudelman 1987). More important, because the firms were operating at less than full capacity, almost all of the 100 women involved in these group enterprises were working only on a part-time basis. The income stream implicit in wages of one to two weeks per month was insufficient to cover their family expenses (Crandon 1984).

Even though bankruptcy is a common fate for many of those setting up small businesses, the question that arises in this case is, when are the objectives of creating an enterprise beyond the realistic capacity of the project implementers and beneficiaries? In several cases in the Pathfinder program, basic feasibility and marketing studies were not carried out before production was set up in the group enterprise. Supplementary literacy and math training were considered essential to allow the women to benefit from skills training. Overall, the women participants undoubtedly benefited as individuals and as members of their community, but they did not benefit significantly from the income generated by the enterprises established.

Studies and evaluations of several enterprise development projects, both women-specific and not, suggest that developing financially viable enterprises is a complex, long-term proposition. Providing training and technical support for enterprise creation directly to the unemployed or to those with no previous experience carries much higher risks than providing support to individuals currently engaged in some form of economic activity. A second issue is the time cost to the participants in complex, long-term group enterprise creation projects. In many cases, it takes two to three years for many of these enterprises to become financially viable, if at all (Crandon 1984; Helzner and Overseas Education Fund 1982; Placencia 1985). For women, the time commitment of long-term training can be excessive given their family responsibilities. The more important issue in the medium term is the time by which the group enterprise will bear a reliable stream of revenue sufficient to provide income for the beneficiary and her family.

The enterprise development methodology designed by the Overseas Education Fund (OEF) for working with semi-literate women in rural areas is the basis for a number of projects targeting pre-entrepreneurs as well as established small producers. The priority in the four phases of the OEF approach—organizing, training, credit, and technical assistance—is to encourage the involvement of the women beneficiaries in the organization and management of the enterprise to a maximal extent (Kindervatter 1987). Nonformal education methods, a strength of OEF work with illiterate women, has been used increasingly in training programs developed for the urban informal sector as well as in solidarity group programs (Corvalan Vasquez 1985; Otero 1986).

The OEF Women in Business project in Central America has focused on providing services to small established home-based firms, instead of creating larger group enterprises. The high cost per beneficiary and the longer time horizon of group enterprise creation have encouraged the project manager to limit support for group enterprises to less than ten percent of the portfolio. This microenterprise credit program targets established enterprises as clients, because this group has already been prescreened for their motivation and basic skills. Even though low-income women not currently engaged in economic activity will be excluded, a criterion targeting women already economically active increases the potential for an improved income stream for a larger number of women in a modest time horizon (Kelly 1987).

New courses for existing small-scale and microenterprises are also being designed by training institutions (for example, the National Training Service in Colombia, SENA) to upgrade or improve the skills of owners, particularly in accounting, marketing, management, and even community development and leadership training. Working alone or in coordination with microenterprise programs, these institutions hope to be able to provide short, part-time courses that will be more useful to owners/operators of informal-sector businesses than the typical offerings of training centers, which are oriented toward providing technical production skills to formal sector workers.

The cost effectiveness of recent training programs directed to the informal sector is still undetermined. A study of SENA programs in Colombia found that the economic benefits of courses for informal sector workers were considerably less than those for the modern sector. Still, the per unit cost of formal sector training is much higher than training for the informal sector (SENA, Sistema de Planificación de Recursos Humanos, Bogota, 1982, p. 189, cited in Corvalàn Vàsquez 1985, pp. 159–77). We must also keep in mind that many of these training initiatives for the informal sector are directed toward promoting new enterprises, including small home-based firms, microenterprises, and associative forms of production, an approach that (according to initial results) will have a negative effect on studies of cost effectiveness (Corvalàn Vàsquez 1985, p. 161). The project's experience in the informal sector to date indicates that the risks of enterprise creation may outweigh the potential benefits to the participants.

The efforts on the part of the mainstream training institutions such as SENA, which capitalize on the more successful training initiatives of small and microenterprise credit programs, appear to hold greater promise than enterprise creation activities and may be carried out at lower cost. However, given the limited track record of these programs, it is too early to evaluate their success.

INDUSTRY- AND TRADE-BASED INITIATIVES

As we have reviewed, a favorite solution to increase access to small and microenterprise programs particularly for women beneficiaries is to provide them with training and business extension. The assumption is that these individuals suffer from a lack of skills and managerial ability. However, several studies have demonstrated that the skill level of small producers is often not a primary constraint; in some cases, it may even be a source of strength (Schmitz 1984, p. 179; King 1975). The individual skills of microentrepreneurs may not be as important as factors that are beyond the control of the individuals in determining their ability to stabilize or increase their incomes and expand production and employment. Schmitz's study of the small-scale weaving and hammock industry in Brazil found that many small producers were skilled workers, and that access to raw materials was a more important constraint for them than additional training. The significant increase in beneficiaries' income in "minimalist" microenterprise credit programs also suggests that training and technical assistance inputs may not be as essential as many assume. Organizational and management assistance to individual firms is most useful in certain situations, particularly when a firm is expanding.

In a number of women-specific small business programs, the promotion of training as a solution to problems of program access may be a problem in itself. Several of these programs, such as MUDE in the Dominican Republic, Women's World Banking in Cali, Colombia, and PAME in Ecuador, consider social and female consciousness-raising as an important tool for managerial reorientation (see Chapters 7 and 11 of this volume). Although the training itself may be valuable in changing women's attitudes and increasing their self-confidence and participation, the final effect may be the diversion of attention from some of the fundamental external constraints of these small producers.

Emphasis of a lack of individual entrepreneurial or management skills places the blame for the failure of small enterprises on the people who run them, rather than on the environment in which they operate (Schmitz 1982, p. 179–80). Recent studies of small and microenterprises increasingly demonstrate the value of analyzing the constraints on these firms in terms of the external factors influencing their development. Analyzing external factors, such as raw material supply, access to technology, or product markets, is best approached by starting with the industry subsector or trade in which the small firms operate. Trade or industry subsector-specific studies have been used increasingly as a means of identifying points of intervention. The objective has been to analyze the forces in the industry that determine the position of small enterprises, such as the pressures of competition, access to raw materials, and subcontracting relations, and then to develop interventions to alleviate the most serious constraints (Schmitz 1982; Boomgard et al. 1986; Cohen 1984; Tendler 1987; McKean 1987).

One type of project activity based on this "subsector" approach is of direct relevance to low-income women. Most often, subsector-based interventions involve studies of economic activities in which women predominate, such as the garment and weaving industry, or the street food and prepared food trade (Schmitz 1982; EPOC 1985; Cohen 1984). A project activity found responsive to these women's needs is trade-based organizing and targeted responses to specific obstacles. Schmitz's study of the hammock industry found that the lack of access to raw material was the principal constraint, and that setting up a raw-material deposit would be the most viable solution. However, women who finish the hammocks in their homes would most likely be excluded from benefits. Given the large number of workers and the lack of work alternatives, trade-based organizing, although a difficult objective, was found to be the most advantageous solution for these women (Schmitz 1982). EPOC's 1985 review of the street food trade, in which women predominate, also found that police harassment and the lack of legal recognition were major problems. An analysis of EPOC's street food activity concluded: "Perhaps the most important assistance that can be given to vendors is help in organizing" (Cohen 1984).

A review of a series of similar Ford Foundation projects found that the better performing organizations "concentrated on a . . . particular trade, sector or income-earning activity (for example, garbage collectors, food preparers, dairy producers, vegetable vendors, landless groups owning tubwells). The narrow sectoral focus of these organizations forced them to tailor their interventions to the needs of that particular sector of trade" (Tendler 1987, p. 9). It is likely that the bulk of the food preparers and vegetable vendors cited above are women, given gender breakdowns by subsector found in similar projects (EPOC 1985).

In Latin America, vendor and trade-based associations of microenterprises are slowly growing and expanding the provision of services. In Cartagena, Colombia, stall vendors have formed an association to limit police harassment (Otero 1986). In the Dominican Republic, the Asociación de Tricicleros, a trade association with a predominantly male membership, has an insurance scheme and provides representation in negotiations with the municipal government (Reichmann 1984a).

The stimulation of brokering between buyers and producers is another type of sector-specific assistance to small enterprises, but the results of project experience in this area have been limited. In one case, an attempt to link up groups of small handicraft producers directly with buyers has allowed buyers to conduct on-site training in product design and quality control, which led to contracts for several groups of small producers. Women, in this case, were the primary beneficiaries (McKean 1985). Technical assistance has been targeted to small furniture enterprises to strengthen their access to buyers, and to shrimp farmers to improve the quality of their production in Indonesia. However, it is unlikely that these types of interventions will have a direct effect on income of the beneficiaries in the short term. Again, as in complex enterprise development projects, the risk of failure is inherent in efforts requiring the provision of multiple inputs over a long period of time.

CONCLUSION: HOW CAN LOW-INCOME WOMEN
BEST BENEFIT FROM TRAINING AND TECHNICAL ASSISTANCE?

Several factors influence the capacity of low-income women to benefit from training and technical assistance inputs. Illiteracy and lack of education are fundamental constraints. Second, the very tiny size and commerce base of the enterprises most commonly managed by women limit their motivation and capacity to absorb complex technical training or business extension. Third, time is a scarce resource particularly for the growing number of Latin American women responsible for both providing for their family and managing a household.

Solidarity group lending has given economically active women in the informal sector access to credit for working capital. Minimal training and technical assistance inputs have permitted the loan guarantee mechanism to work and have provided some skills upgrading in order to improve the businesses and to solve other problems. However, there is the risk of overloading the system. Using the solidarity group mechanism for providing supplementary training in organization, or even nutrition, may unintentionally add unsustainable costs to the credit program. Microproducers and vendors may want training in record management, nutrition, or even in business strategies. Managers also consider training an integral component of the solidarity group strategy. Yet the danger of responding excessively to these demands within the context of the solidarity group credit program is that expectations grow, objectives multiply, and capacity diminishes. The costs of providing these services have the strong potential to overwhelm a self-sustaining credit mechanism and to reduce the ability to lend, thus interfering with the primary focus of the program.

Market vendors and home-based producers, many of whom are women, may have little capacity to absorb training and technical assistance aimed at separating household and business accounts. Illiteracy, minute scale, and lack of time can make such efforts a waste of resources. Credit- or trade-based organizing for established producers or traders may be more immediately relevant to their experience. Training in accounting, business extension, and production-specific assistance have the greatest impact on microenterprises with the capacity and desire for expansion. Still, for women managing these larger microenterprises, time is a constraint to the benefits of valuable accounting assistance. Family obligations and household duties may continue to restrict women's ability to access such services.

The opportunity cost of participation is even higher in the case of projects that seek to develop new enterprises. The priority here for programs targeting women in the informal sector is not to attempt the impossible. Concentrating on economically active women, for whom a limited number of inputs are required, is a more realistic approach. Targeting illiterate women who are not economically active for the creation of new group enterprises may result in more failures than successes. As Kilby has argued, supplying the "missing ingredient" is the project activity with the greatest potential for generating income for beneficiaries in a relatively modest time frame (Kilby 1979).

Finally, it is important to transcend the mindset that sees factors internal to the firm, such as lack of skills, of management capacity, or of a social consciousness, as the primary constraints. Subsector studies identifying critical external obstacles in the industries and trading activities, in which women predominate, can lead to effective interventions for women in the informal sector.

NOTES

1. The term "informal sector" is used here to refer to economic activity characterized by "ease of entry, reliance on indigenous resources, family ownership of enterprises, small scale of operation, labor intensive and adapted technology, skills acquired outside the formal school system and unregulated and competitive markets" (ILO 1972; see Hart 1971 for original definition).

2. Dipak Mazumdar documents the preponderance of women in the informal sector in his article, "The Urban Informal Sector," in *World Development,* p. 660. See also Chapter 1, the Introduction to this volume, and Lycette and White, Chapter 2.

3. The term "pre-entrepreneurs" refers here to individuals not currently economically active, who have been identified as interested and capable of undertaking activity to generate income. Some projects of the Overseas Education Fund, the Pathfinder Fund, the ILO, and other institutions have targeted pre-entrepreneurs as beneficiaries.

4. The term "minimalist" credit is used by Judith Tendler in her recent review of Ford Foundation programs for poverty alleviation. See Tendler 1987.

7

Training and Credit Programs for Microentrepreneurs: *Some Concerns about the Training of Women*

MARÍA MERCEDES PLACENCIA

Socioeconomic conditions have been critical in Ecuador since the early 1980s, worsening over time in the context of a recessionary economy. Employment statistics indicate that open unemployment has doubled in the past ten years, with a rate of 12 percent forecast for 1987. More than 50 percent of the economically active population (EAP) is considered underemployed according to income criteria.

There are no national measurements of the urban informal sector; but, according to estimates of the International Labour Organization's Regional Employment Program for Latin America and the Caribbean (PREALC), more than one-third of the urban EAP is included in this category, equivalent to approximately 600,000 people. Analyzing El Guasmo, one of the largest shantytowns of Guayaquil, with approximately 200,000 inhabitants, the International Labour Organization (ILO) estimated that in 1982 of the population of active or working age (124,000, or 61 percent) only some 50 percent were employed. Of that total (61,800), 40 percent worked in the formal sector—in low-income occupational categories—and about 60 percent worked in the informal sector, in activities with low capital-labor ratios, that is, low-productivity and low-income work.

Women's participation in this sector of the economy is significant and varies from region to region. For example, research carried out in Quito and Guayaquil has indicated that, although women account for 70 percent of petty traders in Quito, in Guayaquil the figure is only 30 percent (Farrell 1985). In any event, women comprise about 50 percent of the total labor force in that part of the informal sector that encompasses tertiary-sector economic activities (commerce and services) and some productive activities such as garment-making and baking. In this context, it is particularly important to consider the possibilities for women to improve their quality of life and their incomes.

This chapter describes the operation and some of the achievements of programs to support microentrepreneurs, based on the experiences of the Center for Informal Sector Promotion and Employment (Centro de Promoción y Empleo para el Sector Informal-CEPESIU) and the Fundación Guayaquil, in which ILO-PREALC is implementing an integrated informal-sector development project that includes assessment and training activities, advisory services and credit. The methodology of this program will be analyzed, and within this framework the question of whether it is necessary to develop training specifically for women will be addressed.

DEFINITION OF THE INFORMAL SECTOR

To understand the whole set of actions of the program cited, it is best to begin by characterizing and conceptualizing the urban informal sector (UIS). In effect, the range of activities geared to supporting the UIS is based on the notion of the informal sector as a set of microentrepreneurial units, be they commercial, productive, or service-oriented, which develop with their own particular features. On the whole, this group is made up of the surplus labor force—those workers who are not absorbed in the formal labor market and have to find alternative ways to survive and generate incomes. Thus, the UIS is a strategy for employment and survival (see Chapter 3 by Jaime Mezzera).

Although there is not yet a consensus regarding the conceptualization of the UIS, there is a trend toward viewing it as a structural phenomenon—an approach that has been advocated by PREALC after years of research and studies. According to this definition, the UIS is identified with productive units based on heterogeneous technological and occupational structures, which have been created by that part of the labor force that is excluded from the modern sector. Despite this differentiation, multiple and complex relationships exist between the modern and informal sectors.

The urban informal sector is generated out of the need to survive, and vis-á-vis the lack of an alternative in the shape of a formal-sector job. It is a universe of productive units with specific characteristics, which distinguishes them—in a disadvantageous fashion—from the productive units of the modern capitalist economic sector. These small firms—most of them run by a single person, sometimes with relatives—have several common denominators. Among the most important are their economic limitations—minimal or no access to capital and credit, and therefore limited use of appropriate technologies, which is reflected by the low levels of investment per worker; technical limitations—major gaps in terms of quality control and design, low technical qualifications, and little or no productive organization; legal and administrative limitations—lack of a legal and organizational framework, lack of basic accounting records; and social limitations—lack of insurance and other benefits, and relatively frequent use of unpaid family labor.

Considering that these productive units are self-generated by a poor population that has little capital, it is not suprising that their main limitation, at least at the outset, is a low capital/labor ratio (K/L), which implies low profits. Women, who historically have had less access to productive resources in Ecuador and other countries of the region, are even more capital-starved. If one of the most limiting factors for developing an informal firm is a low capital endowment, support strategies should aim to eliminate this restriction, or at least diminish it, by gradually fostering an increase in the capital/labor ratio, and raising productivity.

But in addition, given the characteristics of these firms and of those who run them, support for increasing their assets must be accompanied by a process of technical and managerial training and advice, to allow for an integral transformation of the proprietors and the productive units themselves. Comprehensive and coordinated support should lead to enhanced productivity and incomes for a significant part of the "functional" informal units, that is, those that manifest possibilities for growth in the short and medium term. The microenterprise support programs discussed here were designed and implemented according to this perspective and its focus on integral support.

A comprehensive approach and self-management should be the pillars of support for a microenterprise development methodology geared to a group in which the contribution of the owner-operator is so important. In the case of women microentrepreneurs, recognizing the need for both comprehensive and specific support implies recognizing the existence of problems and needs that women entrepreneurs share with their male counterparts in the informal sector. But it also implies taking into account the age-old discrimination against women, which has blocked their access to better training, capital, employment, income, savings, and decision-making authority. Also, given their roles of mother and wife, women have often had to combine their domestic activities and their economic activity in the home, which can be an obstacle to their full social and economic development.

In sum, attempting to establish a specific methodology for training women microentrepreneurs necessitates recognizing and accepting that the state of subordination and discrimination against women is a class problem and a sex problem, manifested in social and economic life in general, albeit taking on different forms and varying in intensity. Enabling women to achieve social and economic self-realization will thus require more specific attention, as their problems are also specific.

THE MICROENTERPRISE SUPPORT PROGRAM

The main obstacles faced by informal-sector activities, or microenterprises, are two: training and credit. If these are the main hindrances to greater de-velopment and growth of microenterprises, then any strategy for support and promotion should contribute to eliminating or at least limiting these obstacles in the establishment of new firms, and in the strengthening of mi-croenterprises that already exist. This is the approach taken by the program described here, which is based on an integral, complementary, and par-ticipatory methodology geared to the small-scale producers of the UIS.

Enterprise Creation Subprogram

The International Labour Organization's program concept and methodolog-ical design for microenterprise support (PAME) goes back some four years, and has grown out of research and studies carried out in poor urban areas of Guayaquil where the microenterprise situation was assessed for different activities. Implementation of the Microenterprise Support Program began in December 1985, with selection, assessment, training, advising, and exten-sion of credit. The Fundación Guayaquil is in charge of the program. Al-though at this stage it is still too early to assess the program's results and impact, this chapter will describe the key aspects of the program as well as trends emerging after a few months' work.

The Microenterprise Support Program has two subprograms. One is aimed at generating new employment by creating small cooperatives. This program was initially intended to serve as a methodology for massive job creation. But in practice, after a tremendous effort had been made—espe-cially of a technical nature, which required giving two cooperative firms con-siderable support—it was concluded that this was not the best way to create jobs on a massive scale. In any event, it was not possible with the methodol-ogy adopted, in which the support organization was to start from zero—that is, choosing the activity, developing an investment profile and getting the firm started, and culminating in initial management and then co-management as steps leading to the total transfer of the property and man-agement of the firm by the workers.

Clearly, a program to generate new microenterprises, if it is going to function with lower costs and less expenditure of energy, should be attempted only when certain preconditions are met. Training a relatively homoge-neous, pre-existing group, even if the group is incipient, is easier than start-ing from scratch. Investing capital in a productive initiative that has been studied, planned out, and backed by the basic nucleus of potential entrepre-neurs who will operate it will also facilitate launching and setting such an initiative on a sound course.

Notwithstanding these difficulties, two firms were established within this first subprogram, a bakery and a luncheonette, both of which are located in downtown Guayaquil in a highly populated shopping area. The bakery works very well; it employs twenty-three workers, six of whom are women. One of the women is the general manager. All the workers receive at least the minimum wage, in addition to those benefits mandated by law. To date they have paid off approximately 50 percent of the cost of the firm's total assets, such that the business operates with adequate profit margins. It operates with a capital-to-labor ratio that is under US$2,000, showing that it is possible to establish firms whose investment costs per worker are considerably lower than they would be in the formal sector.

Although it was an extremely costly experience, this subprogram yielded many lessons regarding self-management including the idea that this type of firm can be used as a technical and managerial training ground or workshop for informal-sector entrepreneurs.

Subprogram of Support to Existing Microenterprises

The second subprogram is geared to supporting already existing productive units, as it is obviously much easier and less costly to support activities that have already been initiated, whether they are small-scale commercial operations or small workshops. First of all, those who operate these businesses wanted to start their own business, even though ultimately they were driven to do so by social conditions and lack of opportunity in the formal labor market; but they had a drive, and they thought and behaved like entrepreneurs. Given their predisposition, it was easier for them to absorb technical knowledge and support in the form of credit.

The informal businesses receiving assistance are located in Guayaquil's shantytown areas, particularly in the populous Febres Cordero parish, and in some areas on the periphery of the city center. Within the city some marketplaces where large numbers of women work have also been supported. To date there have been 390 beneficiaries, 67 percent of whom work in production (that is, manufacturing) and services, and 33 percent in commerce. This breakdown corresponds to an institutional policy that tends to place priority on the productive sector, in which activities are assumed to be more dynamic, and which is considered to have greater potential for growth in the short and medium term. Indeed, the seeds of training and credit planted in the productive sector will yield better and longer lasting results in terms of productivity, employment, and income.

From an economic standpoint this approach diminishes the possibilities of supporting women, who have only minimal access to productive activities and are mainly involved in the tertiary sector, that is, commerce and services. Seeking another priority does not mean that the economic participation of women should not be reoriented; it should. However, in the meantime, it is important to support the economic activities in which women are already involved.

Microenterprise Assessment

Within the ILO program, the methodology for enterprise support is integral; it includes an initial step for assessment through application of a questionnaire for microentrepreneurs that reveals information about the owner of the shop and about the firm. This step enables the program to work with an advanced basic knowledge about the firm's status, which in turn makes it easier to determine the firm's training, technical assistance, and credit needs. This first phase of assessment is done with a computerized data-processing system, increasing efficiency, reducing costs, and facilitating to a certain extent "massification" of the program. This novel technique was partially applied by CEPESIU and was further developed by the Fundación Guayaquil. Although these programs will probably require midstream adjustments, they already constitute a significant methodological contribution.

The program is being carried out on an experimental basis to demonstrate that implementation of a relatively simple, quick, and low-cost methodology for assessment of microenterprises is feasible and replicable. To assess and support firms whose investment-per-worker range is from US$300 to US$2,000, alternative methodologies that take little time and that can be implemented with properly trained mid-level technical personnel had to be developed. By use of these methodologies, the cost of the assessment per firm is estimated to be about US$30. The cost of training ranges from US$30 to US$100. Thus it is possible to operate the support program at a cost that is generally not greater than 5 percent of total investment.

Training and Technical Assistance

Once the assessment phase concludes, the training program begins with eight workshops. Training is provided in general accounting principles (inventory, balance sheets), costs (profit and loss statements, break-even point), and investment. In addition, this phase includes tasks relating to individual assistance, that is, field visits to each of the microentrepreneurs attending the training workshops. The fundamental objective of these visits is to reinforce the skills taught in the workshops.

Through the training program the microentrepreneurs learn to take inventory, calculate production costs—including in some cases the break-even point—and, finally, to produce profit and loss statements. This type of training adds a technical business-oriented dimension to the microentrepreneur's own self-improvement efforts. The program is predicated on the belief that training is fundamental. If after several months or a year of participating in the program the entrepreneurs are unable to manage their firms on their own, and to make business decisions—whether to expand, or to diversify production or clients—very little will have been accomplished. In that regard, the organization strives to ensure that training be highly participatory and concrete, easy to understand, and accessible, taking into account the skills and needs of the entrepreneurs themselves.

If training is designed not only to bring about immediate improvements or changes in the microenterprise, but also to affect the transformation and sustained development of the microentrepreneur, training must result in a qualitative leap of advancement for the individual. That is, it attempts to convert him or her into a true entrepreneurial manager, capable of analyzing a business situation and of finding ways to develop permanently his or her establishment, always seeking optimally to administer the firm's economic and human resources. With this as the goal, active participation of the people who are being supported is a key training strategy.

A training program for informal-sector producers who have the characteristics and needs described—minimal level of general knowledge, material and economic limitations, little or no knowledge of management and business administration, and limited availability of time—requires a nontraditional methodological approach, taking as its starting point the real conditions these individuals face. At the same time, it should be a catalyst for involving the trainees as a creative force in their own training process. Thus, parallel to training courses, a process of individual technical assistance is put into motion, for follow-up of the initial training. This methodology arose because the ILO found that, when there is training with no follow-up, it is very difficult for the microentrepreneur to absorb all the information, as he or she enters the course with a bare minimum of entrepreneurial knowledge. If there is no follow-up, what was gained can easily be lost. In the case of the Fundación Guayaquil program, technical assistance consists of field visits to each enterprise, which are followed in turn by new workshops in which the microentrepreneurs assist in the assessment of their progress, in particular in using the accounting tools. The Fundación wants to ensure that they keep a daily record of cash flow that will enable them to calculate, at the end of each month, how much they sold, how much they bought, and how much their personal expenses came to.

Results of the Training Component.   Some of the early results of the training and technical assistance follow:

- Seventy-nine percent of the microentrepreneurs identified and invited attended the training sessions, and of these approximately four-fifths passed the course.

- Of all those trained, 82 percent were male and 18 percent female. This mix is explained by the low percentage of women in manufacturing activities, upon which the Fundacíon places greater stress.

- There were no differences in methodology or training contents for men and women microentrepreneurs.

- A comparative analysis between those invited and those who attended indicates that women are relatively more interested in training than men, as a higher proportion of women who were invited actually attended.

- There were no major differences between men and women in numbers of dropouts.

Credit

A credit program is closely linked to the training program. The credit system involves small loans that increase in size in correlation to the repayment of earlier loans; the loans also grow in accord with the firms' needs, which mainly involve covering working capital, increasing liquidity, and increasing sales capacity and, thus, income.

The loans are divided into two types: working capital and investment capital. The first provides small loans (between S/5,000 and S/50,000, equivalent to approximately US$17 to US$170) mainly to members of solidarity groups of three to six microentrepreneurs for a period of fifteen days to four months. Fixed investment loans can be used only for the purchase of new machinery, for incorporation of new production techniques, or for the expansion or improvement of the workshop itself. To apply for an investment loan, the microentrepreneur must receive prior training and prepare an investment plan. The size of these loans is larger (between S/50,000 and S/300,000, equivalent to approximately US$170 to US$1,000), and repayment periods are longer than those of the working capital loans. Interest rates for both programs correspond to prevailing commercial rates and vary according to market conditions.

An attempt is made to enable the firm, in the initial training and credit support stage, to maximize use of installed capacity, without adding, for the time being, new fixed investments. At the conclusion of the credit and training stage, the project permits the more dynamic firms to advance to a second credit stage geared mainly to manufacturing units that have some potential for expansion, and that can thus justify increased credit for fixed investment to improve existing equipment or to add new machinery.

Results of the Credit Component.   The results of extending such credit follow:

- Up to September 1986, credit was extended to 283 firms, 42 percent of which are in manufacturing, 18 percent in services, and 40 percent in commerce (see Table 7.1).

- The average size of loans was approximately S/20,000; the largest loan granted has been for S/100,000 (approximately US$336 at the current exchange rate).

- Given the high rate of turnover of credit to commerce activities, this sector received the largest number of credits, even though the total amount extended to commerce was roughly the same as that which the manufacturing sector received.

- Seventy-eight percent of credit recipients were male, and 22 percent female. Women accounted for a small share of those involved in manufacturing and services, constituting only 6 percent. This small representation is due to women's more limited access to technical training; their minimal, or lack of access to start-up capital; differentiated sex roles established by society; and their other roles and responsibilities. All of these are obstacles to equal opportunity for women in the labor market, and in the manufacturing sector in particular.

TABLE 7.1
Activities for Which Credit Has Been Extended

	No. of Microenterprises
Manufacturing and Services	
Cabinetmaking	66
Autoshop	36
Locksmiths	35
Foundries and workshops	5
Sewing and tailors' shops	8
Shoemaking	2
Restaurants and related services	11
Bakeries	1
Cement block-making	1
Handicrafts	2
Electrical appliance repairs	3
Beauty parlor	1
Commerce	
Food staples	49
Butchers, shellfish, and fruit vendors	31
Hardware outlets	2
Miscellaneous supplies	20
Clothing	8
Watches and jewelry	2
Total	283

Implications for the Woman Microentrepreneur

The program described above is geared to both men and women. At this time no preferential treatment is accorded to women. The project has been centered in the southwestern part of Guayaquil, and to some extent in Guasmo, these being the poorest parts of the city. Surveys are taken and firms are approached—independent of the proprietor's sex—both in markets and among small workshops, with emphasis on the latter. No explicit effort has been made to work with trade associations or organized groups. Nevertheless, in the context of the work described, some concerns must be expressed regarding women's participation and specific additional training for women.

As a starting point, we must recognize that the problems of male and female microentrepreneurs—that is, lack of training in management and lack of credit—are identical. In this respect, there is no major difference between men and women. As entrepreneurs they share similar problems, even though the origins of these problems are different in some cases. Nonetheless, the fact that women are concentrated in certain branches of production implies that the training they receive in production techniques might be different. But, even taking these technical differences into account, if we only consider women as microentrepreneurs there would be no justification for promoting programs specifically for women.

However, the experience of PAME has given rise to the question of whether it is important to add something more to technical, entrepreneurial, and management training. Perhaps there is a need for training related to the fact that the entrepreneur is a woman, and all its implications—the discrimination, exclusion, and historic subordination to which women have been subjected. In this context it makes sense to expand training to include a component on analysis of the national reality, so as to enable female entrepreneurs to place themselves within the overall context of the microenterprise sector and their respective firms, as well as to advance toward an analysis of their role in society, and their role and potential within the firm, as individuals who generate employment and produce wealth. Needed is a type of training that is geared to an appreciation by women of their value as human beings and as part of a labor force responsible for their own production.

The aim of PAME—and of most other programs—in trying to help firms become dynamic, is the conversion of both women and men into true entrepreneurs. This goal requires a qualitative leap on the part of the individual, which involves creating or strengthening his or her entrepreneurial outlook. If such an approach is to be successful, it may at times require special consciousness-raising in the case of women who have not been socialized to have such attitudes.

Training for entrepreneurial reorientation should also be designed specifically for women. Without this, microenterprise programs will indeed continue supporting for many years, or even decades, women's activities marked by very low productivity, which yield very low incomes. Entrepreneurial reorientation should offer women the chance to redirect their businesses, that is, to have access to knowledge of what other types of firms they might establish, their real capabilities, costs, and alternative lines of work available to them even within the commercial sector. With such orientation, there will continue to be high percentages of women in nonproductive informal-sector activities, and inequality of incomes between men and women will persist.

As regards credit, it is important to recall that women often use microenterprise loans to address needs that are not exclusively entrepreneurial, and that nonentrepreneurial use is practically inevitable given their responsibilities of caring for children and maintaining the home. In any event, provided that they pay their debt in a timely fashion—and there are indications that women are more responsible than men in doing so—they should be served on a basis equal to that of men, to the extent that, as entrepreneurs, they need this service.

Finally, one important step that can be taken to promote women's participation in microenterprise programs is the creation of a subcomponent for women within the program as a whole, to serve an advocacy role as well as monitoring women's participation and progress. The subprogram should be carefully designed, to take into account the specific characteristics of women's businesses in the area, the existence of other complementary programs, and the costs of such an intervention.

8

Women's Participation in Two PVO Credit Programs for Microenterprise: *Cases from the Dominican Republic and Peru*

REBECCA REICHMANN

Thus chapter examines the level and quality of women's participation in two programs supported by ACCION/AITEC, a U.S.-based private voluntary organization (PVO) that provides technical assistance to microenterprise programs in Latin America. ACCION is dedicated to testing and applying new credit methodologies in an attempt to overcome traditional constraints faced by the poor, including poor women, in securing access to credit and recognition as productive contributors to their local and national economies.

The chapter presents two parallel cases: The Association for the Development of Microenterprises, Inc. (ADEMI), in the Dominican Republic, and Progreso, a project of Acción Comunitaria del Peru in Lima, Peru.[1] These cases illustrate the degree to which integrated (that is, non-women-specific) microenterprise assistance schemes can be effective in reaching women, and highlight the benefits women derive from participating in such schemes. Although they have many similarities, the two programs are also greatly influenced by the different national environments in which they operate. They have distinct organizational and operational features, yet both programs share an emphasis on trying to reach the smallest businesses in the microenterprise sector, targeting assistance directly to the self-employed poor. In part, this approach helps to explain the high proportion of women borrowers in both credit schemes.

The chapter will first briefly review the data on women's economic activities in the project areas, Santo Domingo and Lima. Second, it discusses the scarcity of credit options available to marginalized women in Latin American cities, along with the special constraints faced by women who wish to obtain formal credit. Next, the chapter describes each of the credit programs, examines their experience in lending to women, and makes an initial assessment of their impact on women. The final section summarizes the strengths and weaknesses of the projects and provides some recommendations for improving their effectiveness from the point of view of women beneficiaries.

WOMEN'S ECONOMIC ACTIVITIES

Santo Domingo

The level of women's productive economic activity in the city of Santo Domingo is not accurately reflected in official statistics about women's labor force participation.[2] This discrepancy is due, in part, to their predominant involvement in "informal-sector" economic activities: vending (of charcoal, firewood, foods, flowers, and cigarettes) from the house or in the street, clothing production, food production, cottage crafts, and services such as hairdressing.

Nonetheless, data do show that the informal-sector activities of women have multiplied in recent years because of the large numbers of urban migrants in Santo Domingo. In 1983 one-quarter of the total population of the Dominican Republic resided in Santo Domingo (Duarte 1983), and that number is steadily increasing, as noted in a recent study by the Inter-American Development Bank (IDB 1987). Over the past twenty years the female labor force has been increasing rapidly. In 1960 only 22.1 percent of women over age fifteen were considered economically active; by 1980 the proportion had risen to 39.3 percent. Urban migration resulted in the tripling of the population of Santo Domingo between 1960 and 1980, while the numbers of economically active women in the city quintupled during the same period (Bàez 1983, p. 3). Growth in female labor force participation has been greater than that of males, especially in urban areas.

Rapid rural-to-urban migration has also been associated with rising rates of urban unemployment and underemployment in the Dominican Republic, and women are affected more than men. In 1983 unemployment in Santo Domingo was 19 percent for economically active men and 25 percent for women (Duarte 1983, p. 35). Women who are employed are often found in more precarious jobs than men (Bàez 1983). In 1983, 45 percent of the total female labor force was made up of either domestics or informal workers who work in establishments with less than five employees (Duarte 1983).

The self-employed workers whom ADEMI seeks to assist increased from 14.4 percent to 17.7 percent of the total working population in Santo

Domingo between 1980 and 1983. Women represent 25 percent of the self-employed (Bàez 1983). Women are overrepresented in certain sectors of the economy, particularly services (where 50 percent of the economically active women are employed, compared to 36 percent of men) and commerce (accounting for 19 percent of women and 7.5 percent of men). Only 11 percent of working women are in the manufacturing sector, as are 14 percent of working men.

In Santo Domingo, women's salaries are lower than men's across the board, even when the level of education is the same. In 1983, 58 percent of the working women in the city earned less than the minimum salary established by PREALC of RD$125 per month (or US$42 at the exchange rates of that time—US$1 = RD$3). Twenty-six percent of the men were below this poverty line, and 31 percent of the microenterprise women earned less than RD$50 (or US$17 at 1983 rates). More recent estimates reflecting increases in the cost of living show that as many as 81 percent of women may be living below the poverty level.

Lima

One study undertaken in the 1970s found that women accounted for 40 percent of the informal-sector labor force in Lima, even when domestic servants were excluded. Of the self-employed in that sector, 61 percent were women (Mazumdar 1976). More recent labor force surveys estimate that women constitute 34.5 percent of those working in informal-sector activities of the Peruvian economy. Hernando de Soto reports that 70 percent of women working in the informal sector are involved in commerce, 22 percent in production, and 8.2 percent in services.[3]

Census data show that, overall, women are 23.1 percent of the self-employed in the Department of Lima and they are heavily concentrated in commerce activities, where they account for over one-third of those employed in the sector. Women are disproportionately represented among vendors who borrow from the Progreso microenterprise loan program (they are 80 percent in that category) and under-represented among producers (they account for only about 17 percent of clients). However, Progreso's married female microentrepreneurs tend to earn more than their husbands, who earn laborers' or even semi-skilled salaries. Most of the women interviewed for a 1984 study of Progreso reported that either they were the sole source of income for the family; their husbands were sporadically employed; or they made significantly more money than their husbands, because of extremely low wages.

Constraints to Women's Access to Credit

In spite of their major contribution to the economies of Latin American countries, women are virtually excluded from credit opportunities with formal-sector institutions. Interviews with local credit institutions and development programs in the Dominican Republic, for example, revealed that few credit options are available to urban women with incomes below the upper-middle-class level of RD$10,000 (or US$3,333) in that country.[4] One woman with a small ceramics manufacturing business noted: "Here in the Dominican Republic, the people who are able to borrow money are those who already have it."

Several programs combining credit with technical assistance (handicrafts, livestock raising, clothing production, or other cottage industry) work with rural women's groups in the Dominican Republic, but these programs reach limited numbers of women and often assume responsibility for obtaining production materials, supervising technical inputs, and marketing the finished product—in short, controlling all aspects of business management so that beneficiaries serve primarily as labor inputs and learn very little about managing their own productive activities (Kelley 1983). In urban Santo Domingo, even programs of this sort are scarce. The Dominican Development Foundation provided credit and technical assistance to small numbers of microbusinesswomen, but it was unable to meet the needs of the vast numbers of potential beneficiaries in the city and has since ceased these operations.

In part, their exclusion from access to formal credit sources is due to the fact that the specific credit needs of women entrepreneurs often differ from the credit options available through formal-sector lending institutions. Their businesses require smaller amounts of capital than are customarily lent, and repayment and collateral requirements must be fairly flexible. For these reasons informal lending flourishes at the marginal level. The most common form of credit utilized by lower income Dominican women is the *prestamista,* the informal moneylender who charges 10 to 20 percent interest on small, short-term (one- to six-week) loans. This credit is generally used for emergencies and day-to-day survival, rather than for investing in the expansion of productive activities. The *prestamistas* will lend small amounts on a short-term basis; they are local, accessible, available day or night, and flexible about repayment; and their collateral requirements depend primarily on the level of his personal acquaintance with the borrower. Of course, the tradeoff for the microentrepreneur is the *prestamista's* usurious interest rates.

In Lima, women's informal enterprises—dressmaking, knitting, food production, or even a small electrical parts manufacturing business, for example—do not qualify for loans from traditional lending institutions. With no collateral and only her word to guarantee a loan, a resident of one of Lima's *pueblos jóvenes,* or squatter settlements, must depend upon family members or friends for informal loans, or upon moneylenders (locally called *usureros*), who charge up to 20 percent per week for small loans. Another informal source of credit is the *junta* or *pandero,* an informal revolving savings/credit association in which members of a small group of friends or neighbors contribute weekly to a common fund, and the money is distributed to each of the members on a rotating basis.[5] ACCION's interviews revealed that very few of Progreso's female clients had borrowed either formally or through moneylenders before receiving their Progreso loan. Many reported having participated in *juntas* or borrowed from family and friends.

In Peru, the Dominican Republic and, elsewhere in Latin America, efforts have been made to overcome these constraints to women's access to credit by use of a group credit mechanism, through which either a small group guarantees its individual members' debts or production groups borrow together for their collective business activities. ADEMI and Progreso have chosen to adopt the former, a "solidarity group" credit mechanism that alleviates collateral problems to assist microbusinesses at the lowest economic levels. At the same time, these programs try to address the problems encountered by women at a slightly higher economic level by making individual loans to them. In their "microenterprise" components, the previous track records of the businesses and their potential capacity for increased production and marketing replace collateral requirements.[6] Below we will examine how ADEMI and Progreso have incorporated design features that remove some of the constraints to women's access to credit.

PARTICIPATION OF WOMEN
IN TWO MICROENTERPRISE PROGRAMS

The history of the ADEMI and Progreso programs presents an interesting study in contrast in microenterprise assistance. Although they arose out of different institutional experiences, the two programs began with very similar mechanisms for providing credit and technical assistance to microproducers and vendors. They both utilized two well-known lending methodologies to reach different types of beneficiaries. Individual loans, guaranteed by cosigners, were offered to microenterprises involved primarily in manufacturing, and to a lesser extent, services. Borrowers with small-scale sales operations were only eligible for credit as part of a "solidarity group" whose members mutually guaranteed each other's loans. Table 8.1 compares the key features of these two credit mechanisms.

In early 1984, when studies of women's participation in the two programs were conducted (see Reichmann 1984 and 1986b), both were still using the two credit mechanisms. However, over time different problems faced by the institutions led each to focus on a different methodology: ADEMI has virtually eliminated solidarity group loans while Progreso now organizes its program almost exclusively around solidarity groups, regardless of the borrower's economic activity. These changes have had an impact on women's participation in the two programs, which will be explored in greater depth after the following background discussion of the programs.

TABLE 8.1
Comparison of Two Credit Methodologies

Solidarity Group Loans	Individual Loans
Promotion	
Word-of-mouth: informal conversation among friends, relatives, and workmates	Word-of-mouth: generally informal conversation between project participants and other business owners
Selection	
Consensual selection of group: members share responsibility for loan payment	Suitability of client is determined by the project staff through an economic analysis of the business
Mechanism	
Clients form their own credit groups of five business owners	One-on-one assistance to individual clients
Assuring Payback	
Group structure ensures that those who do not pay will be pressured by other group members	Staff keep records of repayment schedules and control their loan portfolio
If this fails, program staff can, as a last resort, repossess property purchased through the loan	Staff members are advised of late payments and visits are made to the business; if this is not enough, legal steps are taken
Management Assistance	
Exchange of ideas about improving business practices occurs informally through conversations with groups members	Program personnel teach clients how to improve their businesses in one-on-one sessions
Beneficiary's Role in Program	
Clients can assume increasingly important roles in meeting program goals	Aside from clients' activity in program promotion and training, their role is limited
Membership	
Informing others about the program	
Taking an active role in the credit group	
Becoming a group coordinator	
Appropriate Client Population	
Very small businesses	Manufacturing shops with at least one employee
May be appropriate for larger businesses but this needs to be explored	Probably not suited for the smallest businesses, as cost per beneficiary is higher and the supportive structure of the groups is absent

Source: Ashe 1984.

PROGRESO

Acción Comunitaria del Perú (ACP) created Progreso to fortify the numerous businesses of the informal sector in Lima's squatter settlements, with long-range goals of increasing income and creating new employment at the lowest levels of the economy. Because of ACCION International/AITEC's Latin American experience with microenterprise development programs, Acción Comunitaria del Perú expressed interest in working with AITEC advisors to implement a similar methodology in Lima's southern cone. The program has now expanded to include offices in each of the four "cones" of Lima's *pueblos jóvenes*. During the period December 1986–January 1987, a total of 2,217 clients were assisted.

Progreso combines characteristics of informal lending practices with elements of a formal lending institution. A frequent repayment option for market vendors, elimination of the collateral requirement, reduction of client paperwork, transaction time, and costs, and regular meetings for program beneficiaries in the Progreso offices all contribute to client perception that Progreso is informal and therefore accessible. The philosophy of a "line of credit" for each client encourages Progreso clients to begin long-range planning for their businesses and to think critically about how to increase production.

Progreso's main formal credit characteristics are competitive interest rates, integration with banking procedures, and legal protection. Timely loan recuperation is essential to Progreso's continued ability to extend credit to the poor in Lima. When payments are overdue, a fine is charged for every day that a payment is late, which averages 2 percent of the amount due plus a late payment fine. Progreso's seriousness in collecting loan payments is reflected in high repayment rates. As of December 1986 the on-time repayment rate was 93 percent for individual and 96 percent for solidarity group loans.

Progreso's loan program originally had two components with contrasting methodologies: individual loans for microenterprises, mainly oriented to very small manufacturing businesses; and solidarity group loans for street and market vendors and owners of very small manufacturing or service businesses. The vendors reinforced collective responsibility through a highly participatory process, whereas the methodology of the microproducer component emphasized one-on-one technical assistance and had limited associative objectives.

To qualify for participation in the Progreso loan program, a business must demonstrate a capacity to invest effectively in materials, equipment, machinery, or inventory, and, for microproducers, to employ more workers. A business must be at least two years old and be located in Lima's *pueblos jóvenes*. There are restrictions on the size of businesses that may apply for

Progreso loans; in 1987 new clients had to have assets valued at less than US$1200. Normally, microproducers must be engaged in manufacturing because it is generally agreed that these activities have a greater potential for expansion, but some service businesses are included in this category. There is no minimum income level for either program, but monthly income of clients cannot exceed a certain level (S/100,000 per family member—or $33 per capita—in 1984).

In order to borrow from Progreso, eligible microentrepreneurs must form a "solidarity group" of five to eight members, all of whom are willing to guarantee each other's loans. Originally, the solidarity group mechanism was used only with vendors. The methodology was tested among microproducers and service businesses, and its success has recently led ACP to phase out its individual loans and shift all new loans to the solidarity group methodology. Only twenty-nine participants received individual loans in 1986. There were two major reasons for this change in policy. First, administering credit to groups is far more cost-effective than it is to individuals. The groups become promotional vehicles for expanding the program's reach; technical assistance can be extended to small groups in one member's shop, rather than individually; and finally, group coordinators facilitate the attendance and participation of their groups' members in the ACP training courses.

Progreso's policy is to try to reach a ratio of 80 percent women/20 percent men among beneficiaries. Women were targeted in this program because: they represent the great majority of market vendors; they are among those who suffer the greatest impediments in their access to credit; they are viewed as more responsible; and it is assumed they will channel new income to their families rather than spend it irresponsibly. Despite efforts to target credit to them, the current level of women's participation in Progreso is only 52 percent.

First loans to vendors from Progreso, fixed at the equivalent of US$25 per group member, are generally used for working capital. All group members are expected to attend a Progreso meeting when these first checks are disbursed. The loans are repaid on a weekly basis over eight weeks (for some groups borrowing larger amounts, over ten weeks); a flat transaction fee charged each week includes all interest costs. The coordinator or president of each group collects the payments and deposits the weekly quota at the bank, or the job is rotated among group members.

First loans to microproducers begin at US$98 and may be increased by up to 50 percent with each successive loan. Payments are made on a monthly basis over a period of one to six months. Maximum loan sizes for producers currently equals US$975 (1987).

Progreso disburses checks for the groups from the Progreso office and collects payments at the local branches of Banco Weise, a private bank, each week. The bank advises Progreso of late payments and Progreso follows them up, charging a fine for each day the payment is late after an eight-day grace period. Interest charges are currently based on a 32 percent annual rate.[7]

If a group applies for its next loan two weeks before the final payment is due on the previous loan, and if that group's payments have been on time, the group will receive its next loan check on the same day final payment is made. Progreso has set fixed increments with each new loan of approximately US$12 per group member, but no member is required to borrow more; many opt to borrow at fixed or lower levels, depending upon their business activity. Within groups, members may borrow different amounts after the initial loan. After a group has successfully repaid its third loan, members may opt for a ten-week repayment period. So far no upper limit has been set on the amount a group may borrow.

In 1987 the loan repayment rate averaged 97 percent.[8] A strong incentive incorporated into the Progreso program design is the automatic lending of a slightly larger amount once a loan is paid; if a member or group has been late in making payments, the subsequent loan may be delayed for a few weeks, depending on the staff's assessment of the reasons for the group's tardiness. In all but the most extreme cases (a group member's death, for example), a fine is imposed for late payments among microproducers. Vendors are not fined for late repayment.

All clients attend a series of three introductory meetings before they receive their loans. During the first meeting, the program philosophy and policies are presented. The second meeting incorporates technical assistance. Dividing the group of twenty to thirty potential clients into smaller work-groups, staff members help participants to outline their production objectives, their accounting system, and working conditions in their workplace; identify their markets and suppliers; account for costs, sales, and long-term production plans; and set goals for their family and community. At the third meeting clients receive their loan checks. Between the first and second meetings, about 25 percent of the prospective clients drop out, either because of disagreement with some aspect of program policy or lack of the required qualifications or commitment.

After a potential client has applied for a loan, a Progreso staff analyst visits the business to see if more working capital can be invested effectively in production and to assure that the business has been in existence for at least two years. If the analyst approves the loan application, then the Progreso Director, technical assistant, and a staff committee review the application. If it is accepted at this stage, it is officially approved by a representative of Banco Weise, the Director of Acción Comunitaria del Perú, and an ACP board member. The entire process takes twelve days for a first loan.

Technical Assistance

For both commercial and productive enterprises participating in the Progreso program, the original philosophy governing technical assistance was that it should be extremely simple—informal advice to clients or management hints offered in a group setting—both through Progreso group meetings and through the vendors' self-initiated group meetings.

But some staff members found that client need and desire for technical assistance exceeded the limits that the staff's crowded schedules would allow. They believed that, because clients were paying commercial interest rates, they were entitled to efficient and high-quality services. In addition, needs for technical assistance in business management were universally reported by program beneficiaries and other local experts working with similar groups. Particularly among women, lack of literacy[9] and education make even simple accounting a relatively rare occurrence. At the time of the interviews (1984) microenterprise staff advisors had no idea how many of their clients used an accounting system, but the program director estimated that only about 2 percent were using an account book.

Early in 1984, Progreso planners decided that more formal technical assistance should be offered to microproducers so that they could make more effective use of their loans. Progreso policy was changed to require that all first-loan clients pay for monthly technical assistance visits, during which business analysis, accounting, production plans, and organization were introduced. Since mid-1987, Progreso has implemented a full-scale training program for all program participants. With the services of professional outside trainers, ACP holds four to six courses per month in each of its four offices; approximately 25 participants attend each course. The first course, called "Entrepreneurial Development," is composed of six modules of four hours each: introduction, accounting, marketing, costs, financial controls, and human relations. These courses are attended by vendors and producers together. Additional seminars with each of these groups are held separately on a monthly basis. The three-hour seminars focus on business planning. Each module of the Entrepreneurial Development course costs US$2.44 and each seminar costs US$1.22 per participant.

Program Costs

Based on Progreso's annual report for 1986, loan sizes averaged US$938 per group. During 1986, the ratio of self-sufficiency, which measures the program's ability to cover administrative costs out of revenues, was 187 percent for the solidarity group program but only 64 percent for the few remaining individual loans. In 1984, program costs per new job created for the microenterprise component averaged $512. Today, solidarity group loans cost about two cents per dollar loaned; individual loans cost seven cents per dollar loaned.

Characteristics of Beneficiaries

Progreso works with clients in each of Lima's four "cones" of *pueblos jóvenes,* the city's densest concentrations of urban migrants involved in informal-sector businesses and trade. But Progreso beneficiaries are not the poorest of Lima's poor; although their monthly family incomes are below the level necessary to buy the basic basket of essential goods, many of these people are residents of established *pueblos jóvenes* that receive electrical, drainage, sewage, and water services and have more adequate housing than do many residents of Lima's other *pueblos jóvenes*. The information given below is based on interviews conducted in 1984 with borrowers from the southern cone of Lima, mainly in San Juan de Miraflores. However, it probably gives a fairly accurate reflection of the current beneficiary population of the program as well.

In 1984 virtually all women participating in Progreso were mothers. Although the general consensus among women and men interviewed was that child care services or even educational activities for their children would be highly desirable, child care was not a major preoccupation among Progreso clients, as the majority of their children are old enough to be left on their own. A few women do pay for child care, usually in combination with housekeeping help, but these few women are earning enough so that it makes sense economically to hire someone to help with household tasks and child care while they dedicate themselves to their businesses.

Microvendors

Although it has now been extended to other borrowers, the solidarity group credit component of the program was originally designed to meet the credit needs of the predominantly female food vendors in the local markets of the *pueblos jóvenes*. In 1984, 80 percent of the vendors borrowing from Progreso were women. Often with their younger children in tow, these women work from 5:00 A.M. to 12:30 P.M., first buying their produce or staple products in the central market, then transporting their goods to a local market. They attend their closet-sized market stalls through the morning. Making an average of $6 a day, many of these women are the sole income earners for their families. Of fifty women market vendors who were interviewed for this report in 1984, 40 percent reported being heads of household. The women market vendors have an average of six years of education, while men have eight-and-a-half years. The average age of the women is thirty-seven years, slightly above the men's thirty-five years, but both have about the same amount of business experience between seven and eight years.

Microproducers

In general, women have fewer manufacturing businesses, and they are more difficult to reach because they are almost exclusively located in the business owners' homes, they are smaller scale, and the purchasing and marketing networks they rely on are more informal than those of male producers. Data from the 1984 study of Progreso (Reichman 1984a) show that women's manufacturing businesses that received loans from Progreso primarily produced food or clothing; on average, they generate the equivalent of US$163 in monthly income and employ one person in addition to the owner.

The average age of female producers who borrow from Progreso is thirty-four years, close to the male average of thirty-six years. In our interviews with female microenterprise clients, 39 percent reported being heads of household. Both males and females had studied for an average of nine years and had an average of three dependents. The women averaged nine years of business experience, while men averaged eleven years. When they applied to the program, the average income for women was the equivalent of US$139 monthly and for men was US$160, and they each employed an average of 1.5 permanent workers and an average of 1.5 temporary workers. Female employers among Progreso clients tended to pay their workers less than did the males—the equivalent of US$72 per month on average versus US$95 for men's employees; both compare favorably to the minimum wage of US$50. Half of the male microentrepreneurs interviewed and 13 percent of the women reported having borrowed previously through moneylenders or other sources, including mutuals, cooperatives, and *juntas*.[10]

Impact on Women's Businesses

Women's participation in Progreso has been remarkably strong, especially among vendors. On the whole, women's businesses assisted by Progreso are faring almost as well as men's, in terms of relative increases in income and generation of new jobs. In addition, women have gained confidence by participating in the program, which may help them improve their businesses. Finally, for both program components, women's repayment behavior is more responsible than men's, according to Progreso staff.

Microvendors

Between November 1982 and April 1984, a total of US$345,467 was lent by Progresso to 560 female and 140 male market vendors. As of December 1986, the total loaned to solidarity groups since November 1982 was US$4,430,982 with each loan averaging US$938 per group (or US$188 per person). Women's average daily income was approximately $3.40 in 1984 (however, men's was higher, averaging $5). An ACP study conducted in the fall of 1983 showed that vendors' incomes increased an average of 43 percent.[11] Men's incomes increased much faster than women's: they rose by 205 percent compared to pre-loan levels; women's incomes rose only 41 percent.

Updated qualitative information from spring of 1984 (Reichmann 1984a) showed that, despite decreased or leveled-off sales activity, vendors' income were generally improved. In the samples of vendors, one-half of the men and one-third to one-half of the women reported increases, if modest, in income. Another one-third of the women reported that their income was stable at pre-loan levels.[12] Both men and women who were interviewed had borrowed an average of six times. Of these clients, 42 percent of the men and 30 percent of the women had savings, but very few kept their savings in a bank. Forty-six percent reported that they were better off than before participating in the program.

One-quarter of the vendors interviewed worked longer hours than before they received loans, presumably because they had more to sell. According to their own reports, the vendors carried more merchandise and more variety on their shelves, and many had fixed up or enlarged their market stalls. Three-quarters of the female vendors reported buying in larger quantity, half were making at least some of their purchases on credit, and three-quarters extended interest-free credit to their regular customers. Most of these vendors, especially those dealing in *abarrotes* (rice, beans, and other staples), had traditionally purchased on credit as well as extending credit if at all possible. After the loan, slightly more flexibility in obtaining and extending credit was possible with the extra capital it provided. None of the vendors reported selling their products at lower prices.

Microproducers

The equivalent of US$40,350 was loaned to female microproducers between January 1983 and April 1984, and US$267,601 to male producers. Average size of first loans for women was lower than for men—$572 versus $611—and for the 14 percent of women and men who have received second loans, the difference was similar—$917 versus $957. Given the total average monthly income for these business owners ($163 for women and $198 for men), the difference of $30–$40 in the average loan size was proportional to the difference in male and female actual income (Reichmann 1984a). As of December 1986, a total of US$401,027 had been loaned to individuals over the life of the program; the average loan size was $1,186.

Although the women business owners who were surveyed in 1984 experienced an increase of 25 percent in their incomes since receiving credit,[13] 28.5 percent reported that they were earning *less* than they had before the Progreso loan. Unfortunately the male sample was too small to compare income figures. Fifty-two percent of the women and 42 percent of the men had savings, and three-quarters of each group reported that the credit allows them to live better.

Forty-eight percent of the female sample reported increases in income of more than 50 percent. Of these, half experienced increases of more than 100 percent. Table 8.2 reveals characteristics of these business owners. Virtually all of the nontraditional women's businesses (for example, baking soda manufacture, stove parts, and dish-soap packaging) were among the most successful businesses. But 60 percent of the women's businesses with more than 100 percent increases were in clothing manufacture.

Microproducers reported that most of their loan money was invested in materials, but about 20 percent of both men and women also invested in

TABLE 8.2
Characteristics of Successful Women Microproducer Clients in the Progreso Program, 1984

	Income Increase of 50–100%	Income Increase of 100 + %
Average age	33	32
Average years of business experience	9.4	4.8
Percent head of household	40%	40%
Average years of education	9	(not enough data)

machinery. The average workday was about eight hours for half of both the men and women. However, 35 percent of the women reported that they worked longer, averaging eleven hours per day.

ADEMI

The Association for the Development of Microenterprises, Inc. (ADEMI), was founded in 1983 to assist informal-sector businesses in Santo Domingo, Dominican Republic. ADEMI originally operated two credit schemes: one for individual microenterprises and a solidarity group component directed at smaller businesses, primarily in trade. Like Progreso, ADEMI has completely phased out one component, but ADEMI has begun to focus on assistance to individual entrepreneurs—primarily producers. In November 1987, its outstanding portfolio of only thirty solidarity groups was handed over to a more grassroots-oriented development institution in Santo Domingo, the Instituto de Desarrollo Integral.

In order to qualify for participation in ADEMI's loan program, a business must demonstrate a capacity to effectively invest more capital in equipment, machinery or services, and to employ more workers. There is no minimum income level, although the business must demonstrate a good track record. Credit is given for new productive activities if the client has proved him or herself a good candidate through previous ADEMI loan repayment. For example, a baker (working out of her kitchen at home) who has a good repayment record at one loan level may be lent a larger amount of money to establish a bakery in a separate location. If a series of small loans is repaid on time, field staff do not spend much time investigating *how* the money is spent; this is left up to the business owner.

The loan approval process is slightly simpler than that of Progreso; it usually takes no more than a few days. Clients hear about the program either through contact with a staff member or through word-of-mouth. Following inquiries from a prospective client, a staff person visits the client's business and assesses the capacity for investment in materials, inventory, or equipment. With the staff person, the client completes an application that requests all relevant details about the business and its owner. The client or group of clients and staff person determine the size of loan and repayment schedule according to the particular business requirements. The application is then assessed by the manager of either the solidarity group component or the microenterprise component and the ADEMI director, who may incorporate some modificatons.

The loan is usually disbursed within a few days in the form of a check from ADEMI's account at a private bank, the Banco Popular. The client or group receives the check at the ADEMI office and cashes it at one of the Banco Popular branches in the city. A staff person accompanies each client or group of clients to the bank for the first time to assist them in using the bank's services and to open a savings account. All clients are encouraged to deposit a portion of each check in a savings account. Savings are required of all clients and are recorded each time the client returns for another loan.

One innovation of the ADEMI program is that initial loans are very small. First loans for microenterprises are US$50–$250, repayable in three to twelve months in monthly installments. Interest rates are 24 percent annually, which includes a 6 percent fee for technical assistance and closing costs. The largest loan administered is equivalent to roughly US$4,000. ADEMI hopes that, after reaching such a level, clients will be able to "graduate" to a bank or other formal lending institution.

Timely loan recuperation is essential to ADEMI's continued ability to extend credit to the poor in Santo Domingo. When payments are overdue, a fine averaging 0.5 percent of the amount due, is charged for every day that a payment is late. ADEMI's seriousness in collecting loan payments is reflected in a relatively high repayment rate, 78.6 percent as of December 1986.

Solidarity Group Loans

As noted, the thirty remaining solidarity groups participating in ADEMI were transferred to another Dominican development institution in November 1987. ADEMI shifted away from lending to vendors in order to support businesses that generate more employment. Because most solidarity groups were made up of vendors, ADEMI has essentially stopped supporting them. Unfortunately, as the great majority of these participants are also women, they were effectively marginalized by this step. ADEMI also cited the greater mobility and instability of this sector of the population as a justification for the withdrawal of its assistance.

However, in 1984, just before austerity measures were imposed by the International Monetary Fund (IMF), the solidarity groups were not viewed as suffering from a precarious situation. At that time, solidarity groups were an important part of ADEMI's loan program and the groups included many women vendors among their members. As of March 1984, there were seven all-female solidarity groups and 138 mixed groups, of a total of 215 solidarity groups. Of the mixed groups, most were dominated by men, but 25 percent of the mixed groups were more than half female. Female coordinators were heads of up to 28 percent of the mixed groups. At present, only 22 percent of all of ADEMI's loans go to women.

Technical Assistance

ADEMI's advisors offer technical advice on business organization and simple administration, budgeting, and other skills through on-site training of clients at their places of business. ADEMI staff members are proud to report that they often teach their clients to sign their names as the first step in assistance. Although field visits are not recorded, ADEMI staff members estimate that they spend 50–70 percent of their time in the field and visit each client at least twice per month.

Overall, the microproducers interviewed in 1984 (Reichmann 1984b) were visited more often than vendors; of these, the male clients receive proportionally more assistance. Fifty percent of these male clients reported receiving a visit from staff at least once per week, whereas none of the female clients reported being visited that often. Fifty-eight percent of the female microproducers reported being visited two or three times per month. Among solidarity group members, 47 percent of the women and 71 percent of the men interviewed reported that their advisor visited them once per month or less.

ADEMI may face a greater demand for technical assistance in the future. The 1984 survey indicated that many microvendors (47 percent of the men and 3 percent of women), and most microproducers (50 percent of the men and 66 percent of the women) would like to participate in some kind of training in administration or business management. To date, individual assistance is offered informally, but no training courses have been organized for ADEMI clients. This informal approach is consistent with ADEMI's "minimalist" philosophy of focusing strictly on credit.

Program Results

ADEMI's achievements in its first three years indicate that the program design has been effective. One aspect of ADEMI's success, its ability to reach large numbers of businesses, can be attributed in large measure to the previous existence of a microenterprise program run by the Dominican Development Foundation (DDF). Great numbers of people in the *barrios* of Santo Domingo were already familiar with the microenterprise credit concept through DDF promotion of its program.

As of June 1987, ADEMI's overall performance has been encouraging, with 11,661 loans disbursed to 3,391 individual microproducers and to vendors in 270 solidarity groups. Over 2,500 new jobs have been created, and the equivalent of US$23,700 has been deposited in client savings accounts. ADEMI currently operates with a monthly portfolio of approximately US$656,000. ADEMI has achieved 100 percent self-sufficiency, covering its administrative and overhead costs with interest earnings. As of June 1987 the cost per dollar loaned averaged ten cents.

Women's Performance in ADEMI

The level of women's participation in ADEMI primarily reflects women's overall level of self-employment in manufacturing and services in the informal Dominican economy.[14] As of December 1986, 22 percent of ADEMI's total client population was composed of women, or 19 percent of all individual borrowers (primarily microproducers) and 40 percent of all the solidarity group members (who are mainly vendors).

Women microproducers interviewed in 1984 (Reichmann 1984b) had an average of sixteen years of experience in their businesses, and most were heads-of-household responsible for supplying the bulk of the family income. They were involved in businesses such as food production, clothing production, ceramics, woodworking, and rugmaking and had an average of six employees. Their business earnings averaged RD$460 per month (equivalent to US$153). The female solidarity group members were primarily involved in vending from their homes or in the street, earning an average of RD$238 (US$ 79) per month. This compares favorably to the present minimum wage salary of RD$125 (US$42) per month for a laborer in the Dominican Republic.

Women clients in general differ from men clients in that they are a few years older (on the average), and the women microproducers have an average of one more year of business experience and one more employee per business. But they earn slightly less per month from their businesses than do the men. Among both microproducers and microvendors, women and men have similar educational backgrounds: among those interviewed in 1984, microvendors had an average of four years, and microproducers an average of eight-and-a-half years of education.

Microproducers

Women's patterns of borrowing—both amounts and frequency—are close to the men's patterns, as is their repayment record. By March 1984, both male and female microproducers who had participated in ADEMI for six months or more had borrowed an average of five times; microvendors with ADEMI six months or more had borrowed an average of eight times. Women producers had borrowed about the same amount as men (average RD$540 in 1984—US$150) and their cumulative payback rate (89 percent) was 1 percent lower than that of the men at the time of the interviews.

Although women's borrowing patterns are similar to men's, the increases in monthly income generated by their businesses appear to differ.

Only 58 percent of the women interviewed in 1984 reported an increase in monthly income since they began to participate in the program. Overall, the average increase in all women's businesses' monthly income was 66.5 percent, while men's was 99 percent. Table 8.3 illustrates how different types of businesses operated by men and women compared in terms of average increases in income since they entered the program six months earlier.

Women microproducers interviewed had hired an average of two new employees per business since joining the program, while men had hired just one. The salaries of all clients' employees fluctuated around the minimum wage. But the average salaries of the women's employees (RD$117) were lower than those of men's employees (RD$145) by 19 percent, an amount that reflects salary differences in the country as a whole (Baez 1983, p. 17). Savings by women microentrepreneurs, averaging RD$162, were slightly higher (18 percent) than those by men.

TABLE 8.3

Change in Monthly Income by Gender and Type of Business Among ADEMI Clients, 1984

Type of Business	Men		Women	
	Percent	No.	Percent	No.
Food production	104	46	127	13
Ceramics/crafts	115	49	89	8
Clothing production	154	41	128	48
Upholstery	199	28	− 67	5
Furniture making[a]	148	113	− 40	2

[a] The small number of women furniture makers' businesses (two) makes a comparison with 113 men's businesses very tenuous.

Microvendors

Microvendors who had participated in ADEMI's solidarity group program for six months or more by March 1984 had borrowed an average of eight times. The average size of the most recent loan for all-female groups interviewed in 1984 was slightly higher (averaging RD$500 total, or RD$100 per member) than for either all-male or mixed groups. The all-female groups had a better on-time payback record as well: 89 percent versus 87 percent for all-male groups and 85 percent for mixed groups. In the savings category, the all-female groups had saved more—an average of RD$32 per member, while the all-male groups had saved an average of RD$27 per member and the mixed groups an average of RD$22 per member.[15]

ADEMI did not record changes in income levels for microvendors, and estimates of their incomes upon entering the program (submitted with their initial loan application) did not significantly differ from estimates given during the 1984 interviews. Of the microvendors (male and female) interviewed, 24 percent reported increases in income since their participation in the program, 35 percent reported decreases in income, and 41 percent reported no change.

STRENGTHS AND WEAKNESSES OF PROGRESO AND ADEMI: LESSONS FOR PROJECT DESIGN AND MANAGEMENT

Given their specific goals of job and income generation, the initial successes of Progreso and ADEMI have been significant. In addition, many constraints to women's access to credit were successfully overcome, mostly because of the following program characteristics:

- Women's businesses are recognized as creditworthy.

- No collateral is required.

- Interest rates and frequent payments (for vendors) are believed by clients to be appropriate.

- The program offices are located in the community.

- Transaction time is minimal.

- There is social support for women's participation, particularly through the solidarity group mechanism.

- Program promotion and technical assistance are located in the markets or place of business.

- Program methodology is fairly simple, although literacy is virtually required for microenterprise clients.

In both programs, the participation of women was much higher in solidarity groups than in individual loan components. In the case of Progreso, women are specifically targeted as beneficiaries in the solidarity group program. Women were not specifically targeted by ADEMI as potential clients in either component, but many aspects of the program design are conducive to their participation. Overall, the income level and types of businesses represented by women clients are on target for the type of client ADEMI has sought to reach.

Unfortunately, it seems that both Progreso and ADEMI are withdrawing support for the poorest female business owners. Both organizations are conforming to the policy of one of their major funders (the Inter-American Development Bank) to prioritize manufacturing businesses over commerce. In effect, this approach serves to exclude large numbers of economically active poor women. ADEMI's termination of the solidarity group component further reduces women's access to the support they might find necessary to participate in a credit project, even as microproducers.

Nevertheless, the programs have offered security and more stability to local vendors and microbusiness owners. Flexible repayment schedules and small loans on an escalating scale have allowed clients to introduce new capital into their businesses gradually while learning how to manage increased scale and administrative problems. This is a very effective way for women inexperienced with large-scale commerce or production to grasp concepts of efficiency or economies of scale.

From an institutional point of view, the major achievements of Progreso and ADEMI are: first, the ability to lend to larger numbers of small borrowers than is possible under less "agile" programs; and, second, the ability to cover operating costs out of revenues from the project, adding a dimension of self-sustainability previously absent from many PVO programs.[16]

Efficiency

Both programs have been able to achieve these results, in part, by streamlining staff functions for greater efficiency. With Progreso, staff time per client is greatly reduced by the practice of filling out loan applications in group meetings. Each staff person thereby assists up to twenty or thirty clients; although a site visit will recheck details about the businesses, the meetings eliminate much of the informational time a strictly one-on-one methodology requires. The slogan and concept, "you approve your own credit," strengthen beneficiary self-sufficiency in the ongoing loan application process; clients can fairly accurately predict whether or not their application will be approved, based on prior repayment performance and a realistic appraisal of their own businesses. The rudimentary accountkeeping and management advice proffered during those initial meetings also make staff time more efficient during the technical assistance visits.

By June 1987 ADEMI had achieved 100 percent self-sufficiency, covering all its operating costs through interest income and fees. Progreso reached 64 percent self-sufficiency in its individual component and 187 percent in the solidarity group component at the end of 1986.

Promotion

Both programs are promoted almost exclusively by word-of-mouth. Although it is a low-cost way of attracting clients, this promotion approach may also tend to "select out" certain potential beneficiaries, mainly those who are not tightly linked to informal information networks. These are often recent migrants or those who live in less accessible areas of the cities' outlying slums. Women may also be unduly neglected by this approach, especially those who operate "invisible" manufacturing businesses inside their homes.

This tendency may be counteracted by active marketing of the programs' services to women, as in the case of Progreso, which has a target of 80 percent female borrowers. Progreso tends not to reach the very poorest residents of Lima's *pueblos jóvenes,* primarily because of its two-year requirement for loan eligibility. Lima's poorest residents are newly involved in economic activities in the urban area. In the past, the failure to reach the poorest was also due to another shortcoming of the program—the virtual necessity that individual borrowers be proficient at reading and writing. The intake process for these loans hinged on the ability of clients to work independently on their own applications. However, in more recent years, Progreso's greater emphasis on solidarity group lending, which makes fewer demands for literacy, has resolved this problem.

Promotion of the ADEMI program has focused more actively on men than on women. Of the clients interviewed in 1984, two-thirds of the male microenterprise owners had been approached by ADEMI staff members, whereas only one-third of the female microenterprise owners had heard about the program in this way. Among solidarity group members, field staff had originally contacted 43 percent of the men interviewed and only 6 percent of the women. Ninety-four percent of the female solidarity group members and 58 percent of the female microenterprise clients reported that they had heard about ADEMI through word-of-mouth.

Transaction Costs for Borrowers

Transaction costs, including time lost from other activities, have been identified as major constraints to women's access to credit. ADEMI is one of the most successful programs in Latin America in minimizing these costs with rapid application and disbursal systems. In fact, in most cases loan processing time has been reduced to less than three days. Administrative efficiency is heightened by the credit advisors' field work and their personal knowledge of individual businesses so that loan applications need not be scrutinized in a lengthy loan approval process as in traditional institutions.

To eliminate both waiting time and clients' need to make several trips to the downtown office, administration of ADEMI's program has been streamlined for maximum advisor-client time at the client's place of business or home. Banco Popular, in coordination with ADEMI, shares the tasks of loan disbursal and recuperation, a proces that minimizes congestion in ADEMI offices. Because the fourteen bank branches are located in all zones of the city, decentralization eliminates long lines and waiting time.

In the case of Progreso, microenterprise loan disbursement time, although reduces from twenty to twenty-five days in late 1984, and to twelve days in 1987, is still too long and the process too complex to be able to administer the numbers of loans required to impact the informal sector economy even in the targeted local area. The limitations of the collaborating bank's infrastructure prohibit faster loan disbursal, just as they eliminate the feasibility of short-term loans added to microenterprise clients' regular longer-term loans.

Technical Assistance and Client Follow-up

Neither program has yet developed an extensive technical assistance component, although efforts are underway. The relationship between staff and clients is constrained by the relatively large scale of the projects; staff client time is limited and some advisors are overburdened. For ADEMI's microenterprise component, the ratio of staff to clients was 1 to 82; for the solidarity group component it was 1 to 383 in 1984. Today Progreso serves over 800 businesses with a staff of twelve promoters/advisors.

Given the large population of women in the vendor components and the commitment to bring women into the microproducer component, a serious weakness in both Progreso and ADEMI is the absence of female field staff. Program staff, as well as beneficiaries, concur that a female staffer would serve as an important channel of program accessibility to women, as well as a role model for the young. The great majority of the women market vendors who borrow from Progreso commented in interviews that they would prefer to work with a female staff person, although 61 percent of female producers (and 83 percent of the men) interviewed said that the staff's sex did not really matter.

Training and Skill Development

Through participating in formal institutions such as Progreso and ADEMI, women who have never used a bank account or been familiar with an office setting are learning a number of new skills. All of the tasks required of new clients are simple to learn. ADEMI advisors introduce their clients personally to the bank, taking them step-by-step thorough the check cashing and depositing procedures. When necessary, they even teach their clients to sign their own names. ADEMI helps integrate the many women who are nonliterate or unfamiliar with procedures of this kind into a different sociocultural world and a new level of economic participation.

At present, women's businesses cluster around clothing, food production, and vending; as women's experience and success with their present business activities increase, ADEMI and Progreso should encourage them to move into diverse kinds of activities. Women clients generally reveal that their goals for their businesses are similar to men's—to expand production or scale, and eventually to diversify. However, about one-third of the women borrowers interviewed from ADEMI said that they were satisfied with their present level of production and did not intend to modify their business practices.

Participation and Organization of Beneficiaries

One of the anticipated results of programs like ADEMI and Progreso is that women will come to sense increasing power and autonomy, both within their communities and in the larger economic world. The solidarity group mechanism has the capacity to preserve and maintain existing social support networks because it involves a mutual commitment by people who know each other well and live in close proximity. Solidarity groups might also become a forum for community organizing or information sharing and networking, but these are now only potential capacities. ADEMI policy has been one of allowing these kinds of activities to shape themselves.

Progreso has established an effective feedback system for beneficiaries to participate in program decisions. The regular meetings function as a sounding board with project director and/or staff. With similar policy concerns, clients lobby at beneficiary meetings for policy changes, and Progreso staff are compelled to consider the issues seriously. However, no formal mechanism for client input and participation in program policy development has been implemented.

In the fall of 1983, women from Progreso attended the first staff-initiated "microbusiness association" meeting proportionate to their representation in the microproducers' program; 15 percent of the 200 meeting participants were women. At that meeting, participants talked of putting on trade fairs to market their products, of organizing to legalize their businesses, of implementing mutual aid benefits as an association, and of addressing other common concerns they faced as informal sector residents and business owners. Women, in particular, had hoped to organize bulk purchasing, as many are involved in similar businesses. Women had also expressed an interest in a microbusiness association as a context for organizing to receive family planning, medical, and hygiene information and services.

The market vendors held a similar program-wide meeting in 1983, in which 300 attended, the majority women. Their hopes and concerns were similar to those of the microentrepreneurs; however, in our interviews the vendors seemed less motivated to continue organizing common activities, at least through a vendors' association.

As an outcome of participation in the survey conducted by an Acción Comunitaria social worker during the 1984 evaluation, women microenterprise clients initiated a microbusinesswomen's association. Because the program-wide meeting in 1983 hadn't resulted in concrete activities, the women decided to take matters into their own hands to organize a fair to sell their products and to promote popular education courses among Progreso's female business owners.

SUMMARY OF DIFFERENCES BETWEEN ADEMI AND PROGRESO AND IMPLICATIONS FOR WOMEN

Even at first glance, ADEMI and Progreso are extremely different institutions, although they share similar microenterprise lending methodologies.

Acción Comunitaria del Perú had already had fifteen years of experience in community development when it created the Progreso program in 1982. It had developed extensive expertise in integrated community development in the urban *pueblos jóvenes* of greater Lima, supporting grass-roots groups to obtain housing, water, sewage, drainage, electricity, and other services, as well as organizing legal assistance, literacy, and other educational programs. One old-timer at ACP notes that Progreso's goals are "integrated . . . to help people to change their socioeconomic situations," in sharp distinction to what he perceived as ADEMI's goal of ever more efficient and expanded lending services.

Acción Comunitaria's long history of involvement in community organization and education influences its work with microentrepreneurs: a strong value is placed on training and education of beneficiary groups; existing local organizations (for example, associations of market vendors) are used for promotion and dialogue within the communities; and the solidarity group concept is consciously built upon a relatively well-established tradition of local organization.

ADEMI, on the other hand, was created in 1983 specifically to administer credit using what Tendler (1987) has termed a "minimalist" model, and it has never pretended to offer any other services. ADEMI's values and management style are modeled after the private sector: fees for services, efficiency, measurable results, an incentive structure to motivate employees to produce more, and a "trickle down" concept of social effects.

A striking difference between Progreso and ADEMI is Progreso's emphasis on training. Several years ago, ADEMI contracted a private technical assistance team to work with microenterprise clients but found that this program was not cost-effective. Since that time, in keeping with its "minimalist" philosophy, ADEMI has not offered client training courses; instead, its staff provides one-on-one technical assistance on a fee-for-service basis.

Progreso's training courses are also offered on a fee-for-service basis, but it is not yet known whether the courses are financially self-sustaining. In any case, the seminars and extensive training schedules planned for upcoming months are consistent with Progreso's more integrated approach to microenterprise development.

Despite their differences in style, ADEMI and Progreso promote similar values: accessible credit for the poor, minimal time and transaction costs, agility, and personal relationships as a principle basis for credit guarantee. In ADEMI, the personal relationship is that between staff and client, whereas at Progreso the relations between members of the solidarity group serve as the loan guarantee. In both cases, character judgments must replace business analysis as the criteria for credit approval, as most businesses at the informal level keep poor written records, if any, and have little access to property to post as collateral.

Given the common values guiding their lending to the poor, ADEMI and Progreso started out in 1982–83 with strikingly similar programs. Both worked with solidarity groups comprised mainly of market vendors and operators of other commerce activities, who were among the poorest of the economically active, and both also loaned to individuals whose businesses were somewhat larger and usually involved manufacture or service. In both ADEMI and Progreso, the solidarity group programs reached mainly women, and the individual loan programs primarily assisted men. During their first several years each program was influenced by at least two factors: (1) its own experience in lending to both sets of clients, and (2) the Inter-American Development Bank's lending policy of targeting a so-called pro-ductive (that is, manufacture and, to a lesser extent, services) enterprises. These factors led each institution to modify its lending practices in very dif-ferent ways, but surprisingly, the net effect on women's participation may have been similar in both cases.

The first factor—institutional experience—is probably more signifi-cant. Progreso integrated the solidarity group concept into its established *modus operandi* and found the groups to be low-cost, effective vehicles for training, technical assistance, program promotion, and most important, payback. Solidarity group repayments were far better than individual rates; therefore, the individual lending component was gradually phased out, and productive businesses and services were incorporated into the solidarity group program.

At the same time, ADEMI had trouble with solidarity groups. The project director began to look askance at the groups just after the IMF adjustment in April 1984 reflecting austerity measures. Urban vendors and marginal busi-nesses were hardest hit by the recessionary effects of the adjustment policies. There were riots, during which 100 people were killed; many people left the city to return to the countryside where they believed food would be cheaper, and some of the solidarity groups refused to pay back their loans. The situation became politicized, and at that point the director and Board of ADEMI decided to cut off all lending to street vendors. They gradually began to cut out market vendors too, and just a few of the older, more stable groups were still participating by 1987.

In 1987 ADEMI handed its solidarity group portfolio over to IDDI (In-stituto Dominicano de Desarrollo Integral), a development agency with a more grass-roots, integrated development philosophy. Today, ADEMI makes new loans only to individual businesses, the great majority of which are pro-ductive enterprises. ADEMI's director notes, "We have more control over in-dividuals" and points to the Board's discomfort with the concept of "solidar-ity" and its potential implications for politicization.

The second factor that influenced changes in ADEMI's and Progreso's methodologies was the Inter-American Development Bank policy of sup-porting lending only to enterprises that transform raw materials or recycle goods. Because the IDB supports both projects, both have developed policies that severely limit loans to commerce. This policy effectively excludes women, who are predominantly represented in the commerce sector.

Typically, loans to commerce are much smaller than those extended to productive businesses, because informal commerce rotates capital on a daily basis and needs capital primarily for inventory. Correspondingly, solidarity group loans are generally very small, beginning at about $30 per group member. Therefore, we can correlate small loan size with vending activities and women's participation. A review of changes in average loan size over the past few years indicates how the changes described above have had an impact on women. Table 8.4 sketches the changes in the average loan size for each program component between 1984 and 1986.

It is evident that while ADEMI's few remaining solidarity group loans may have grown larger to meet the capital needs of productive enterprises, the size of individual loans has also risen by 21.7 percent. The average size of loans to groups has also increased (by 469%), to accommodate small producers who require larger loans. The few remaining loans to individuals participating in Progreso have been made to older clients whose businesses have grown. In each of the four program components discussed above, women's participation has dropped as larger, more stable businesses were assisted (among individual borrowers) and as assistance to commerce was phased out to accommodate productive enterprises.

If we compare the two programs, Progreso now assists microentrepreneurs who are significantly smaller-scale than those assisted by ADEMI, if we take loan size as a valid indicator. Given that ADEMI now loans exclusively to individuals, and Progreso to groups, Progreso has defined its target businesses as smaller scale, administering loans averaging approximately $200, in contrast to ADEMI's average loan of approximately $500. ADEMI's loan ceiling is also much higher than Progreso's: $4,000 repaid over a three- to twelve-month repayment period, versus Progreso's ceiling of $1,000, repaid over one to six months.

In part to sustain its rapid expansion, ADEMI has tended to work with larger, more stable businesses, because their repayment is more consistent.

TABLE 8.4
Average Loan Size, 1984–1986

	1984	1986
ADEMI		
Solidarity Group (per member)	$ 62	$ 232
Individual	$395	$ 486
Progreso		
Solidarity Group (per member)	$ 33	$ 188
Individual	$655	$1,186

ADEMI also continues to assist businesses as they grow. With its shift away from lending to commerce, ADEMI has stopped loaning to the poorest of the poor—the majority of whom are women. Progreso, however, has intensified its focus on the poorest by eliminating the individual borrowing component. Although Progreso also continues to work with successful clients as they grow, it has maintained its focus on assisting the smallest businesses. However, Progreso's shift in priority toward producers may contradict this policy, and it will be interesting to observe whether it maintains a beneficiary population among the poorer of the economically active.

The termination of the solidarity group component in ADEMI and its expansion in Progreso can be considered separate from its implications for the types and size of businesses that is assisted. It has been argued that the mechanism itself, as a social intervention, is more conducive to women's participation than the individual loan mechanism, as the group can be a supportive context for women who otherwise have had no experience dealing with institutions (see Otero, Chapter 5 of this volume). Furthermore, a group context has been shown to enhance the benefits of credit for poor women. Till and Chaudhuri (1986) found in Honduras that a woman's ability to manage credit was correlated with her participation in a group. A woman has a better idea of credit and its ramifications, they found, if she belongs to a supportive group. In addition, the greater the level of organization that is achieved, the more cognizant women appear to be of the use of credit for productive activities.

In conclusion, although the Progreso and ADEMI programs were both originally designed to help women overcome barriers in obtaining access to credit, much of their early (and significant) achievement in this respect has been undercut by their shift in lending priority to service and productive sectors and, in ADEMI's case, by the termination of the solidarity group program. A critical examination of women's participation in these and other microenterprise programs is needed, particularly with an eye toward discerning the viability of supporting microvending or commerce activities. Using one or more samples of female vendors, documentation of the expansion of internal markets and backward and forward linkages is necessary to make a stronger case for assisting commerce.

Launching start-up businesses with women's groups and training women for nontraditional productive activities have become acceptable alternatives to lending to commercial enterprises, but neither strategy has enjoyed remarkable success in increasing incomes or creating stable new employment. Assistance to market vendors—who represent the vast majority of economically active poor women in the urban world—must become a priority if women are to be included in the emerging campaign to address the needs of the world's ever-growing informal sector.

NOTES

1. This chapter synthesizes the findings of two earlier reports by the author: "Women's Participation in Progresso: A Microenterprise Credit Program Reaching the Smallest Businesses
of the Poor in Lima, Peru" (Cambridge, Mass.: ACCION International/AITEC, October 1984),
and "Women's Participation in ADEMI: The Association for the Development of Microenterprise, Inc." (Cambridge, Mass.: ACCION International/AITEC, March 1984).

2. For example, a boy who sells fried yucca as an ambulatory vendor is included in labor force
statistics whereas his mother, who prepares the yucca in her kitchen, is classified as an un-
salaried *ama de casa* (housewife); see Bàez 1983).

3. In the Progreso program, 90 percent of the women clients are vendors and 10 percent are
involved in productive activities.

4. Programs like the Central Bank's FIDE and Women's World Banking serve as intermediary
credit guarantors for women's businesses with a minimum annual net income of
RD$10,000 or above. Their first loans average RD$2,000 to RD$3,000 and require that busi-
nesses demonstrate the capacity to expand production. These programs are organized like
ADEMI, in the sense that they investigate the client's creditworthiness and provise some
technical assistance to business owners, while the actual loan transactions are carried out
at the bank of the client's choice.

    ADEMI works strictly with Banco Popular and lends from its own funds rather than
guaranteeing bank monies, but a mutually profitable reciprocal relationship with the bank
has been arranged so that all loan payments are made at the bank, along with the required
savings deposits; checks for loans approved by an received from ADEMI staff are cashed at
one of the Banco Popular's fourteen branches by clients, so that no cash is actually handled
by ADEMI staff.

5. Based on a similar concept, the Progreso credit mechanism is familiar to residents of *pueblos jóvenes.*

6. For some businesses, machinery and/or equipment serves as a guarantee.

7. Compare this amount to commercial bank annual interest rates of approximately 60 percent. Profits generated from the vendors; component are directed to Progreso's Reserve
Fund, which serves as "protection against devaluation, general expenses, bad debts, and
incontingencies," according to ACP Director.

8. "Repayment rates" refer to on-time loan payments. Actual recuperation rates (including
late payments) are much higheraveraging 99 percent. Repayment rates are calculated according to the following formula: total amount of loan payments due (unpaid)/portfolio
(loans disbursed) = percent unrecuperated. As of December 1986 the repayment rate was
96 percent.

9. The literacy rate of women attending the meetings averaged 60 percent.

10. Additional information on these women is provided in Reichmann 1984a.

11. Sample size: twenty males, eighty females. Because of the small male sample size, the male/
female differential may not be accurate. The ACP report does not disaggregate data for
which types of products are more frequently sold by males than by females. However, the
male/female income differential reported by ACP differs significantly from our interviews
with vendors of *abarrotes* (rice, beans, and other staples), who represent 42 percent of the
market vendors interviewed. Of these vendors selling more or less the same products, 83
percent of the women and 55 percent of the men reported increased income. All of them

reported slight increases. Across all vendor businesses, 30 percent of the men and only 6 percent of the women reported decreases in income.

12. Forty-seven percent of the nineteen men interviewed by a staff member reported that income has increased and 60 percent of the women he interviewed reported "a little bit more" income than before. One-third of the fifty women interviewed by the outside evaluator reported that their incomes had increased, one-third that they were the same, and one-third reported decreased income. Our third sample set, those attending *encuestas participación,* reported income increases for about one-third of their businesses.

13. Income data are figured by translating initial and current income figures into the appropriate dollar equivalent, but, as mentioned, this method is problematical because the sol's real buying power does not keep pace with inflation.

14. Bàez 1983. Anexos Cuadro no. 1.

15. These savings figures are calculated in mid February and the balances in members' accounts fluctuate almost daily. Often members draw their accounts all the way down when they make their repayment.

16. Because the loan funds themselves currently come from monies that were donated or obtained on concessional terms, these programs are not yet covering all of the costs implicit in such a lending activity.

9

The Experience of MUDE Dominicana in Operating a Women-Specific Credit Program

LUZ MARÍA ABREU

The structural and political shortcomings responsible for poverty and underdevelopment in the Dominican Republic can be summarized as: acute concentration of power, limited participation of the great majority of the population, and various forms of external dependence.

- At the economic level, there are an unfair land tenure system, a defective financial-industrial system, and a poor technology with low productivity and income levels.

- At the social level, there exist a lack of institutional stability; insufficient education, health, housing, transportation, water, electricity, and recreation services; and a high rate of malnutrition.

- At the agricultural level, the poor endowment of resources, unsatisfactory work conditions, and poor quality of life among producers limit progress.

One of the population groups most drastically affected by the impact of underdevelopment is that of poor women, and among poor women, rural women in particular. As a result of the large rural-to-urban migratory flux affecting mainly women, particularly those in the 10–24 year age group, women comprise only 47.2 percent of the population in rural areas.

In these areas, 18 percent of the households are headed by women, and 21.9 percent of agricultural workers are women, but only 3.8 percent of the rural workers who own land are women. The unemployment rate among rural women is 53 percent, and only 14 percent for rural men. Forty percent of adult rural women are illiterate.

In the 1960s it was recognized for the first time that rural women make an important contribution to production. During this period, international organizations and Third World governments started to promote rural projects in which groups of women produced goods for their own consumption or for the market. Despite these advances, women's participation in development is still limited today because of the persistence of stereotyped roles and the lack of educational activities to help women organize and develop their creativity and critical capacity.

WHAT IS MUDE?

Mujeres en Desarrollo Dominicana (MUDE) was created in response to the limitations listed above. Founded in 1977 as an affiliate of an international organization called "Women in Development," MUDE became a national organization on October 23, 1979, in the midst of a period of profound political change in the Dominican Republic. Today its activities have been extended to six provinces—four in the northern part of the country and two in the south—and they reach about 4,000 women organized in approximately 175 groups. MUDE is a nonprofit, nongovernmental organization that promotes the social and economic development of low-income women in order to improve their standard of living and that of their communities, encouraging women's active participation in the development process of their country. Its philosophy is based on a set of closely interrelated principles that relate to different aspects of its institutional mandate.

Concept of Development

MUDE is a development agency, and its concept of development is an important factor affecting the design and operation of its programs, including the credit program. For MUDE, development is an essential means to promote the basic principle of human equality. Such development must seek to overcome marginality and poverty through the active participation of the grassroots in the definition of the objectives, strategies, and means involved in the development process. Development activities should extend to the restructuring of the economic and social system, and to the creation of a more balanced and just society, in which there is support for the basic values of dignity, solidarity, justice, and participation.

Target Population

In order to achieve its basic objectives, MUDE promotes, supports, and advises organizations of rural women; sponsors equal, informed, and organized participation among women and men in the solution of community problems; facilitates access of women's groups to specialized technical assistance; sponsors the use of appropriate technologies; and funds the implementation of small productive projects through a credit program. MUDE conducts programs directed to other sectors of the poor population, particularly working-class women. It also seeks to create alternative jobs for young women. MUDE's financing activities fulfill a social and cultural function that strengthens women's individual participation and responsibility, self-management in women's groups, family unity, and the improvement and collective participation of the whole community.

Within this framework, the practice of giving credit to rural women is encouraged; it extends to servicing the needs of urban women as well. As a priority, MUDE promotes the participation of women in nontraditional agricultural projects. Furthermore, it encourages handicraft manufacturing on a profitable scale, marketing projects, and the development of agroindustries.

THE STATUS OF DOMINICAN WOMEN

In the Dominican Republic, the development process has had implications for the emergence, strengthening, and persistence of ideas that consider women as marginal to income-generating productive activities. However, some socioeconomic indicators provide a more objective view of the status of these women.

Population and Migration

According to the National Bureau of Statistics, in 1981 the Dominican Republic had a population of 5,647,977, with 2,817,782 women and 2,830,195 men. Some 42 percent of rural families now have no access to land. This loss has contributed to the progressive increases in rural-to-urban migration and has resulted in a decline in the rural population from 70.3 percent of the total population in 1970 to 48 percent in 1981. Urban population growth during this period was 52 percent, and women accounted for 52 percent of that growth.

Education

According to the National Population Census of 1981, illiteracy rates for the population fifteen years old and above vary greatly according to area of residence. In urban areas about 15.1 percent of the men and about 18.9 of the women are illiterate, whereas in rural areas, about 40.1 percent of the men and about 40.7 percent of the women are illiterate (Bàez 1982).

The proportion of women fifteen years old and above who have never attended school is higher than the proportion of men in that age group who have never attended school. In urban areas around 63 percent of women over fifteen years of age have never attended school, in contrast with only 37 percent of the men in that same age group. This difference suggests that Dominican families still favor sending their sons to school, but not their daughters.

Economic Participation

In spite of the great number of population censuses and household surveys conducted in the Dominican Republic, both the undercounting of women's economic participation and the changes in indicators and categories of analysis between different survey periods make it difficult to formulate comparisons. According to a study by Bàez, "although it is true that Dominican women now [1982] tend to participate more in the formal labor market, they have historically been engaged in household activities such as handicrafts, commerce or food production, which have little visibility for the purpose of statistical accounting." However, even when these activities are not paid, they imply major economic transfers for the family unit.

According to official statistics, during 1960–80 the economically active female population showed a sharp increase. Its growth rate was 10.1 percent, much higher than the 2.8 percent rate for the male population. The economic participation rate for women increased from about 11 percent in 1960 to 37.5 percent in 1980. However, there are still significant differences in participation by sex, with a ratio of forty-eight women for every one hundred men.

An analysis by type of activity for 1980 shows that 13.2 percent of the female labor force was employed in manufacturing, 16 percent in agriculture, and about 66.2 percent in the tertiary sector (services, businesses, and financial institutions). In 1980, 25 percent of the economically active female population worked in domestic service occupations. Domestic service is the sector that employs the highest number of women in the country but offers the lowest wages and few social or legal benefits.

The proportion of women working as unpaid family workers rose from 4 percent in 1960 to 25 percent in 1980, mostly because of increases in the number of women helping in family economic activities. Among occasional workers, about 55 percent were women in 1980. These figures indicate that the economic crisis that the Dominican Republic has been facing in recent years has prompted a growing number of women to turn to activities that allow them to supplement insufficient family incomes. The economic situation is even more difficult for the 342,171 households headed by women. These households include 1,539,770 members who depend on the support provided by women.

Income Levels

In the Dominican Republic, as in many other countries, the earnings of women workers are lower than those of men across sectors of activity. In

1980, 59 percent of urban women did not receive the minimum wages required by law. In rural areas, 88 percent of women are in this situation, because of the widespread prevalence of very low income levels, which in most cases are below the absolute poverty line (Bàez 1982). Despite the fact that a high proportion of the employed population receives low wages in the Dominican Republic, the ratio of male to female income levels is striking. As Bàez notes, "Whatever the indicator selected, wages for men are significantly higher. They are 1.1 to 6.9 times higher. In terms of percentages, this means that women's wages vary between 14.6 percent and 95 percent of those of men" (1983).

Legal Status

It was not until July 1978 that a new law was passed governing joint responsibility in the family and giving more parental authority to women. Under this law the rights of married women were expanded, making them more similar to those of single women and requiring the same obligations from the spouses with respect to the upkeep and maintenance of the home and the children's education. At the same time, certain legal restrictions were removed, for instance, those preventing married women from obtaining, without their husbands' consent, documents such as passports, the opening of banking accounts, and the right to sell, transfer, or pledge their personal property. Before the new law was adopted, married women had to obtain their husbands' consent to make any commercial transaction. These and other cultural mores have limited women's access to commercial, entrepreneurial, and credit activities.

There are still very few real opportunities in the Dominican Republic for women who want to undertake economic activities on their own. It goes against the Dominican tradition to see women as clients eligible for credit. In addition, formal credit possibilities are minimal and of a discriminatory nature—for example, as land reform programs apply only to men, women do not even have land to offer as collateral.

ECONOMIC CHARACTERISTICS OF THE TARGET POPULATION OF MUDE'S CREDIT PROGRAM

From a socioeconomic perspective, the population MUDE works with can be considered very poor. However, different levels of poverty exist, particularly between groups in the central region, abounding in natural resources, and those of the dry, arid southwest.

A survey of the target population of the economic development services shows that 87 percent of the women who participate in MUDE development programs are in what are considered the economically active age groups; of the rest, 2 percent are minors and 11 percent are older women who remain economically active or are willing to become active.

About 76 percent of the participants in production projects have husbands, most of them in consensual union. Two-thirds of the husbands are
engaged in agricultural activities, and half of them belong to some type of
organization. It is estimated that most of these organizations are farmers'
associations. Approximately 23 percent of female respondents do not live in
a conjugal union. However, over 90 percent of these women reported having children. The average number of children in each of the surveyed households is 6.26. Nearly half of the households have six or more children.

The poverty levels of the participants in MUDE-funded projects have
been measured according to family income (see Table 9.1). Over one-fourth
of the households surveyed depend on the joint income of the father and
the mother. In 60 percent of the households the total monetary income
comes from the father. Furthermore, one-tenth of the families depend exclusively on the mother's income, and 6 percent of the households receive contributions for the family expenses from the children and members of the
extended family.

TABLE 9.1
Family Income of Participants in MUDE Programs

Monthly Income	Percent of Respondents
Up to RD$60[a]	11
$61–$100	39
$101–$200	30
$201 +	10
Did not respond	10
Total	100

[a]   At the time of the survey in 1983, the exchange rate stood at approximately US$1 = RD
    $1.73. Although this was not the official rate, it was tolerated by the government.

OPERATION OF THE CREDIT PROGRAM

MUDE's credit program is exclusively oriented toward women's associations that are devoted to agricultural, handicrafts, and/or industrial tasks but
have no access to credit from formal banking sources. The participants are
involved in other MUDE programs, particularly organizational and training
programs. Priority is given to those groups with the highest degree of organizational and managerial capacity, sharing of leadership, and community
involvement. These groups should have at least six members; an average of
13.7 women participate in each project.

In 1987 the annual portfolio of MUDE devoted to credit amounted to
RD$2 million (equivalent to US$445,000). In eight years of operation, approximately RD$2,484,098 has been invested by MUDE in projects providing

direct benefits to 3,622 participants. Including the women's contributions, the total value of these projects amounts to RD$5 million.

The population receiving credit represents, at this time, nearly 45 percent of all the *campesinas* (rural women) receiving services from MUDE. Approximately 17.8 percent of these women have received loans on at least two occasions; 3.7 percent on three occasions; and about 1.2 percent on more than three occasions.

The largest amount of credit is RD$30,000 (equivalent to US$6,666). The size of the loans varies according to the type of activity that is being financed. They are payable over a sixty-month period, and carry a 10 percent annual interest rate. As mentioned above, the only collateral required is the applicant's reputation. The main endorsement of the group requesting credit is its record of responsibility and struggle for individual and collective improvement. Disbursements to cover the investment on a project are generally made by MUDE to the suppliers of machinery or raw materials. This procedure gives the group better control and gives MUDE the assurance that the money is being used as stipulated in the investment plan. The borrowers, of course, identify the supplier of inputs and services, conduct the negotiations, and request MUDE to issue a "purchase order" through the area representatives. When the item or service has been purchased, the *campesinas,* usually through the president or the treasurer of the group, request MUDE to make payment to the supplier by signing the bill. The suppliers then collect from MUDE. There is an average interval of thirty days between the time when the item or service is requested and the time when payment is made to the supplier. This is a short interval—a great advantage when there is a lack of liquidity.

A significant part of the credit, approximately 20 percent, is disbursed on behalf of the group, or rather, of its representatives, because these associations do not have legal status. Disbursements made in the name of the group representatives are used to hire additional labor.

The group is required to keep bookkeeping records of the project operations, for which they receive training. This measure is based on the precept that a mismanaged project or a questionable system of management can generate mistrust in the members and erode the strength of the group.

MUDE provides continuing supervision of the project. We should note that this supervision is seen by MUDE and by the *campesinas* not as a tool of surveillance, but as a mutual commitment to carry out a successful project. Everyone knows that the *campesinas'* success is MUDE's success, and that, conversely, a failure adversely affects both the *campesinas* and MUDE.

LESSONS FROM EXPERIENCE WITH THE CREDIT PROGRAM

From its founding in 1977, MUDE has been operating a credit program and offering training and technical assistance, as well as financing, which was the core program of the institution. However, the crucial problem facing the institution in the early years was the low demand for the loans available. The credit performance during the pioneer years is illustrated in Table 9.2. This first experience was very useful for a reorientation of the program. Attempts to find a causal explanation for the low demand for loans over these years focused on a number of elements:

- the *campesinas'* lack of confidence in the institution, aggravated by the presence of foreign staff, including MUDE's top officials;

- lack of understanding on the part of the *campesinas* about the credit program, compounded by the use of complex concepts such as "grace period," "closing costs," etc.;

- interest rates that were considered to be too high;

- mandatory signature of a contract containing unintelligible terms;

- lack of integration of the credit program into a broader social and human strategy;

- lack of identification of the *campesinas* with a rotating credit fund;

- no tradition in associative credit among rural women; and

- the sociocultural patterns characteristic of patriarchal and "machista" societies, which unfortunately still persist.

The conclusions of this analysis led to a general review of the regulations and procedures of the credit program, which was accompanied, beginning in 1981, by a redefinition of strategies, frameworks, and the development of a process for working with women. The first step was to change the "contract" system between debtor and creditor, eliminating the collateral security or mortgage and replacing it with the moral collateral and organizational soundness of the group. The document that records the amount of the

TABLE 9.2
The MUDE Credit Program: The First Years

Year	No. of Loans Extended	No. of *Campesinas* Receiving Loans	Amount of RD$[a]
1977	1	100	1,000.00
1978	2	170	10,945.70
1979	3	130	8,550.55
1980	6	365	12,879.41

[a] US$1 = RD$1.00 in December 1980.

debt and repayment obligations was reformulated to eliminate difficult terms. It became what in the *campesino* culture is called *vale,* and in the formal system *pagaré* (promissory note).

Why did MUDE abandon something that appears to be so logical as the collateral security? There were several reasons. First, most of the population with which it works does not own property on which a claim can be placed. Second, the risk of losing what is owned is undoubtedly an obstacle in any investment, and at this level it becomes a weapon in the hands of husbands who resist the participation of women in income-generating programs.

There were other changes in the loan regulations, both in form and content. To be sure that the target population would fully understand those changes, MUDE first discussed them with some of the women, and then incorporated their suggestions. The first big step for women was to believe that they were participating in the development of the "rules of the game" to obtain credit. After being adopted by the Board of Directors, the new regulations were widely disseminated among the *campesinas,* who acknowledged and accepted them.

Another task had to be carried out in order to increase and reorient the demand for credit. Credit was intended to be a means and not an end. Also needed within the legal-statutory framework was a philosophical shift to change MUDE's image from that of a credit institution to one of a social promotion and development organization. In this context, credit becomes a valid tool because it allows the development of productive projects by women's groups. Productive projects developed by women have a social, psychological, and economic impact. They provide an opportunity for income generation. By itself, generating income is not a sufficient condition for improving the status of women, but it is a necessary condition to expand their economic and social roles. And changes in the performance of roles have profound implications for the attainment of equality between the sexes.

Credit must be used as a tool for the human growth of women, and their association with and control of the production processes in which they are involved; a greater and more accurate understanding of the reality surrounding them; a clearer view of their future; a greater solidarity with their own social class; the strengthening and cohesion of their organizations; and the development of their communities.

As a result of these changes and the greater availability of resources, the demand for credit showed a significant increase (see Table 9.3). MUDE made loans of more than one million Dominican pesos in 1987.

In 1981, a line item in the amount of RD$5,000.00 was earmarked for credit from the global funds of the institution; the Inter-American Development Bank (IDB) gave a first loan of RD$250,000.00, which together with repayments from the *campesinas* made up the basic portfolio. A second loan from the IDB for US$250,000.00 was received in 1985.

TABLE 9.3
The MUDE Credit Program: Recent Years

Year	No. of Loans Extended	No. of *Campesinos* Receiving Loans	Amount in RD$[a]
1981	8	640	19,245.16
1982	13	920	53,397.83
1983	37	2,305	167,196.65
1984	38	2,035	200,306.92
1985	41	2,835	367,256.50
1986	61	3,950	581,780.00
1987	75	5,846	1,031,182.00

[a]   The evolution of the exchange rate has been as follows:

Year	Dominican Pesos per US$1
1983	1.7
1984	2.7
1985	3.0
1986	3.0
1987	4.5

This support from IDB to MUDE was considered "successful" by the formal banking sector, and its impact on the institution goes beyond the financial aspects. The loan not only assured the availability of more resources for credit but also affected the internal management of MUDE because of the Bank requirements and the nonreimbursable technical assistance component of the loan. The reputation of the institution was enhanced among important national entities such as the Dominican Government itself. In fact, many national institutions began considering MUDE a sound project only after the agreement with the IDB.

DIFFICULTIES OF THE CREDIT PROGRAM

Some of the main obstacles MUDE has confronted are the cultural constraints discussed by Lycette and White in their study for this volume (see Chapter 2). One of them is the negative attitude of husbands, particularly at the beginning of their wives' experience as producers; with time, however, they often stop criticizing and start working at their side. Another obstacle is the low esteem men have for women—the belief that women lack ability, either based on their biological nature or linked to their roles as mothers and wives. Furthermore, many *campesinas* are very much afraid of being in debt, even if only for a small amount of money.

The low levels of formal and functional literacy among *campesinas* represent another serious obstacle, further exacerbated by the relative lack of information they have about the world surrounding them, as a result of their confinement in a restricted spatial and social circle.

From the point of view of the program's operations, the main difficulty lies in the lack of qualified staff to work with the *campesinas;* this often results in the wearing of different hats by the same person, who must work as project promoter and supervisor, and as service referral aid. Second, despite many efforts, MUDE has not yet succeeded in getting all the credit applications processed on time. There have been instances in which one of the members of the group, in order to gain time, has borrowed money from a moneylender who charges high interest rates before the group formally submits the application for a loan, which then may not be enough to pay the interest.

There are also obstacles related to functional-structural issues:

- lack of *de facto* or *de jure* ownership of land; this is the case for most of the rural population, but particularly for women;

- unreliable marketing of products and strong dependence on intermediaries; and

- widespread impoverishment which is exacerbated by the growth of the external debt, and a resultant policy of adjustment bringing the poor to the brink of despair and absorbing any economic benefits resulting from these projects.

PRINCIPAL ACHIEVEMENTS OF THE CREDIT PROGRAM

We can unmistakably claim that the credit program has helped generate more income for the very poor rural women who participated in it, and that this increase in their income has improved their standard of living. Furthermore, even when they have not been economically successful, the projects financed have still been useful in training and motivating the participants.

Credit obtained by women for income-generating purposes has raised their status within their families and their communities. Women now bring new attitudes to the socialization of boys and girls. The social dimension given to credit by MUDE leads to the development of solidarity among women, and to a reevaluation of their self-esteem. Credit has opened the door for convincing both men and women that, despite the stereotypes and the lack of equality between the sexes, nature has certainly endowed women with the ability to work, think, and improve themselves.

Credit as a Generator of Other Programs

Besides the direct economic results of the program, credit has made it possible to conduct other activities contributing to women's development, strengthening at the same time the credit program itself. Based on the program experiences, and particularly because there is now a better understanding of women's reality and the methodology to work with them, MUDE has redefined their objectives to go beyond simply improving the economic status of the target population to reach a broader, ultimate goal: women's social and economic self-management.

MUDE believes that education and production are the basic aspects of promotion and development. These aspects go hand in hand when a group decides to carry out an economic project. Production is essentially a means to generate income, but the process of production should be accompanied, in turn, by education if solidarity and individual and collective strengthening are to be achieved.

Into this new conception of work MUDE has integrated with the credit program other programs that will permit it to offer a range of services to women, including the following:

- *Group Development:* to raise women's organizational levels, to promote the creation of women's groups, and to support the strengthening and improved operation of existing groups.

- *Leadership Development and Strengthening:* to educate and train women so that they can work as promotion and development agents in their own communities and neighboring communities.

- *Social Services:* to meet the basic needs of women in the areas of health, education, and development of infrastructure. The program includes specific activities such as the construction of Lorena stoves and individual humus-producing latrines, reforestation and environmental conservation education, and legal services for women.

- *Publications:* to keep consistent and continuing communication with the beneficiaries, donor agencies, and supportive institutions. One publication, *Mujer y Desarrollo,* is regularly sent to women's groups, in support of and as a complement to their training activities. MUDE's publications also include booklets for the general public that serve as guides for training efforts in production technology, processes, and quality control in the areas of agriculture, fishing, and agro-industries.

- *Cultural Expression:* to add a cultural dimension to the daily implementation of programs of social promotion and economic development.

CONCLUSION: SUGGESTIONS FOR OTHER PROGRAMS BASED ON MUDE'S EXPERIENCE

The experiences of MUDE have led it to conclude that by combining the credit program with other complementary programs, and by redefining its philosophy and regulations, which were adapted to the specific conditions of a target population, it can revive and expand the demand for credit services and increase the participation and raise the social consciousness of women.

This experience with the implementation of a credit program for very poor *campesinas* in a Caribbean island permits us to draw some lessons that might be useful to other institutions attempting to develop credit projects oriented to poor women. First, MUDE believes credit does not have any validity in development when it is not accompanied by an integrated development process including the understanding on the part of the target population of the social and economic reality in which they live. The MUDE experience has shown that individual loans lead in the long run to the isolation of the beneficiary, and potential incorporation into an exploitative system that once victimized him or her. On the other hand, associative credit is a positive force because it helps people to organize.

Associative credit, and especially credit targeted to the rural sector, must have the effect of increasing a borrower's ability to generate and keep a surplus. Only in this way can he or she expect to develop a "capitalization capacity" and, consequently, self-reliance. Credit should ensure, by itself, surplus generation, retention, and capitalization. Furthermore, this last element, used in an associative way, multiplies the productive and social benefits of the investment.

The organizations responsible for the management of credit funds must resist the temptation to design projects before women can have a say in them. The beneficiaries cannot skip any stage of project development if it is going to be successful. The design should be within the implementation capacity of the group, should respond to local peculiarities, and should be free of foreign stereotyped influences. Organizations managing credit funds should also resist the temptation to promote nontraditional projects if the groups responsible for their implementation are not yet ready.

Credit programs should be accompanied by appropriate technical assistance, organizational support, and previous training on the type of activity to be carried out. A method should be developed to allow participants to communicate their own experiences to other groups. MUDE's experience was that the *campesinas* who participated were the best trainers of the other *campesinas*. Furthermore, they were often excellent public relations agents.

Finally, we have to be cautious about the risk of concentrating credit in "elite" groups, or in groups capable of monopolizing leadership and power. We should seek to overcome a severe bias within many development organizations: the tendency to reach only those among the poor who already have had some opportunity of organizing themselves and do not fare as badly in their communities as others with no such experience.

10

The Credit Guarantee Mechanisms for Improving Women's Access to Bank Loans

WOMEN'S WORLD BANKING

W omen's World Banking (WWB)[1] was founded in 1979 by a small group of women from diverse cultures to provide a global support network for women entrepreneurs. WWB was chartered as a nonprofit organization in the Netherlands, under the name Stichting Women's World Banking. Its objectives are: to help create an environment in which women have equal access to the benefits of the modern economy; to build within individual countries local support bases that can respond to the specific needs of its own entrepreneurs; to establish a global network of women leaders in banking, finance, and business; and to encourage women's confidence and trust in themselves as capable, professional businesspeople.

Women's World Banking shows preference to no group—regional, ethnic, religious, or political—nor is it beholden to any special interest group, agency, or nation in determining how best to meet its objectives. Its financial and social approaches are sound ones. WWB charges going market rates of interest and expects an adequate return on the loans it guarantees or makes to local borrowers.

WOMEN'S WORLD BANKING AFFILIATES

WWB encourages entrepreneurial women in any country to join together as WWB affiliates and thereby assume responsibility and authority for their local programs. The men and women who establish an affiliate are self-starters who care about their society and their countrywomen.

To acquire funds for an affiliate's capital base and start-up costs, its members donate or risk their own resources and convince others to commit theirs. They must know their community and have a broad knowledge of the economic and technical assistance needs of local women. They must have organizational skills and understand markets and marketing. They must be able to communicate with various sectors of the community such as government officials, bankers, donors, other local leaders, and the women they seek to serve. The affiliates are also responsible for working with financial institutions, helping banks work with women, and negotiating a rate of interest no higher than the going market rate.

Affiliates select an appropriate legal structure, whether a nonprofit or for-profit private sector organization. They create their own charter, bylaws, and governing board. Because they are incorporated and operate in their own countries, they must adhere to the local laws and regulations. No country is limited to a single affiliate. The affiliate functions independently of WWB's international office in New York and is responsible for its own administration, financial viability, and plan of action. However, it must agree to conform to WWB goals and rules, and to maintain open lines of communication with WWB/New York and the other WWB affiliates. During the formation period, and at any time thereafter, the affiliate can call upon WWB/New York for assistance and advice.

To generate financing for small-scale enterprises, many affiliates utilize the WWB loan guarantee mechanism. For each loan an affiliate sponsors, WWB guarantees 50 percent of the principal amount, the WWB affiliate guarantees 25 percent, and the remaining 25 percent risk is borne by the bank. Spreading the risk among the three institutions creates an incentive for lending institutions to expand their pool of women borrowers. For many borrowers, the loan guarantee program provides credit for the first time and is a key element in their path to self-sufficiency and participation in the formal economy.

Some WWB affiliates have created other credit programs, such as direct loans for animal husbandry and revolving loan programs to provide working capital for businesses. Many WWB affiliates have also established training programs that provide basic business skills to their loan beneficiaries. Others provide free management consulting services to help women expand their enterprises. They link local women with the informational, technical, marketing, and other production elements necessary to their business development.

The affiliates understand that their assistance should go beyond direct business needs. Some have established inexpensive health care programs for clients and their families. Others help women work through the conflicting demands of family and business. They hold local seminars and workshops, encouraging women entrepreneurs to share their experiences and business problems, and to help each other find workable solutions.

WWB/New York

The international office in New York is the service and communication hub of the WWB global network. WWB/New York facilitates the exchange of ideas among affiliates and the WWB network, thus enabling affiliates to benefit from each others' insights and experience.

To promote the WWB concept and to reinforce each stage of the affiliate development process, WWB/New York is establishing regional operations around the globe. It also holds international workshops for women leaders in banking, finance, and business. These workshops and regional meetings offer opportunities for members of the WWB global network to exchange ideas on a personal basis.

From the time that a local group indicates its interest in forming an affiliate, WWB/New York can offer advice on its organization and operation, its incorporation as a legally recognized entity in its own country, and its contractual negotiations with local financial institutions. Once an affiliate is chartered, however, WWB's policy of local authority and local responsibility takes over. WWB/New York limits its collaboration to:

- matching the amount that the affiliate places in its loan guarantee fund, two-to-one;

- creating prototype programs that affiliates can adapt to their needs;

- providing management and technical assistance workshops and materials, at the request of the affiliate; and

- identifying potential partners, markets, and resources—local and international.

Women's World Banking/New York also oversees a capital fund, which supports local program development. The capital fund is the heart of WWB, providing financial stability for the WWB network and an endowment for the future. Its steady growth gives WWB credibility as a financial intermediary with local banks and financial institutions around the world. All monies contributed to the capital fund are invested conservatively at a reasonable rate of return in socially responsible investment vehicles. These investments serve as a reserve for loan guarantees. Portfolio income helps pay administrative and program development expenses, augmenting revenue from other contributions and fees that WWB/New York charges for guaranteeing loans and arranging management assistance programs.

The concept of leverage is key to the efficient use of capital fund monies. By leveraging the use of its capital, WWB multiplies the effect of its monies. As WWB's name and credit become more firmly established, the leverage effect will expand: WWB will be required to collateralize a decreasing fraction of its guarantee liability and thus will be able to support more loans with fewer dollars.

Since its founding only a decade ago, WWB, through its affiliate programs, has facilitated the start-up and expansion of thousands of woman-owned businesses and cooperatives. These businesses, in turn, have generated new employment and new money in the local economies.

WWB has demonstrated to financial institutions that they can profit by working with women clients. Urged by WWB, some banks have installed women's credit desks, with funds for use by women only. By working with governments, foundations, and financial institutions, WWB has helped change laws that restrict women's activities in private enterprise. Through such collaboration, local laws prohibiting women from having bank accounts in their own names have been changed; contractual requirements, forcing women to produce certifying signatures from a husband or male lawyer before they are allowed to sign contracts, have been revoked. Because of the success of their enterprises, women in dozens of less developed areas are experiencing a growing sense of independence.

WWB Affiliates in Latin America and the Caribbean

At present, WWB-affiliated organizations are operating in a variety of Latin American countries, including Brazil, Colombia, Costa Rica, the Dominican Republic, Haiti, Honduras, Jamaica, and Uruguay. Affiliates are also being formed in the following Latin American countries: Barbados, Bolivia, Ecuador, Mexico, Paraguay, Peru, and Venezuela.

In Colombia, a client of a Women's World Banking affiliate in Cali has received a loan making it possible for her to double the size of her bicycle manufacturing and repair business. In the Dominican Republic, WWB-backed loans are assisting women who operate small clothes manufacturing concerns to improve their buying and marketing skills and organization. In Haiti, residents faced a serious loss of important health care when the only dentist in a small community closed his clinic and moved on. The town's dental hygienist, however, went to Women's World Banking with a plan to keep the clinic open. The institution, dedicated to "women helping women," came through with enough money to restock the clinic and put the hygienist in business for herself. These are only a few examples of the achievement of clients of WWB affiliates. The list below reviews the progress of ten WWB affiliates in the Latin America and Caribbean region.

Highlights of 1986

Banco Brasileiro da Mulher.   Banco da Mulher started its first loan program in Rio de Janeiro in 1986 with thirty-eight loans totaling US$15,267. The affiliate is opening eight new offices to reach women entrepreneurs in other regions of Brazil.

Fundación Banco Mundial de la Mujer—Bucaramanga. The Colombian affiliate in Bucaramanga, established in 1986, has begun raising funds for a local capital base to support its program plans.

Fundación BMM–Banco Mundial de la Mujer—Cali. WWB's affiliate, BMM/Cali, provides loans to individuals and solidarity groups in Colombia. It also assists women through management training programs, a medical insurance plan, and a savings program. By December 1986, the affiliate had made 14,575 loans for a total amount of US$1,485,983. An overview of this affiliate and the results of its activities are presented in Chapter 11 of this volume.

Corporación Banco Mundial de la Mujer—Medellín. During its first year of operation in 1986, BMM/Medellín made eighty-five loans to solidarity groups totaling US$38,915. This Colombian affiliate provides management and skills training programs and a medical insurance plan. It also serves the community by operating a first-aid kiosk at the local market on weekends.

Credimujer (Costa Rica). Credimujer manages both a short-term and long-term loan program. The affiliate made a credit line of US$100,000 available to women in Costa Rica and disbursed 101 loans totaling US$54,000 by the end of 1986.

ADOPEM: Asociación Dominicana para el Desarrollo de la Mujer. Working with WWB and Banco del Comercio Dominicano, ADOPEM has made loans for the equivalent of US$391,247. During the year, this affiliate started a new savings program and a new loan program that granted 268 loans to solidarity groups totaling US$39,040.

FHAF: Fonds Haitien d'Aide a la Femme. By December 1986, FHAF had made US$96,000 available through its loan guarantee program with WWB and Banque Nationale de Credit and had disbursed 184 loans totaling US$163,700. It provides loan beneficiaries with training in fundamental business principles, offers a health insurance plan to its clients and their children, and expects to start a savings program. In early 1987, FHAF opened a branch office in Cap Haitien and started negotiations with a multilateral institution for a major loan to expand the affiliate's program threefold.

FUNHDEMU: Fundación Hondureña para el Desarrollo de la Mujer. In 1986, the Honduras affiliate's loan portfolio was comprised of 346 loans totaling US$81,933. FUNHDEMU provides a training program for loan beneficiaries and is starting another program to extend housing loans to women.

Friends of Women's World Banking Jamaica, Ltd. Through a 1985 loan guarantee agreement among WWB, FWWB/Jamaica and the Worker's Savings and Loan Bank, US$150,000 was made available for loans; however, because of the high interest rates prevailing in Jamaica, the program was not activated. The affiliate has made three loans for US$9,875 with local funds.

Fundación Uruguaya Women's World Banking. This affiliate has raised capital of US$62,000, which it uses to guarantee loans to women entrepreneurs in Uruguay. By the end of 1986, twenty-two loans had been guaranteed to individuals and cooperatives.

The Dominican Republic: A Country Profile

The Asociación Dominicana para el Desarrollo de la Mujer (ADOPEM), like many of the other affiliates of Women's World Banking, was initiated through the active commitment of a few women. Mercedes Canalda became the driving energy behind the organization of ADOPEM, following her attendance at a WWB Latin American regional workshop held in Cali, Colombia, in 1981.

The initial capital for the local portion of the guarantee fund came from 263 founding members' certificates. The Board of Directors of ADOPEM is made up of professionals who are committed to the goals of WWB and who work as volunteers. The Board meets once per week to discuss WWB programs, prepare monthly reports, and monitor loans. Members of the Board visit the borrowers' businesses themselves to monitor progress periodically and offer assistance where needed. The personal contact with loan recipients and the reputation for reliability that ADOPEM has established have been important to its success.

Other factors have contributed to the success of ADOPEM: the women of ADOPEM began to work immediately with businesswomen, and to learn from them; they set up a system that allows continual feedback from each case; they screen each loan applicant for credit and follow up with constant evaluation and assistance. Advice and training in accounting, sales, and business management are also provided to the borrowers.

Haiti: A Country Profile

The Affiliate

The Fonds Haitien d'Aide a la Femme (FHAF) is the affiliate of Women's World Banking in Haiti. It is a nonprofit organization created for the purpose of promoting the integration of small-scale Haitian businesswomen into the mainstream banking and business community.

In July 1983 a contract was signed by WWB, FHAF, and a local bank in Haiti, the Banque Nationale de Credit (BNC), to establish a guarantee fund to permit the BNC to grant credit to small businesses owned and/or managed by women. WWB covers 50 percent of the risk on each loan made through the BNC; FHAF covers 25 percent, and the BNC assumes the remaining 25 percent of the risk.

Guarantees are provided for short-term loans, over a maximum of twenty-four months. The interest rates charged by the financial intermediary fall within established commercial rates. Each loan is subject to an ex-ante evaluation by FHAF. FHAF not only conducts a financial and technical evaluation of each loan request that is submitted, but also includes in each evaluation some specific recommendations regarding technical assistance that will be needed by the prospective borrower.

The Projects

In the first year since the signing of the agreement among WWB, FHAF, and the BNC, a number of women's businesses in Haiti have received loans and flourished. For example, Mme. Rafino obtained a loan that will enable her to purchase two new sewing machines and expand her home-based garment manufacturing and retail business. The FHAF officer who evaluated Mme. Rafino's application concluded that she is a serious woman who knows her business, maintains a high quality standard for her products, and is open to suggestions and technical assistance on the part of FHAF. FHAF recommended that Mme. Rafino develop a system for the inventory and the control of raw materials, as well as a more detailed bookkeeping and budgeting scheme.

Dr. Nazon, a dentist who graduated from the University of Haiti, has been granted a loan to open her own dental clinic. The loan will pay for a complete set of new equipment for her clinic, which will be established in a building in which she already has some space. FHAF has approved Dr. Nazon's application for a number of reasons: she is a young and competent professional whose work is greatly needed, particularly in the provinces; she has already invested US$2,000 of her own money in the construction of the clinic; and the future of the clinic is promising, as are the opportunities of creating new jobs. Dr. Nazon will receive assistance from FHAF in setting up bookkeeping and accounting procedures.

Mme. Turenne runs a small garment manufacturing business in her home. She specializes in the production and sale of women's lingerie and caters to the local market (80 percent), as well as to the Dominican Republic (20 percent). FHAF has approved Mme. Turenne's request for a loan to expand her business through the purchase of new equipment and raw materials. Mme. Turenne was found to be a capable businesswoman who is able to sell all that she produces; by reinvesting profits, she has increased the value of her business tenfold since its establishment four years ago. FHAF will also assist Mme. Turenne in marketing and accounting techniques.

GUIDELINES FOR ESTABLISHING
AND OPERATING A WWB AFFILIATE

The following guidelines have evolved out of the practical experience of regional operations. They are not *official* strategies for establishing affiliates, but they will be helpful for giving organizations an idea of the elements of preparation that are involved and the steps that should be taken if a group is serious about establishing an affiliate.

Socioeconomic conditions, as well as political and cultural factors, vary from country to country; thus, it is most important that WWB promoters respond to women's economic needs in ways that are practical, appealing, appropriate, and socially relevant to the specific country. However, a number of basic organizational elements, along with a few initiating steps, are essential to assure that an affiliate operates efficiently and effectively. These include the following twelve items.

Associate

The key local individual, or individuals, who often provides the spark to get a WWB affiliate started is generally called the associate. She or he should be well acquainted with WWB objectives and goals; have a broad appreciation and sensitivity to the economic and technical needs of women in her (or his) country; and have organizational skills and ability to communicate with various sectors of the community, including government officials, commercial bankers, donors, women leaders, and entrepreneurs.

Working Committee

The associate must assemble a Working Committee made up of people with a commitment to the goals of WWB and a sensitivity to women's socioeconomic problems. Committee members should also possess a variety of skills, including those of a banker, lawyer, social worker, fundraiser, and accountant. A diversity of skilled personnel will facilitate more efficient, effective establishment of the affiliate. Eventually, the Working Committee may become the affiliate's Board of Directors or Trustees.

First Steps.   The first steps a Working Committee needs to take before an affiliate can become operational entail:

- officially registering with the government as a nonpolitical, for profit or not-for-profit organization with a legally registered charter or status;

- writing up an internal set of rules or bylaws;open a bank account in the affiliate's name; and

- preparing a tentative program design that includes identifying target groups, outreach and fundraising strategies, screening and loan review procedures, and technical training programs.

Keeping the WWB Regional Operation posted on the affiliate's progress is expedient, as WWB can offer advice, encouragement, and practical assistance.

Research

The Working Committee must also gain practical knowledge of: women's financial and technical needs; government policies and laws affecting women; climate and character of the financial and banking community; and scope and character of women's organization and leadership in their country.

Fundraising

Fundraising is required as a means to generate support for administrative costs of an affiliate office, including staff and a local contribution toward the WWB Loan Guarantee Program of no less than 25 percent. Once that sum is raised, WWB/New York can provide 50 percent of the loan guarantee through letters of credit and/or deposits to financial institutions. The remaining 25 percent will be assumed by a local financial institution after negotiations for the program have been completed.

A number of innovative means have already been used by affiliates to raise funds, including: issuing memberships (both corporate and individual); holding dinners, dances, charity balls, film shows, and festivals; and approaching local and international donor agencies for assistance.

Donors

WWB affiliates are encouraged to be self-sufficient economically, although donors can play a constructive role in affiliate formation, especially in the initial stages.

Donors who have assisted WWB in the past include governments and UN agencies, corporations, foundations, private organizations, and individuals. Especially when dealing with international donor agencies, affiliates should be sure to inform the WWB/New York Office, as it can assist on behalf of the affiliate at the international level.[2]

Banks and Financial Institutions

To identify the bank(s) and other financial institutions that would be willing to participate in the WWB Loan Guarantee Program requires some research and diplomacy, but once these institutions have been identified, negotiations can begin. A WWB negotiator need not necessarily be the local associate but she (or he) must have a working knowledge of the national banking laws and practices, a statement of the affiliate's financial status, and an ability to negotiate a rate of interest that is no higher than the current commercial one.

When negotiating with banks, affiliates must feel confident that they are offering the banks an opportunity to expand their commercial scope and cultivate new markets that hitherto have been untapped. WWB is not asking banks to do women a favor; rather, it is conducting a business deal.

Legal Incorporation

Once an affiliate is legally registered, has raised its financial contribution to the Guarantee Fund, and has found a bank willing to participate in the Loan Guarantee Program, it can sign the formal agreement with WWB/New York. A draft copy of the model/agreement is available through WWB/New York.

Affiliate Structure and Procedures

An affiliate may consist of a Board of Directors and various committees and an administrative staff, including a General Manager.

The Board.   The Board formulates policy and programs; delegates authority to various committees, such as a Program Committee, Client Training Committee, Loan Review Committee, and Fundraising Committee; helps implement and monitor client's loan disbursements and collections; and evaluates the impact of loans on women's projects.

The Administrative Staff.   Initially, affiliate members may serve the organization on a voluntary basis but, within the first year, sufficient funds should be raised to cover the cost of operating a small staff.

The administrative responsibilities include: implementation of the policies and programs of the Working Committee, which has become a Board elected by members; staff recruitment and training; personnel policies and office systems; development of an annual work plan and projected budget; fundraising, including building strong links with donors; establishing a working rapport with banks and negotiating for the WWB Loan Guarantee Program; provision of support services for the affiliate's Board and committees; and administration of client technical training programs.

The administrative staff works closely with the committees, especially in the implementation of the Loan Guarantee Program. Together they ensure that: women's projects and loan proposals are viable and well presented; timetables for loan repayment are set and followed; loans are used for the purposes specified; and final evaluation reports are kept, including highlights of positive effects of loans to women entrepreneurs.

The staff may include a General Manager, Training Officer, Accountant, Extension Worker, and Secretary. The criteria for staff selection should be flexible to suit local circumstances, although staff, especially the General Manager, must have initiative, imagination, social sensitivity, and management skills. They must be able to project an image of WWB that is both professional and socially concerned about the needs of women in development.

Training Programs

Most affiliates include a business training program for prospective clients as part of the criteria women must fulfill prior to participation in the Loan Guarantee Program. The training program, devised by a Training Committee, should include information on business planning and management, the use of credit and the responsibility for loan repayment, and marketing.

Publicity

A WWB affiliate may wish to launch a promotional campaign designed to reach the target group of small businesswomen in both urban and rural areas or to reach out to the larger public—such as bankers, policymakers, and donors—through the local media. The campaign might include holding press conferences announcing the affiliate's formation and activities, inviting journalists to write feature stories on affiliate activities, and preparing scripts for radio and television programs on women and economic development.

Networking

Networking is a means for women to exchange ideas and valuable experience that can help other women advance in affiliate development. Exchange of ideas can take place at forums or seminars, as well as through a WWB Newsletter. Because it is distributed not only to affiliates, but to representatives of government, donors, and the financial community, the newsletter is especially important in this regard.

NOTES

1. The reader can obtain additional information on Women's World Banking or assistance in starting an affiliate by writing to WWB at the following address: Women's World Banking, 104 East 40th Street, Suite 607-A, New York, N.Y. 10016.

2. For guidance in the preparation of funding proposals, WWB has prepared a Fundraising Manual for Affiliates, which is available through WWB/New York.

11

From a Women's Guarantee Fund to a Bank for Microenterprise: *Process and Results*

MARIÁ MARGARITA GUZMÁN and MARÍA CLEMENCIA CASTRO

T he Banco Mundial de la Mujer (Women's World Banking—BMM) opened its doors in Cali in 1982 as a source of guarantees for bank loans to individual microenterprises. It now has a variety of programs for men and women microproducers and microvendors. By July 1987, loans totaling 341,873,621 Colombian pesos (equivalent to more than US$1 million) had been made to 19,025 microentrepreneurs. At present in Colombia, the Bank has operations in Cali, in Popayàn (the capital of the Department of Cauca), and in the rural district of Puerto Tejada. Although it works with both men and women, the Bank is specifically committed to bringing formal credit to women operating in the informal sector. It meets this commitment by targeting its programs to the poor, and adapting its credit mechanisms to the various needs of both male and female microentrepreneurs, instead of confining its services to women alone.

The first part of this chapter describes the Bank's development, with emphasis on its assistance program for solidarity groups. The second part contains a summary of a recently completed evaluation that measures the program's impact.

DEVELOPMENT OF THE BANCO MUNDIAL DE LA MUJER

Origins

The 1975 international conference held in Mexico City launched the United Nations Decade for Women. In the wake of the conference, a group of women who had participated resolved to set up a mechanism for giving women and their families a more active role in the economy. The main obstacles that they identified were: lack of appropriate credit mechanisms, difficult access to credit, and a lack of guarantees for the support of credit applications to traditional institutions. The next step was taken in the Netherlands in 1979 with the birth of Stichting Women's World Banking (WWB). Its first project was the establishment of guarantee funds to encourage the traditional banking sector to invest in enterprises owned by women. Toward the end of 1980 a group of women in the city of Cali, with the assistance of WWB, decided to form a group of "Friends of WWB" and launched the Banco Mundial de la Mujer/BMM (Spanish for Women's World Bank). The WWB approved a line of credit for up to US$10,000 as seed capital for the group in Cali and as a counterpart to the US$5,000 put up by the local group.

In 1981 and 1982 the Friends of WWB met regularly to plan the program and raise the local donations that became its contribution to the Guarantee Fund. In this formative stage the BMM had the good fortune to receive support from the Fundación para la Educación Superior (Fund for Higher Education, or FES), which lent its name for the raising of the donations that then completed the local contribution to that Guarantee Fund. The FES also served as a backer in agreements to be concluded with private banks for the making of loans guaranteed by the Banco Mundial de la Mujer, and it provided resources to complete the local counterpart contribution to the Guarantee Fund. Another piece of good fortune for the BMM was the existence in Cali of a pioneer operation specializing in technical assistance to microenterprises, the Programa de Desarrollo para la Pequeña Empresa (Small Business Development Program, or DESAP) of the Carvajal Foundation. The Banco Mundial de la Mujer benefited from this foundation's experience through its system of instruction and support in the monitoring of loans secured by the Guarantee Fund.

In 1982 Banco Mundial de la Mujer gained its legal status under a law that permits it to operate as a foundation (hence, its formal name, Fundación Banco Mundial de la Mujer). The Bank formally initiated operations in June 1982.

Purpose and Functions

The basic purpose of the Banco Mundial de la Mujer is "the creation of financial mechanisms for enabling women and their families to participate in economic activity." Its specific function is to establish a bank for the family-based informal sector. Because the informal sector embraces 60 percent of the economically active population of Cali, of which 54 percent are women and 46 percent men, the Banco Mundial de la Mujer cannot exclude male heads of household from its programs. Up until 31 July, 1987, however, 68 percent of the beneficiaries of the lending programs of the Banco Mundial de la Mujer were women.

The Bank has accomplished its objective through three programs:

Guarantee Fund.   The BMM's first operation was the establishment of a fund to guarantee loans made to microentrepreneurs by regular lending institutions. Under this project, loans for up to $3,970,700 and averaging $113,448 per loan in Colombian pesos (the equivalents of US$21,121 and US$603 respectively) have been guaranteed for thirty-five microenterprises. In the first year seventy-five jobs were generated at a cost of C$52,942 (US$281) per job.

In 1982 the Colombian Government issued regulations for the Fondo Nacional de Garantías (National Guarantee Fund) and set the charge for this service at 2 percent. The BMM decided to channel the applications of microentrepreneurs through the Fondo Nacional de Garantías and, having secured a replacement for its program, began a second stage of development. For its solidarity groups the BMM has set up another Guarantee Fund that currently totals more than two million Colombian pesos.

Credimicros.   The BMM has established *Credimicros,* a credit card for microentrepreneurs, which gives the microenterprise access to working capital up to an approved limit for a period of one year. The facility may be drawn on as often as desired, each amount drawn to be repaid in four months. The guarantee provided is the post-dated checks that microentrepreneurs receive from their customers. This arrangement has given microenterprises standing access to working capital, allowing them to avoid stoppages in their operations, which have been one of their main problems. *Credimicros* is backed by a Credit Fund of which the Banco Mundial de la Mujer and FES have each put up 50 percent.

However, *Credimicros* and the Guarantee Fund were failing to meet the full credit needs of low-income women running their own small businesses. The Banco Mundial de la Mujer made a careful study of the situation in the informal sector and found a large number of workers (especially women) existing far below the parameters defined for microenterprises and hence left without access to any organized credit program. As a result, it entered the third stage in the development of its projects.

Solidarity Groups.   A Solidarity Group Program for self-employed workers in public markets was begun in September 1983 with fourteen groups and in May 1984 was extended to include groups of microproducers. In July 1987 there were already 5,872 groups enrolled in the program. The purpose of the groups, which have a minimum of three to five members, is to guarantee loans made to their members, who have no access to conventional guarantees.

The program is aimed at two basic groups: microproducers—small entrepreneurs working as seamstresses, shoemakers, woodworkers, dollmakers, and the like—and microvendors, who include holders of stalls in markets, dry goods dealers and grocers, shopkeepers, and street vendors. The general objectives of the program are to provide advisory services, training, and credit to self-employed low-income workers, raise family incomes, emphasize the need to save, and encourage associative forms of organization among self-employed workers.

To accomplish these objectives the Bank engages in training work, for which it employs specialized personnel and teaching materials (audiovisual aids, games, and so forth) to impart such concepts as solidarity, cooperation, leadership, group objectives, and accounting. This work affords ongoing contact with beneficiaries and makes them feel that they are part of the program. Besides, the structure of the program allows beneficiaries to become "subscribers" of the Bank, a status that instills a deeper sense of responsibility to an institution that, in this sense, belongs to them.

The "Registro de Seguimiento" (monitoring record) provides a running account of the economic situation of the group. At first, this monthly information was gathered by BMM advisors during their visits to homes or at the Bank's headquarters, but now it is prepared by each participant before his or her loan is renewed.

Current Operations

Operations are currently being carried out in four areas:

1. *Direction.* The direction of the operation is the province of the Executive Director. The *Credimicros* program and the Guarantee Fund are managed through this office and are approved by the respective committees. In the administrative area there is an accountant who manages the organization's portfolio, and there are bookkeepers in each branch office.

2. *Training.* Training is coordinated by a social worker. The main purpose of training is to give the group cohesiveness. Group reinforcement talks are given on such subjects as "What is a solidarity group?" and "What is solidarity?" Talks are also being started on principles of accounting and business analysis.

The current loan amount runs from a minimum of C$2,000 (US$8) to a maximum of C$100,000 (US$415) and is increased on the basis of an evaluation of the progress of the enterprise in relation to the time of year. Peak sales are obviously made in April (Easter week), May (Mother's Day), June (Father's Day), and November and December (Christmas and New Year's Day).

Groups requiring an amount of working capital larger than US$415 are serviced through the *Credimicros* line. In addition, a line of credit for the purchase of fixed assets, to be run in conjunction with the government or private banks, has been proposed for the near future and is currently under study.

3. *Advisory Services.* In the area of advisory services, coordinated by the Executive Director, each advisor is responsible for the organization of up to sixty solidarity groups in his or her area of action. The adviser contacts the

groups, holds talks initiating them into the program, and then holds monthly follow-up talks with individual groups in which an evaluation is made of the progress of each member's business during the period they have been involved in the Bank's program.

4. *Planning and Research.* In March 1986 the Foundation set up a planning and research area under a business administrator who specializes in research; the result has been the establishment of a system of ongoing evaluation of solidarity group programs. Data were collected first in May 1986, again in November of that year, and most recently in May 1987. Results from November 1986 are presented in the next section of this chapter. The final report on this most recent information is currently being processed.

Other Activities.   The Bank designed a health insurance scheme that covered hospitalization for the entire family. Despite its low cost, however, the insurance company was unable to include out-patient consultations and purchase of medicines, and as a result the program was not as well received as had been expected and had to be canceled. The experience of the program demonstrated that participants are not used to providing against future illness and hence need access to out-patient consultation on a permanent basis. On their own initiative, however, the users have approved a life insurance plan that covers the cost of their loan and funeral expenses, which will go into effect in the coming months.

EVALUATION OF THE IMPACT
OF THE BANCO MUNDIAL DE LA MUJER

The BMM's programs are designed to permit self-evaluation on the basis of a series of indicators that include jobs created, sales, income and profits, the assets of the enterprise, use of credit, and the savings accumulated by the microentrepreneur. In addition, special evaluations are made that yield further economic and social information.

In May 1986 the Fundación Banco Mundial de la Mujer launched an investigation to determine the impact of the Solidarity Group Program on its participants. This investigation was the basis for the institution of an "ongoing evaluation," which is reviewed every six months. In November the BMM gathered fresh data on the persons interviewed in May, and on others, to complete the sample in order to compare the findings over time. It is worthwhile to delve into the impact of this program, as women are well represented in the activities to which the program is directed, an indication that this program might have the greatest potential for benefiting women.

In November 1986 the Solidarity Groups Program reached a total of 581 beneficiaries—68.5 percent of them women—which included 381 microvendors and 200 microproducers. Up until that month, the program had granted a cumulative total of 11,705 short-term loans amounting to C$178,718,708 (equivalent to US$919,902).[1] In November the value of the outstanding portfolio was C$21,774,282 (US$112,083), with a default rate of 14.9 percent. In that month the program was already self-supporting, with monthly income amounting to 114 percent of monthly expenditures.

The impact on participants in the Solidarity Group Program was measured from an economic and social standpoint: the economic impact in terms of loan amounts, sales, purchases, expenditures, profits, savings, administrative organization of the enterprise, job creation, and the improvement of living standards; and the social impact in terms of solidarity, changes of attitude, participation in the program, and involvement in the community.

First, in November 1986, the variables were studied separately in relation to the time that the person had been with the program, the line of business, and the sex of the person. Then, with the data for May and November 1986, a comparative analysis was made of the borrowers in the program for more than six months, in order to determine what development and behavioral changes had taken place. Finally, a profile of the participant was constructed based on his or her time with the program.

The impact study was based on an analysis of information from a random sample of 217 participants in the program.[2] Table 11.1 shows the makeup of the population of borrowers and the sample used, which was drawn from the universe of credit recipients in November 1986.

TABLE 11.1
Solidarity Groups:
Composition of Population and Sample of Borrowers

Time with Program	More than 12 Months				6–12 Months				Less than 6 Months				Total
Line of Work	Producer		Vendor		Producer		Vendor		Producer		Vendor		
Sex	M	F	M	F	M	F	M	F	M	F	M	F	
Population	11	56	23	50	5	45	5	33	32	51	107	163	581
Sample	4	21	9	18	2	17	2	12	12	19	40	61	217

Credit. In November 1986 a majority of participants received loans of less than 30,000 pesos. Over 30 percent received loans of less than 20,000 pesos. However, in that month a great demand for higher amounts was seen as both vendors and producers began to stock up for December, with working capital requirements doubling in some cases.

Sales. Sales of C$10,000 to C$100,000 (about US$50 to US$500, respectively) per month were made by 61.1 percent of the beneficiaries. Only 12 percent had sales above C$200,000. Monthly sales were slightly lower for women than for men. Vendors began offering their goods in November, and their sales began rising before those of producers. Sellers of merchandise began supplying stores and direct retail customers with toys, apparel, and so forth, while producers were engaged in manufacturing.

Expenditures.   Expenditures were highest among participants with less than six months in the program; thereafter, they tended to decline or level off. Wages were more important among producers, with men hiring and paying higher wages at between six and twelve months, while women did so progressively over time. Rentals were of no major significance in this context because such a large proportion of the participants worked in their own homes.

Net Income.   Net incomes of C$11,000 to C$30,000 a month (equivalent to between 0.6 and 1.8 minimum wages) were earned by 35.7 percent of the participants and maintained through all the periods considered (see Table 11.2). Women's net incomes tended to be slightly higher than those of men. Monthly incomes above C$31,000 were attained by 14.3 percent of the participants, especially among those with less than six months in the program, but such a high income could not be sustained throughout the year.

TABLE 11.2
**Percentages of Participants Earning Different
Net Incomes (Minimum Wages) with Different Times
of Participation in the Program, November 1986**[a]

	More than 12 Months of Participation			6–12 Months of Participation			Less than 6 Months of Participation		
	M	F	Total	M	F	Total	M	F	Total
0 to 0.5 × minimum wage	69.4	51.6	60.5	50.0	63.2	56.6	43.3	44.0	43.7
0.6 to 1.8 × minimum wage	30.6	32.9	31.7	50.0	22.5	36.3	42.5	32.9	37.7
1.9 the minimum wage	—	15.5	7.8	—	14.3	7.1	14.2	23.1	18.6

Source: Banco Mundial de la Mujer.
   [a]   Minimum wage in November 1986 = C$16,812 (equivalent to US$70.22).

Savings.   One of the greatest achievements of the program was the education of participants in the need to save, a total of C$12,348,431 in savings (equivalent to US$51,238) having been accumulated to date. This places the beneficiaries in a position to build up their own working capital to guarantee their further development. However, the evaluation data indicate that voluntary savings depended on the time the participant had been with the program, and that only 8.7 percent of the beneficiaries saved more than the requisite minimum.

A comparison of the male and female beneficiaries under the program shows that in the figures for loans requested and monthly sales, there are more men than women in the higher amount catagories. For example, sales of more than C$200,000 were made by 23.6 percent of the men but only 15.4 percent of the women. Among the microproducers, 5.6 percent of the men and 3.5 percent of the women sold more than C$200,000 in the month.

However, these proportions do not hold for net income, in which 14 percent of the female producers attained the highest level (over C$41,000 a month) compared with only 5.6 percent of the men. Among the vendors, 9.8 percent of the men and 14.2 percent of the women reached this income bracket.

Finally, we should keep in mind that the figures for the period considered (November) were affected by the year-end season, a time in which working capital needs rise markedly, but with differences between vendors and producers owing to the nature of their lines of work. We should also note that the participants who had joined the Banco Mundial de la Mujer in the last six months operated enterprises that faced greater demand and hence had higher capital requirements.

A comparison of data for May and November (see Table 11.3) reveals that the participants' working capital in November was higher—as were their sales, purchases, and expenditures—and the average net income ranged between $11,000 and $30,000 a month, while the figures in the other categories fluctuated in response to changes in the economy as a whole. Hence, time appears to have been a determining factor in the participants' development, the impact being strongest at between six and twelve months. We must view these findings with caution, however, as the participant profile has been constructed with the information for May and November alone, and that for the latter month is affected by external and seasonal factors and hence is not representative.

Jobs.   In November 217 jobs were preserved and 126 generated at a cost of about C$21,000 per job (see Table 11.4). Of this total of 343 jobs, 84.5 percent were permanent and 15.5 percent temporary. The data indicate that enterprises run by men generated relatively more jobs. Some 52 percent of the 343 new workers were employed in the microenterprises of men, but men comprised only 32 percent of the beneficiaries.

The highest number of jobs was generated in the group that had participated less than six months, followed by that participating more than twelve months; the former hired chiefly family members (who are unpaid) while the latter had more paid workers, who did not, however, earn more than the legal minimum wage.

As noted, November is atypical for loan size and sales (owing to the December season); therefore, the indicators of credit and sales needed to generate a job are less reliable. However, the resulting cost per job is similar for November and May. In May the average vendor needed a loan of C$18,000 a month with average sales of C$90,000 a month to generate one job. Producers obtained an average of C$18,000 in loans and their sales were C$75,000.

TABLE 11.3

Economic Impact: Comparative Analysis of Borrowers with More than 6 Months of Program Participation, May 1986 – November 1986 (Colombian pesos)

	More than 12 Months of Participation		6–12 Months of Participation		Total	
	May[a] – Nov.[b]		May – Nov.[c]		May – Nov.[d]	
A. Amount of Monthly Credit						
From $5,000 to $10,000	10.7%	1.9%	38.0%	—	18.2%	5.0%
$10,001 to $20,000	77.3	25.0	56.0	36.4	64.0	27.3
$20,001 to $30,000	8.4	23.0	—	24.3	10.8	25.9
$30,001 to $35,000	2.4	11.5	6.0	6.0	2.7	10.0
$35,001 and above	1.2	38.6	6.0	33.3	4.3	31.8
B. Monthly Sales						
From $10,000 to $50,000	36.9	21.2	54.0	42.4	33.4	26.6
$50,001 to $100,000	34.5	44.2	32.0	27.3	32.5	34.5
$100,001 to $200,000	25.0	23.0	14.0	24.3	24.5	26.8
$200,001 and above	3.6	11.6	—	6.0	9.5	12.0
C. Monthly Expenditures						
Less than $5,000	26.2	7.7	34.0	15.2	19.2	10.1
From $5,000 to $15,000	26.2	34.6	30.0	33.3	25.2	29.2
$15,001 to $25,000	22.6	21.2	26.0	27.3	20.3	20.7
$25,001 to $35,000	13.1	13.5	6.0	12.1	18.1	14.7
$35,001 and above	11.9	23.0	4.0	12.1	17.2	25.3
D. Monthly Net Income						
Less than $10,000	44.0	57.7	52.0	63.6	37.8	50.0
From $10,000 to $20,000	25.0	23.1	42.0	6.1	27.8	23.8
$20,001 to $30,000	15.5	7.7	4.0	18.2	12.5	11.9
$30,001 to $40,000	8.3	3.8	2.0	—	11.7	3.4
$40,001 and above	7.2	7.7	—	12.1	10.2	10.9
E. Monthly Savings						
Minimum	90.5	75.0	96.0	75.8	92.0	86.8
Voluntary	2.4	15.4	2.0	15.2	3.1	8.7
No savings	7.1	9.6	2.0	9.0	6.0	4.5

[a] In May 1986 borrowers were in the category of 6–12 months.
[b] In May 1986 borrowers were in the category of less than 6 months.
[c] Refers to the sample participants analyzed in May 1986.
[d] Refers to the sample participants analyzed in November 1986.

TABLE 11.4

Solidarity Group Program: Number of Jobs Generated and Maintained in Businesses According to Length of Participation, Activity, and Gender, 1986[a]

Job Creation	More than 12 Months of Participation				From 6 to 12 Months of Participation				Less than 6 Months of Participation				Total				
	Producers		Vendors		Producers		Vendors		Producers		Vendors		Producers		Vendors		Total
	M	F	M	F	M	F	M	F	M	F	M	F	M	F	M	F	
A. Job Status																	
1. Full-time	13	25	12	19	3	20	2	14	17	24	62	79	33	69	76	112	290
2. Part-time	1	15	2	7	—	1	—	2	3	2	13	7	4	18	15	16	53
Total	14	40	14	26	3	21	2	16	20	26	75	86	37	87	91	128	343
B. Type of Employment																	
1. Paid	13	32	13	22	3	19	2	15	19	25	61	71	35	76	76	108	295
2. Unpaid	1	8	1	4	—	2	—	1	1	1	14	15	2	11	15	20	48
Total	14	40	14	26	3	21	2	16	20	26	75	86	37	87	91	128	343

Source: Women's World Banking.
[a] Sample.

In November the cost per job, or the loan amount required to create one job, was about C$21,000.

Organizing the Enterprise

Accounting System. In November a system of accounts was being used by 79.9 percent of the participants, and especially among those who had been with the program for more than twelve months (see Table 11.5). However, those in the program less than six months were quite receptive to the Bank's requirement of having a simple set of accounts that would reflect the current state of their enterprises, and 77 percent of them kept an account book.

Improvement of Enterprise Premises. A larger proportion of men made improvements in the physical premises of their businesses, and the need to do so was apparently more important after the first year with the program.

Purchase of Machinery and Equipment. In the last six months, machinery and equipment were purchased by 18.7 percent of the participants. Needs in November differed from those reported in May. The behavior of the female producers was changing, with more purchases being made at between six and twelve months; this situation will be considered in detail later on. The vendors made their purchases progressively.

Sales of New Products. As beneficiaries under the program were able to identify new lines of trade or production (through learning the experiences of other participants), they diversified their businesses with the capital supplied by the Banco Mundial de la Mujer. This addition of products and/or changes in existing products happened chiefly in the first six months. At between six and twelve months, 100 percent of the male producers were selling new articles. After twelve months only the women were still making changes, that is, adapting to demands of the market (fashions, seasons, and so forth).

Use of Moneylenders. Financing other than that supplied by the Bank was needed by 9.8 percent of the participants, mainly producers who had been with the program more than twelve months, to support investments other than working capital. Women tended to use moneylenders more often and had less access to suppliers' credits, findings that suggest it may be more difficult for women to obtain all the working capital they need from formal sources.

Purchases from Wholesalers on Credit. Buying on credit was done more often by the vendors. This arrangement was used more frequently in the first months of participation in the program; later on, cash purchases were preferred, the shift of preference being more pronounced among the men.

The situation among the producers differed from that of vendors. In the first months 16.2 percent purchased on credit, in the next period they

TABLE 11.5

Solidarity Group Program: Participation of Borrowers by Business Organization, Time in Program, Activity, and Gender, 1986[a] (in Percent)

Business	More than 12 Months of Participation				From 6 to 12 Months of Participation				Less than 6 Months of Participation				Total				
	Producers		Vendors		Producers		Vendors		Producers		Vendors		Producers		Vendors		Average
	M	F	M	F	M	F	M	F	M	F	M	F	M	F	M	F	
A. Accounting System	75.0	95.2	88.9	83.3	50.0	88.2	—	91.7	91.7	68.4	67.5	82.0	83.3	84.2	68.6	83.5	79.9
B. Improvement of Enterprise Premises	25.0	33.3	22.2	11.1	100.0	23.5	—	25.0	16.7	—	35.0	19.7	27.8	19.3	31.4	18.7	24.3
C. Purchase of Machinery/Equipment	25.0	33.3	22.2	5.6	50.0	11.8	50.0	16.7	25.0	5.3	17.5	9.8	27.8	17.5	19.6	9.9	18.7
D. Sales of New Products	—	28.6	—	33.3	100.0	29.4	—	33.3	25.0	47.4	30.0	32.8	27.8	35.1	23.5	33.0	29.9
E. Use of Moneylenders	25.0	23.8	—	11.1	—	—	—	16.7	8.3	10.5	7.5	8.2	11.1	12.3	5.9	9.9	9.8
F. Purchases from Wholesalers on Credit	25.0	14.3	—	22.2	—	11.8	—	50.0	16.7	15.8	42.5	27.9	16.7	14.0	33.3	29.7	23.4

Source: Women's World Banking.
[a] Sample.

tended to buy with cash, and after the first twelve months 19.7 percent used credit to finance their operations.

Summary.   In the first months the participants saw the need to organize their businesses, that is, to start keeping accounts. In the next period, the focus was on expanding the business, improving the premises, buying machinery and equipment, and offering new products for sale. After the first year the great majority found a system of accounts essential, and growth continued, but more slowly. At first the participants bought on credit, probably because the amount lent by the Bank in the first months is small (the maximum for an initial loan is C$20,000 per month). Later, the participants switched to cash payments for discounts on volume purchases. Finally, they reverted to purchases on credit because they now had a longer-term position, that is, they tried to balance short-term obligations against payments from debtors. Recourse to a moneylender or financing institutions was more or less constant in all the periods whenever net profits were insufficient to cover additional investments.

Not only did the structure of the group of beneficiaries change, but their development tended to vary with the time they had been with the program (see Table 11.5). Thus, the percentage of participants carrying accounts tended to rise in the first months and recourse to moneylenders diminished, indications that advisory services to businesses must emphasize these aspects (accounting and finance). Between six and twelve months the participant gave less importance to accounting and tended to focus primarily on structuring the business; thus the institution should be helpful chiefly in these aspects to participants making changes in such areas as investments and marketing. After the first year, producers tended to turn to sources of credit other than the Bank and to improve their accounting, from which we can infer that a deeper study of the business is needed to help the entrepreneur find a break-even point. In addition, the entrepreneur must begin to take further training in this area.

Standard of Living

The standard of living of participants was measured in terms of improved food, housing, health, education, and recreation, among other aspects. In November 1986, 76.1 percent of the participants thought that they could spend more on food. The greatest increase in this purchasing power came after the first twelve months. Also in November 1986, 61.1 percent reported having houses of their own, and 18.1 percent—chiefly beneficiaries with a year or more of participation—made improvements in their homes.

Although most of the participants said that their living standards had improved since they entered the Bank's program, very few (less than 20 percent) thought the improvement had been considerable.

There were no significant differences between the men's and women's assessments of their situations except in a few cases. While 78.9 percent of the women had homes of their own, only 27.8 percent of the men owned their homes. Only 36.8 percent of the women producers credited the improvement in their incomes to increases in the income of their businesses compared to 72.2 percent of the male producers.

Social Impact of the Solidarity Program

The social impact of the program was measured in terms of solidarity, changes of attitude, participation in the program, and involvement in the community. These variables were rated by the group of advisers and the institution's training officer on a scale from one to five, with five representing a good impact. These effects of the program are very difficult to measure because they are subjective in nature. However, according to the standards of the beneficiaries who were interviewed, the program had helped raise their level of solidarity and their participation in the program and involvement in the community, and had helped change their attitudes and how they presented themselves. These effects may be not very permanent, as is the case of solidarity, which grew considerably in the first six months and then declined somewhat.

CONCLUSIONS AND RECOMMENDATIONS

Summary of Results of the Evaluation

The data show that the time of participation in the program played an important part in its economic and social impact on the beneficiaries. Thus, at the beginning they worked with loans in small amounts because their businesses had not yet developed to any significant extent. After the first twelve months, however, they obtained loans of more than $30,000 (US$150) per month. The situation is the same for the other economic variables: sales, expenditures, net income (see Table 11.6). The impact was similar for both women and men, but men tended to increase sales and employment more than did women, while women increased their net income more than did men.

TABLE 11.6
**Summary of the Solidarity Group Program's Impact
(Colombian pesos)**

Monthly Economic Impact	Initially	After One Year
Amount of Credit	$ 5,000 (US$25)	$ 30,000 (US$150)
Sales	$10,000 (US$50)	$150,000 (US$750)
Expenditures	$ 5,000 (US$25) or less	$ 36,000 (US$180) or above
Net Income	$10,000 (US$50) or less	$ 31,000 (US$155) or above

During this time, participants started to carry accounts, make improvements in their business premises, and purchase machinery and equipment. Before the end of the first year, however, some had to turn to financial sources other than the Bank to cover these purchases and improve their operations. Additional costs after the first year were covered out of business profits. The increase in net income allowed the borrowers to raise their standard of living by having more money to spend on food, health, housing, recreation, and other expenses.

Recommendations for Changes in the Solidarity Group Program

The findings of the evaluation suggested a series of changes in the Solidarity Group Program of the Banco Mundial de la Mujer. In consideration of the socioeconomic characteristics of the program participants, it was recommended that training talks be presented in a format appropriate for the informal sector, giving the process greater flexibility that could lead to greater participation.

To provide better service, it was suggested that the credit lines be diversified along the following lines:

- *a fixed assets line* for the purchase of machinery, equipment, and tools;

- *a home improvement line* for the partial and progressive improvement of production premises and family homes; and

- *a line of credit for individuals* to meet any of the above requirements.

The evaluation has shown that what the participant does depends on how long he or she has been in the program, and it is advisable to generate timely arrangements for the provision of coordinated advisory and training services. Thus, in the first six months the participant should concentrate on putting business records in order, and the program should focus on the design of an accounting system. Between six and twelve months the main emphasis should be on expansion of the business, which implies a diversification of project services—the addition of different forms of credit (for fixed assets, and so forth) and training in specialized short courses in specific areas and advisory services for infrastructure projects, investment, and other purposes. After the first year the participant also requires continuing education. This education could be offered by the BMM in short courses and seminars with voluntary attendance in order to firm up the concepts of accounting, finance, and marketing that the individual has been building in the course of the year.

Finally, it was recommended that the BMM begin a promotion program using such media as the radio (for example, to offer programs for the expression of personal opinions), the press, and other low-cost forms of publicity such as billboards.

Lessons for Other Programs

The study of the Banco Mundial de la Mujer yields recommendations that can serve as guidelines to other agencies interested in carrying out a similar program. The most important of these lessons follow:

1. Any organization that wants to implement a program of this kind must envisage a system of ongoing evaluation that will apprise it immediately of any changes in the beneficiaries so that the requisite modifications can be made promptly.

2. The program must be designed so that every day participants take over functions initially performed by the institution, such as promotion, loan processing, and preparation of the follow-up survey. In this way the participant becomes responsible for the amounts of the approved loan and the final use made of it.

3. The program must also aim at making the informal sector a customer of the formal banking sector, as efforts to assist the informal sector will otherwise remain small and experimental.

4. These institutions must be run as businesses so that they can achieve self-sufficiency and adapt conventional banking services to the informal sector, in order to simplify the precredit processing formalities, and the approval and disbursement of loans.

5. Institutions interested in a program of this kind must have available government or private banks they can rely on to serve as windows and assume the loan-handling costs, such as check cashing, loan amortization, and collection of savings. However, the check must be drawn by the institution, as this function cannot be delegated to traditional institutions.

6. Lastly, it is essential to have a staff that is convinced of the importance of working in the informal sector and of supporting private sector development at all levels.

NOTES

1. The average exchange rate on that date.

2. The sample was determined by the following formula

$$n = \frac{K \times N \times P \times Q}{K \times P \times P + (N-1)E}$$

where N = size of sample
K = degree of confidence (95%)
N = population
P = percentage of men
Q = percentage of women E = standard error or deviation (5%)

The size of the resulting sample is 217 persons, or 37.3 percent of the population, distributed for time of participation in the program, line of activity, and sex.

12

The Rural Development Fund:
An Integrated Credit Program for Small and Medium Entrepreneurs

MARÍA EUGENIA ARIAS

This chapter is based on a case study conducted in 1983 by the Rural Development Fund (Fondo de Desarrollo, Rural or FDR), a line of credit created by the Banco Industrial del Perú (BIP) and aimed at small entrepreneurs.[1] The objective of the study was to analyze how women borrowers benefit from this credit program.

The fund was financed through the Banco Industrial del Perú with a loan from the United States Agency for International Development to the Government of Peru. The purpose of the fund was to benefit small entrepreneurs who did not have access to credit, and consequently to contribute to the generation of employment and improvement in the distribution of income, and to strengthen a comprehensive plan of national development. As in other projects that follow general outlines for country-level or sector development, the beneficiaries were not defined in terms of gender.

Women were considered an integral part of the FDR project, not targets of a special project. In short, FDR was an integrated credit program for small and medium entrepreneurs (not for microentrepreneurs) conducted by a national industrial development-oriented public institution. In view of these circumstances, what were the results of the program? Was it successful in including women? What is the role of a credit program financed by an institution like BIP?

This chapter attempts to answer these questions by using the BIP case to focus on this type of program. It presents the results of the FDR program in the Banco Industrial del Perú; analyzes the role of the credit programs financed by the public sector; and reviews the data on credit extended to women by the FDR credit line. The conclusion contains suggestions about the implementation of credit programs that are successful at including women.

INCLUSION OF WOMEN IN INTEGRATED CREDIT PROGRAMS

A question we must always ask is whether women-specific programs should be developed or whether women should be included in integrated programs as in the BIP's FDR credit line. Buvinić (1986) argues that it is possible to keep the emphasis on women borrowers who are confronting the central problems of poverty and equity without promoting separate, women-specific programs. Women-specific programs may lack access to greater resources and the organizational capacity to implement successful programs, and end up as welfare programs implying a deepening poverty for the borrower and often leading to the failure of the projects.

The author of this chapter suggests that the implementation of projects should be carried out by integrated institutions. However, the success of production-oriented projects that include women is linked to the nature and technical capacity of these institutions. "Where there are no institutions capable of absorbing outside support and implementing successful women-specific programs, qualified technical assistance and generous outside support might have little impact on the promotion of income/employment-generating programs" (Buvinić 1986).

Consequently, it is necessary to persuade integrated institutions to implement programs that include low-income women. This step will require adapting to the financial needs of women, that is, to even smaller loans, reasonable transaction costs, appropriate reimbursement terms, and minimal collateral requirements. Lycette (1984) recommends the integration of several characteristics of informal borrowing systems into project design and an orientation toward appropriate interest rates, several repayment options, and reduced collateral requirements.

Stern, Naranjo & Co. (1984, pp. 9–14), in a study focusing on the micro-entrepreneur in general, also suggest the integration of the following characteristics of informal credit systems:

- establishment of ceiling risk amounts of credit so that the borrower who has grown beyond the microenterprise "graduates" to more appropriate credit systems;

- interest rates that are competitive in the financial market;

- repayment schedules based on the traditional schemes prevalent in the community. The program should start by keeping the weekly, semi-monthly, and monthly payments that are familiar to the potential borrowers;

- use of fixed assets, equipment, and machinery as collateral, supplemented by personal guarantors; and

- informal references from suppliers and members of the community.

Given this global picture, the central questions are, first, why is it that public institutions created to ensure credit access to small entrepreneurs do not achieve their objectives? What barriers in the organizational structure prevent the channeling of funds assigned to these new clients? Second, how can women be integrated into the design and implementation of credit projects for small and microentrepreneurs? In order to answer those questions, let us review the case of the Banco Industrial del Perú credit program, FDR, and identify the reasons for the successful provision of loans to small entrepreneurs, and to what extent this new orientation resulted in an increase of loans to women.

THE RURAL DEVELOPMENT FUND: A CREDIT PROGRAM INVOLVING MAJOR CHANGES WITHIN THE BIP

The BIP case highlights how the Bank changed its loan portfolio from focusing attention on large-scale urban industries to including loans for small-scale rural industries. The credit extended to small businesses increased from 3.4 percent in 1974 to 50 percent of all the new loans extended in 1981. Furthermore, the BIP was able to decentralize authority over the line of credit, giving more responsibility to the local branches, and to diversify the loans on a geographic basis. These positive results were established as project goals and submitted as a condition by the donor agency at the beginning of the loan.

FDR Background

In 1975, BIP received US$6 million to undertake a pilot project aimed at developing small-scale rural enterprises in four provinces in the highlands of Peru. In view of the successful promotion by BIP of this new line of credit, the Agency for International Development gave a new loan for US$8 million to expand and institutionalize the Rural Development Fund in 1979. In order to achieve these objectives, BIP made a commitment to reduce the demands for collateral, streamline the application process, provide loans for working capital, and provide technical assistance. The commitment was a response to the need of reducing the following obstacles faced by low-income borrowers: the demands for actual collateral, the requirements for information and documentation, and the lack of technical assistance.

At the end of the project it was expected that the BIP would be providing services in designated areas of the highlands and the jungle, by extending 4,000 loans in these areas including 1,600 for the creation of new businesses.

The bank made a pledge to open six new offices and to recruit technical and administrative staff to ensure the successful implementation of the project. In 1982, seven years after the project was started, the initial goals had been surpassed. Through the credit line, 4,698 loans were extended, a larger than planned number of branch offices were created, and not only were additional staff recruited, but existing personnel received new training.

Integration of FDR into BIP Operations

During the first phase of the program some problems occurred, and the total number of loans extended was small. One of the apparent reasons for this slow implementation was the collision between the new line of credit and the bank's traditional lines. It was difficult for the managers of the branch offices, credit officials, and other members of the technical team to understand the new FDR loan concepts. The initial response among the bank employees to the new (much more flexible) criteria for giving credit was not positive. Some officials said that they had to spend whole days analyzing credit applications without taking any decision. The observation made by one of the branch managers gives us a better understanding of the dilemma:

> The idea of authorizing credit on the basis of reports from the store around the corner or the village general store about the good behavior of the applicant and the fact that he did not beat his wife was something beyond comprehension for those authorizing the loans. Sometimes those were the only references obtained and the sole criterion for approving the application. Before, we used to ask for a number of business and personal documents, as well as credit and collateral references. The new clients demanded more flexibility in terms of requirements and we had to depend on informal references, accept that the artisan's licence was being processed, and finance the total amount required for the project. For us, this was something completely new, and many of us were accustomed to other things and were somewhat distrustful of all this.

At its beginning the fund was managed as a section under a division; it then became a unit of the Division of Industrial Credit. USAID and the top officers of the bank applied pressure to obtain a closer management of the fund; they succeeded in getting FDR program coordinators appointed at the branch office level. This step led to the creation in each branch of small FDR offices, which in the beginning were not integrated into the branch office. As one BIP manager noted, this type of program, separate from the bank, would not have left any benefit for the bank because all the trained staff and all the experience acquired would be lost once the project came to an end.

In 1980, six years after it started, the FDR program could be institutionalized within the BIP. The bank accepted the new concepts, the FDR coordinators left, and the importance gained by the program encouraged the bank to create a special unit for the Fund. The FDR portfolio was integrated with those of the other BIP credit programs, but its identity was retained for purposes of bookkeeping and reporting.

Characteristics of the Rural Development Fund

Enterprises eligible for the program were cottage industries, including handicrafts, small manufacturing firms, services/trade/tourism, and small agro-businesses. The maximum loan size allowed was equivalent to US$60,000 (1978), to be established in soles and automatically adjusted according to fluctuations in the official exchange rate. All the loans required collateral, and loans for machinery were guaranteed by the machinery itself. Under the FDR line, the collateral was appraised at 100 percent. This differs from other credit lines, for which the bank lent up to only 80 percent of the amount requested, and the collateral was appraised up to 70 percent of its value.

The longest term for repayment of an FDR loan was ten years, with a grace period not exceeding two years. Interest rates had to be close to the rates set for other development credit lines in Peru. Interest rates were always below the inflation rate in Peru during the life of the project.

BIP promoted the program through pamphlets and the communication media. In areas impossible to reach by these means, megaphones were installed by BIP in the town's square and applications were distributed so that future clients could fill them out on the spot.

All the borrowers received some type of technical assistance. An analysis of 2,490 clients showed that 64 percent received help to fill out application forms; 21 percent received assistance for their feasibility studies; 22 percent received assistance in the accounting area; 9 percent for marketing activities; and 4 percent for production. Courses were offered on marketing, management, and production (one of the trainers noted that, in general, few women attended the courses).

Results

The case of the FDR program in the Banco Industrial del Perú allows us to see a successful example of an institution that changed its portfolio from loans for large-scale industries to the inclusion of loans for small-scale rural industries. The Bank achieved its objective of giving access to credit to borrowers who usually did not have access, and through this contributed to the generation of employment, industrial development, and enterprise development of low-income groups, and thus to the national development plan. The Bank attained these goals through a series of changes at the organizational level implemented in response to conditions established by the donor agency.

To change its portfolio, the Bank decentralized the approval of loans and revised the amounts that could be approved at each level, delegating more authority to the branch offices. BIP found different ways of streamlining the application process, providing more assistance to the borrowers in the initial phase, and adding flexibility to the documentation requirements.

Even when institutions like BIP set up policies at the central level to achieve credit objectives such as in the FDR credit program, it is difficult to pass them on to the local level where the new guidelines should be applied. The institution has to ensure that its evaluation and compensation systems strengthen the indicated objectives, that is, they provide training and incentives to its credit officials so that they do not spend their time reviewing applications without taking any decision.

As suggested by Stern, Naranjo & Co. in their "Manual de Crédito para la Fundación Espejo" (1984), the credit officer is being asked to adopt criteria, roles, and decisions concerning the provision of credit to small businesses which in many instances will appear somewhat distinct from the conventional wisdom. They add that the focus on loans in this type of program is based more on experience (learning by doing) than on a previous detailed study (Stern, Naranjo & Co. 1984, p. 11). This approach implies minimizing the necessary procedures without eliminating them completely, while giving flexibility to the process of application, study, approval, and disbursement. In addition, these borrowers (in many instances, having their first experience with a financial institution) are often used to having direct person-to-person negotiations rather than dealing through written documents. Thus, the staff that will be in contact with these clients should be trained so that their interaction, both in content and in form, will be personal and direct (Stern, Naranjo & Co. 1984, p. 114).

Management Costs of the Credit Line

The low rate of arrearage was an important factor in the institutionalization of the program and in its acceptance by the BIP management as a viable banking practice. The number of delinquent loans in the FDR credit line compared favorably to the other credit lines and was generally acceptable. For example, in a sample of eighty-five borrowers, 57 percent of the loans were paid on time (Goldmark et al. 1982b). The management and supervision costs of the FDR credit line were lower than expected. The bank officers first assumed that, given the nature of the small businesses, loan recovery would necessitate high supervision costs. The average cost of each processed and recovered loan was equivalent to US$49, $18.30 higher than the cost of loans with commercial interest rates and normal collateral. The officers believed that in some way the lower delinquency and payment arrears would compensate for the high management costs. Some of the individuals concerned about this facet have suggested establishing more competitive or subsidized interest rates for these credit lines so that the institution would not move away from the really small entrepreneurs because of the high costs and extra work involved in their management.

In short, the FDR was successfully integrated into the BIP's operations because of the large organizational changes (frequently unplanned) that were made. The organizational decentralization was the source of these changes. For example, credit approval was sent directly to branch offices and credit approval ceilings were raised. Branch managers strengthened their positions by receiving increased decision-making power and increased technical assistance. Changes in the central administrative structure allowed for management to concentrate specifically on small and medium enterprises. There was also an effort to train credit officials in helping new borrowers. Another important factor was the new methods of promoting the program. Lastly, the pressure, follow-up, and support of the donor agency were critical factors that were present throughout the implementation of the project.

RURAL DEVELOPMENT FUND: LOANS FOR WOMEN?

To what extent did the BIP's new orientation result in an increase of credit for women? The case study that follows in summarized form was designed to answer this question (for a more detailed account, see Arias 1984).

Methodology

The methodology for the case study included open, semi-structured interviews with officers of USAID, BIP, small entrepreneur support organizations, and women's support organizations in Peru. At the central level, records of the credit program were reviewed, and in the Huancayo branch data were disaggregated by sex and borrowers were interviewed. The interviews were conducted during September 1983. Starting with an analysis of its objectives, interviews were initiated with the donor agency and Peruvian government representatives; subsequently, the different levels at the BIP involved in the FDR line were covered, followed by interviews carried out in two branches and with borrowers.

During the interviews, some officials expressed surprise when they learned about the purpose of the study. For example, in a donor agency an officer said that women should be an integral part of the project rather than the target of special programs, adding that all the projects included a section describing the impact of the project on women, but that this "was not taken seriously into consideration and usually included only two or three paragraphs." Another officer acknowledged that he had not read much about the status of women and that there may be a number of projects affecting women in unknown ways. The reason given for not being seriously concerned about women's participation was that in these large financial projects it was difficult to handle all the small details.

Although it would not have been difficult to disaggregate data by sex for the FDR credit program, sex-disaggregated data were not available at BIP. A more recent BIP credit line called Urban Development Fund (FDU) maintains such data because it was a project requirement and had to be included in the reports to the donor agency. Many of the BIP officers interviewed asked whether an evaluation of the projects was being carried out and whether having women borrowers was a new condition required by the donor agency.

Results

Number and Size of Loans

The FDR credit line granted 4,698 loans between 1975 and 1982; women received 662 loans, or 14 percent of the total: Table 12.1 shows the percentage of the total number of loans extended to women in 1980, 1981, and 1982, as well as the average loan size. The average amount given to women was lower than the amount given to men during those three years.

TABLE 12.1
BIP Rural Development Fund Loans (FDR), 1980–1982

	1980	1981	1982
Number of loans	3,256	1,006	436
Amount in soles (000)	3,390,850	3,270,397	1,490,994
Percent to women	13%	19%	11%
Percent to men	87%	81%	89%
Average amount of loan—women	609,736	2,616,806	2,205,287
Average amount of loan—men	1,165,069	3,368,092	4,508,993

Source: Developed from BIP records, September 1983. The weighted average of the dollar was 289.20 soles per dollar in 1980, 442.30 in 1981, and 697.5 in 1982.

Table 12.2 shows the distribution of loans by size for the 1982 sample. The breakdown of the sample data by loan size shows that most of the loans given to both men and women are concentrated in the two categories representing the smallest loans. Of the total number of beneficiaries, 39 percent receive amounts below $1,800,000 (in soles), and almost 83 percent are the beneficiaries of amounts below $5,407,020. The average amount received by women is lower than the average amount received by men.

From these data, we could infer that few women obtain loans because the type of credit offered by the bank does not meet the needs of these potential borrowers. Specifically, more women (and probably men) would

TABLE 12.2
BIP Rural Development Fund Loans by Gender and Loan Size, 1982

Amount in Soles (000)	Women			Men		
	No. of Loans	Percent of All Categories	Average Amount	No. of Loans	Percent of All Categories	Average Amount
Up to 1,800,000	28	10.0	13,068	117	90.0	117,572
1,800,000 to 5,407,020	33	17.2	99,339	127	82.0	477,111
5,407,020 to 8,651,092	2	7.3	11,861	22	92.7	149,745
Over 8,561,092	3	6.5	36,029	32	93.5	520,651

Source: Developed from BIP records, September 1983. The weighted average of soles per dollar in 1982 was 697.5.

apply for loans if smaller sized loans were available. Other than the size of the loan, the low number of women borrowers receiving such small amounts through the FDR credit line might be due to the kind of activities undertaken by women, the social barriers that they have to confront, and/or the collateral requirements.

Economic Activities

One of the reasons for the low number of women may be the lack of correspondence between the economic activities that receive credit from the bank and the activities that are undertaken by women. As Table 12.3 indicates, most women in Peru are engaged in community service and personal service activities (39 percent), and agricultural activities (20 percent). About 17 percent are employed in the manufacturing sector and are concentrated in weaving and sewing. This finding confirms statements made by the bank officers that "women are involved in handicraft activities such as weaving, knitting and sewing, which are typical of women."

The bank, however, extended most of its loans to small industries. Of the loans given to small enterprises, 59 percent went to manufacturing firms, 26 percent to handicraft enterprises, 10 percent to businesses in the service sector, and 1 percent to tourism businesses. In a sample of eighty-five borrowers in 1982, 61 percent of the loans were given to the industrial sector (Goldmark et al. 1982b).

Social Barriers

The study showed that women are engaged in activities requiring small loans. An explanation of this "preference" is that women take up activities in which they already have some experience. It could also be argued that they do this kind of work partly because of lack of education. The number of men who attend the elementary school is almost double that of women, and at the secondary level it is almost threefold. Among the population aged fifteen or more, the number of illiterate women is more than two times the number

TABLE 12.3
**National Population Employed by Economic Activity,
Gender, and Salary Level**

	Total Employed	Under 500	500– 4,000	5,000 and Over	Not Specified
Agriculture					
Men	19,907	12.0%	45.9%	17.2%	25.4%
Women	2,032	20.8	39.5	12.4	27.3
Manufacturing					
Men	70,063	—	48.7	42.9	8.4
Women	17,433	—	44.3	24.0	11.7
Commerce					
Men	69,593	—	60.0	32.0	8.0
Women	28,116	—	76.2	13.7	10.1
Transport					
Men	38,439	—	59.6	33.7	6.7
Women	5,499	—	72.0	25.1	2.9
Finance					
Men	26,588	—	35.2	61.7	3.1
Women	7,341	—	56.3	40.2	3.5
Services					
Men	204,708	—	44.3	48.4	7.3
Women	125,353	—	68.9	24.8	6.3

Source: *VI National Population and Housing Census.* Instituto Nacional de Estadística, Lima, Peru 1982.

of illiterate men. This limitation may explain in part why the number of women applying for loans is lower than that of men, and why women are engaged in activities requiring smaller loans.

Collateral

In their study on the BIP's Urban Development Fund, Buvinić, Berger, and Gross (1984) found that collateral was the most important factor in explaining the amount of the loan (53 percent of the variation in loan size was explained by this factor); however, it did not equally affect men and women. In a sample of eighty-five FDR borrowers, over 40 percent of the beneficiaries offered not only the equipment bought as collateral (or some other equipment they had), but also other types of collateral (Goldmark et al. 1985).

From these results and those of the Urban Development Fund credit line, we can assume that banking institutions tend to seek the kind of collateral that allows them to minimize risks. Even in the case of BIP, a small enterprise-oriented public institution whose credit programs attempt to reduce the requirements for collateral, the results show that the collateral requirements are still high. Regarding the Urban credit line, for example, actual collateral values exceeded by a wide margin the minimum required by the bank. Even though there is an attempt to be more flexible, a "real" collateral is still required.

Appropriate Institutional Mechanisms to Integrate Women

Just as the BIP was motivated to include loans for small enterprises in general, institutions similar to BIP could be persuaded to direct part of their portfolio to women in small and microenterprises. Private financial institutions may not be willing to lend small amounts of money, but government agencies like the Banco Industrial del Perú are required to do so because of donor agency requests and because it gives them a good image. The Banco Industrial del Perú reoriented its portfolio in response to conditions imposed by the donor agency. For example, donor agencies could include as a condition the promotion of smaller loans and the targeting of those sectors where women are involved. As more knowledge is gained about women's participation in small or microenterprises, objectives specific to women could be integrated into the larger projects. In short, the target project population might be identified in such a way that women are included.

How can this be done? For example, the results from the FDR credit line show that women were engaged in the service and commercial sectors and in the manufacturing sector, but primarily in activities related to weaving and sewing. The BIP loans, however, were concentrated in the small industries. Given this situation, the donor agency could be asked to specify and assign funds to economic activities where women are concentrated.

In view of the findings of this chapter, we can conclude that when conditions are clearly defined, institutions respond. As they obtain more and better information about women, the activities they are engaged in, the amounts of money they need, and their needs in general, it will be possible to start setting parameters for supervision and evaluation that ensure the integration of women into credit programs.

We recommend the integration of women into large projects because it appears that it is possible to integrate women, by specifying the rules of the game, instead of promoting women-specific programs that run the risk of ending up as welfare programs. In this way, institutions such as BIP will be strengthened and be able not only to move up and lend to small entrepreneurs, but also to extend even smaller loans, such as those offered by the FDU credit line. If these changes do not take place, the experience gained by the BIP, its network of branches, and its staff, already oriented toward the new borrowers, would be wasted. The creation of new institutions and foundations to promote credit for women can scatter funds and weaken the institutions already established.

When specific objectives for women are integrated into a project design, or when women-specific projects are created within larger projects that target small entrepreneurs, some precautions should be taken. The risk that objectives will be mixed up or lost during implementation can be minimized by careful monitoring and supervising of the interventions.

Finally, as researchers have noted, mechanisms for the integration of women should include: providing several reimbursement options, reducing the collateral requirements, reducing the loan size, and establishing appropriate interest rates. To attain these goals necessitates shaping the programs in a way to make them more similar to informal credit mechanisms. Women's organizations should also play an important role as intermediaries, participating as well in the monitoring and evaluation of the projects.

CONCLUSIONS

What is the appropriate role for credit programs financed by the public sector? What are the appropriate institutional mechanisms for integrating women into these programs? These are the questions that have guided this study and that the study has tried to answer by using the case of the FDR credit program of the Banco Industrial del Perú.

The literature about loans for small enterprises in general points out that many credit programs channeled through public institutions have not succeeded in providing access to credit to small entrepreneurs (men or women). This lack of success has been attributed, either by the institutions that offer this service or by those requesting the service, to:

- lack of precision in the definition of the target group;

- interest rate policies;

- lending costs;

- transactions costs;

- paperwork and documentation that are required;

- collateral requirements.

To these obstacles we should add the sociocultural barriers against women engaged in small enterprises, which for women in developing countries is an important means of earning income. Furthermore, women are engaged in economic activities like trade and services that require smaller loans.

Because women require smaller loans and take up activities that are not traditionally in the range of institutions like the BIP, the good intentions and generous help of donor agencies are often not enough to give women access to credit. It is difficult and time-consuming to change the traditional approach of an organization. It is not an easy or short-term process to revise the institutional structures that reflect prevailing social norms and that in many cases unintentionally block women's access to credit.

Therefore, the donor agencies should include specific conditions such as those that proved successful in the BIP program. That is, apart from identifying the target population in a way that women are included (smaller borrowers and economic activities involving women) and requiring changes in the traditional credit mechanisms (with respect to documentation, application, collateral, and references), the institution channeling funds should try to change its own organizational structure to accommodate women and smaller borrowers and accompany this change with training of and incentives to its credit officers.

NOTE

1. The study was prepared for USAID, Office of Women in Development, through the Harvard Institute for International Development, Harvard University. The research was conducted during September 1983. The study was published in C. Overhat et al. (eds.), *Gender Roles in Development Projects,* West Hartford, Conn.: Kumarian Press, 1987.

13

Credit and Development for Women: *An Introduction to the Ecuadorian Development Foundation*

JORGE F. LANDIVAR

T hree concerns that the chapters of this book have in common are the promotion of microenterprises, credit to microentrepreneurs, and women's participation in credit programs. All three revolve around a central theme that is implied but not expressed: socioeconomic development. This chapter discusses each of these concerns briefly as an introduction to the next chapter, which presents the findings of a study of the beneficiaries of a microenterprise promotion program carried out by the International Center for Research on Women (ICRW) with the Fundación Ecuatoriana de Desarrollo (FED).[1]

MICROENTERPRISE PROMOTION BY THE FED

The Microenterprise Promotion Program (PRODEM) of the Fundación Ecuatoriana de Desarrollo (FED) is an outcome of eighteen years of experience of credit and promotional work with the marginal population of Ecuador. Established in 1968, the FED has been making small loans for associative and production purposes, accompanied by advisory services and training, to give both the urban and rural poor new opportunities for working to achieve higher living standards, greater social cohesion and integration, and greater participation in shaping the decisions that affect their own development.

After starting with a program with a markedly rural emphasis, the FED decided in 1984 to concentrate new efforts in urban areas, particularly in Quito, the densest population center in the FED's operating region. The

214

reasoning behind the change was straightforward, although it had previously eluded the FED: all development efforts in the countryside imply an increase in the ratio of capital to labor; there is a subsequent process of capitalization to raise productivity, to improve living standards, and to provide incentives for retaining the rural population and stemming its flight to cities. The result, however, is that the success of the capitalization process is directly related to the displacement of casual labor. The program's very success aggravates the national problem by swelling the flow of rural migrants to urban centers. If the aim is national development, the problem must be addressed at both ends. Without neglecting the fundamental tasks in the countryside, efforts must be made to generate employment, housing, and consumer goods and services for the growing urban population.

PRODEM, the FED's program for urban areas, was a response to this belatedly recognized problem. Since April 1984, it has provided loans, advisory services, and training to Quito's informal sector, which was divided into two target groups—microproducers and microvendors—as illustrated by Tables 13.1 through 13.3.

The microproducers who benefited from the program in its first two years of operation were engaged in various occupations (see Table 13.1). The products most frequently dealt in by the microvendors who received loans from the Foundation are presented in Table 13.2.

TABLE 13.1
PRODEM Microproducers by Economic Activity

Activity	Percentage[a]
Garments	22
Shoemaking	12
Carpentry	7
Seamstress	7
Tailoring	7
Unspecified services	6
Bakery	5
Upholstery	5
Weaving	5
Footwear (accessories)	4
Jeweler	3
Printer	3
Manual trades	3
Others	7

    [a]   Because of rounding, figures do not add up to 100.

A total of 6,052 urban loans totaling 156,440,000 sucres[2] were made in Quito from May 1984 to June 1986 (see Table 13.3). A majority of the program beneficiaries are women; they accounted for 59 percent of all microentrepreneurs granted FED loans in the first two years of operation. The proportions differ in the two parts of the program, however: of 652 microproducers

TABLE 13.2
PRODEM Microvendors and Products Sold

Products	Percentages[a]
Prepared food	16
Apparel	23
Foodstuffs	12
Fruit	7
Shoes	3
Others	38

[a]   Because of rounding, figures do not add up to 100.

who received individual loans, 239 or 36 percent were women, and of the 2,277 microvendors who received loans through solidarity groups, 1,483 or 65 percent were women.

POSITIVE AND NEGATIVE ASPECTS OF CREDIT

A second common concern discussed in the chapters of this book is credit. Here, some clarifications are appropriate before we move on to consider the complete working model of the program for women. The optimism imparted by some of the chapters suggests that a loan is viewed almost as a panacea, although it is indeed true that loans are complemented by advisory services and training. It would appear that, with these services, the intrinsic shortcomings of credit are eliminated once and for all.

Behind this optimism there are two convictions, one cultural and the other ideological. The cultural conviction is that anyone becomes better off by obtaining money. The conditions of oneself and one's family are viewed as determined not by accomplishment, happiness, the realization of aspirations, creativity, or improving one's skills, but by the acquisition of purchasing power. In short, the human condition is reduced to the presence or absence of cash. The ideological conviction is more obvious, yet its clarity makes it no less dangerous. It holds that a loan is always a chance to make more money, always a step toward solvency and prosperity, with no regard to the conditions attached to credit in itself.

Table 13.3
Number of PRODEM Beneficiaries and Loans, May 1984–June 1986

	Beneficiaries	Loans	Amount Lent
Microproducers	660	3,214	71,474,000
Microvendors	2,277	2,838	78,814,000
Totals	2,937	6,052	150,288,000

Note: Loans outstanding totaled 24,667,711 sucres on June 30, 1987.

Only in particular circumstances does a loan work as a stimulus to the borrower's economic advancement. First, it must produce an income higher than the cost of the money, not only to pay net interest, but to maintain its purchasing power. No one is going to lend an amount equal to one hundred if, after a time, he or she will receive in return the same amount in absolute terms but with a relative value of fifty or less. The lender insists on "real interest," which covers the loss of value through inflation and the loss of purchasing power of the lent sum. Thus, the borrower must produce much more with borrowed money if any is to remain after repayment of the principal plus real interest.

Second, credit, which is essentially a financial element, serves to link the informal economy to the formal, monetized, capitalist economy. Barter, still practiced among the urban poor, has ceased to be the only mode of exchange; as a result, the poor are finding it necessary to obtain money to purchase the goods and services they need to survive with cash. To obtain money they must sell the one thing of value they possess—their labor—at any price they can get in a market already saturated with a surplus of labor.

Finally, in this monetary economy, a loan must be used to acquire inputs that are produced outside the environment of the loan recipient, with materials either made by domestic industry or, worse yet, imported. The net flow of borrowed money, which must be repaid with interest, is centrifugal; it moves away from the borrower when it is used, and cannot even be turned over to generate additional general wealth in the beneficiary's hands.

Because of these negative intrinsic qualities, credit has to be used with the utmost care by people who do not understand it. If there is no way to take corrective measures to mitigate the negative effects or constructive measures to counteract them, it is preferable not to lend to marginal sectors, because of the risk of leaving the recipients poorer than they already were and leading them into ever-mounting debt.

From another perspective, however, the contradictory nature of credit can actually make it a positive instrument for promotion and development. Its pressure on beneficiaries, the need for concerted action to obtain and repay a loan, the possibility of collective use of loan proceeds, repayment in installments, budgeting, terms with deadlines, are all factors that can prompt changes in cultural outlook and thus help recipients break out of patterns of thought not conducive to self-improvement and the attainment of higher levels of bargaining power.

Viewed from the perspective of development and not just financial input, credit becomes a trigger of social change. Its importance is not so much its economic and financial aspects as the changes in motivation and outlook it can generate. Unfortunately, there does not appear to be any better method or means than credit for bringing about these basic changes in the short run. Awareness-building systems and programs, for example, take much longer and are much less reliable.

It is a great paradox, therefore, that credit, while an extremely dangerous tool if wielded without proper social perspective, can become with that
perspective the best possible instrument for the generation of irreversible
changes in the social fabric. Under well-structured programs it can at least
make a start toward a transfer of economic power when surpluses are generated and retained by producers. But more important is the shift it encourages—with a social perspective—toward attitudes that are more dynamic,
more structured, more focused on attainable goals.

Central to this view is the idea of credit not as an end, a panacea, but
merely as a device whose effects may be beneficial, but are more likely to be
pernicious. We must remember also that, difficult as it is to strike the right
balance among the elements of credit to make it the development instrument and method we seek, no other viable alternative exists for orienting an
organization to find its way in a real situation and to use all its resources to
attain its development goals.

This philosophy goes well beyond that of economic growth, and even
further beyond that of the growth of family income or per capita income. It
is often said, development is the social process of supplying shortages, cast-
ing off dependence, and overcoming social stratification and atomization. It
is in this context that we must weigh the advisability of granting credit: will
it decrease or increase stratification or dependence? Can it or can it not meet
basic needs? Does it integrate low-income sectors or further atomize them?
It is to pursue this broader philosophy that we maintain that the idea of "development" is always implicit in the themes of the chapters in this book.

CREDIT FOR WOMEN

Although the Fundación Ecuatoriana de Desarrollo works mostly with
female microentrepreneurs, it does not give them preference to compensate for the unfair treatment to which they have been too long subjected. But
it does recognize two objective situations that, despite efforts to change
them, remain virtually intact in the social structure.

The first situation is that the rearing of children is left primarily, if not
entirely, to women. They have to play two roles: they must generate income
for the family (because the income of the husband, where one is present, is
not enough to cover the family's expenses) and take care of the home and
the children. The second, and even more difficult, situation is that, in a very
large number of families, the head of the family and sole source of its support is the mother.

Loans to working mothers and female microentrepreneurs, if they are
to have the development thrust we have referred to and to perform the special function that the particular situation of women requires of them, must
have one particular aim: to increase their income and reduce the time they
must devote to complementary production tasks. In other words, produc-

tion loans must be designed to make the production of women much more efficient so that the increased earning capacity will give a woman the option either of working fewer hours so as to have more time for household duties, or of earning enough additional income to be able to pay for any care of her children she is unable to provide herself.

The FED is particularly interested in continuing and intensifying its development work with women microentrepreneurs, both urban and rural, with the goal of finding new experimental solutions to the problem of poverty, and in working with women under this new option of special credit geared to the specific circumstances of the daily lives of mothers who are also heads of households.

In the same spirit, the Foundation has been working closely with the International Center for Research on Women, not only in promoting the sector of women's microenterprises in Quito, but especially regarding the evaluative study of its work in this field. The Foundation gives a high priority to evaluation, for without it projects cannot be assessed, no clear objectives can be charted, and it cannot be known whether a real advance toward development has been made. Superficial or mere institutional evaluation can yield very clear indicators of performance—numbers of projects financed, amounts lent, status of the portfolio, default rates, cost per sucre lent, and self-sufficiency—but only a detailed evaluation directed at determining the situation of beneficiaries can tell us whether the development goals are being met.

Thus, the study described in Chapter 14 is particularly important. Its conclusions are directly related to the aims stated in the FED view of development, and to the new option of loans tailored to the real situation of women. The statistical results of the study show clearly how the increase in the income of the beneficiary women under the microproducers' program went hand-in-hand with a reduction of the time spent on production work in their microenterprises—time they then used for other purposes.

These and similar conclusions indicate that the programs of the FED are on the right track. If the Foundation gained anything in eighteen years of experience, it is the humility of thinking they have not one or more answers, but merely attempts at solutions; and the aspiration that their pioneering efforts may yield working models and records of successes and failures so that other agencies, including the national government authorities, can repeat with greater resources and on a much larger scale the small successes they have had.

CONCLUSION

One last point is particularly important in regard to the FED's working model and its aims. Microenterprises are being promoted chiefly as a strategy for employment generation. Although the ICRW study was done on only a small sample of beneficiaries and an analogous control group, its results—as well as those of similar studies done in other countries—indicate that the promotion of microenterprises should be approached with less sanguine expectations for the generation of employment.

There is definitely no massive employment generation. Several possible reasons might account for the disappointing results in this area:

• In projects in the urban sector, almost all beneficiaries already hold some sort of job. Although these jobs earn extremely low incomes and are impermanent and part-time affairs, in contrast to the more enduring jobs created by microentrepreneurial credit, workers are not actually starting from scratch. There is no net creation of jobs, only an improvement of production and more productive use of jobs that already exist in some form or other.

• The informal economy itself is not altered by microentrepreneurial promotion, and even the jobs created in it by credit and promotion retain a certain impermanence. Many new jobs may be seasonal or may come and go with rising and falling sales; thus it is difficult to perceive them as "permanent."

• Many of the new jobs are taken by members of the beneficiary's immediate family, who were already collaborating without pay in the production work or provision of services, and who, after the loan, become formal, wage-earning employees. Again, strictly speaking, no new jobs have been created.

• Changes in the use of labor cannot be assessed in the short term or solely on the basis of individual microenterprises. Trends must be traced over several years to determine the overall growth of the sector and its capitalization in order to establish that an increase of work for some beneficiaries does not result in a reduction in other areas, for a zero-sum outcome in the economy as a whole.

Despite all these somewhat pessimistic remarks on employment generation, one premise holds firm: it costs far less to create a job in the informal than in the formal sector of the economy. Sucre for sucre, investment for production reaches further and has a greater positive impact on the economy at large and a greater multiplier effect in the microentrepreneurial sector than in the areas of formal investment. The observation that not as much employment is generated as expected is intended merely to warn about the errors of simplistic solutions that cannot succeed and of complacency with small efforts that amount to very little in the overall context.

The tendency to be content with little can come from setting goals in relation to the institution and not in relation to the development of society as a whole. Thus, an institution with only a few years or even months of experience can imagine it has already discovered the great secrets of socioeconomic development and illustrate them with a mere handful of successes. Nevertheless, the new institutions will need such enthusiasm to triumph over the tasks that await them, the full difficulty of which will emerge only with the passage of time.

NOTES

1. Ecuadorian Development Foundation.

2. US$1 equaled approximately 125 sucres in June 1986.

14

Impact of a Credit Project for Women and Men Microentrepreneurs in Quito, Ecuador

MAYRA BUVINIĆ, MARGUERITE BERGER, and CECILIA JARAMILLO

T he Latin American economic crisis has intensified growth of the urban informal sector in most of the countries in the region. In addition, it appears to have led to the decline in average incomes in this sector. According to the International Labor Organization's Regional Employment Program for Latin America and the Caribbean (PREALC), informal-sector employment in the region expanded by 18 percent between 1981 and 1983, while the average income for informal-sector workers declined some 21 percent (PREALC 1985). Recent research in several countries of the region indicates that a significant share of informal-sector workers are women, and that women account for most of the lower-productivity and lower-income jobs in the sector.

Even before the onset of the current crisis, data revealed that women, the self-employed, and those who had not completed primary education accounted for most informal-sector workers in most of Latin America (Mazumdar 1976). For example, Peru's Ministry of Labor estimated that 64 percent of the female labor force worked in the informal sector in 1974. This figure increased to 73 percent in 1978 (Chueca and Vargas de Balmaceda 1982). Approximately two-thirds of the informal-sector labor force in La Paz, Bolivia, is self-employed. Women's share of the self-employed in La Paz increased from 37 percent in 1976 to 48 percent in 1983, while their participation in the formal sector has fluctuated around 32 percent. Seventy-five percent of the self-employed workers in commerce are women; their average monthly income is 62 percent of the average monthly income of male merchants (Casanovas 1985).

Women generally account for most of those employed in smaller-scale commercial operations in the Latin American cities with a growing informal sector; they are also involved, to a lesser degree, in small-scale traditional manufacturing (particularly sewing and weaving) and services. In Ecuador, even though there are no overall data on the size and growth of the urban informal sector, microentrepreneurs are thought to make up the largest single subsector within the informal sector. Women account for a major portion of those who work in micro-scale commerce, but their participation is greater in Quito than it is in Guayaquil (Farrell 1985). In Quito, women account for 35 percent of all workers, 55 percent of informal-sector workers, and 65 percent of street vendors (Household Surveys, Universidad Central–IIE 1985). Table 14.1 illustrates the percentage of women in different economic activities in the informal sector in Quito.

Two independent lines of research have determined that the lack of easy access to credit from the modern banking system is one of the impor-

TABLE 14.1

Informal Sector Workers in Quito according to their Economic Activity: Women's Participation and Income Level, July 1985

Economic Activity	Total No. of Workers	No. of Women	Percentage of Women	Average Monthly Income in Sucres
Sellers, working in commerce and similar activities	10,113	4,328	42.8	8,114
Small merchants and shopkeepers	33,427	21,062	63.0	12,279
Street vendors	2,841	2,063	72.6	5,637
Cleaning service, security guards, and watchmen	11,277	2,962	26.3	9,285
Dry cleaning and laundry personnel	286	75	26.2	5,750
Workers in unclassified services	2,578	717	27.8	11,637
Housekeepers	27,239	26,365	96.8	4,031
Shoeshiners, deliverymen	953	171	17.9	7,168
Prepared food workers	1,712	571	33.3	10,414
Weavers, textile workers, and assistants	2,285	1,333	58.3	9,845
Leather craftsmen and workers	4,843	665	13.7	9,772
Wood and paper craftsmen, carpenters, and workers	6,277	656	10.5	12,403
Goldsmiths, silversmiths, potters, and jewelers	1,987	358	18.0	11,081
Mechanics, blacksmiths, locksmiths, and plumbers	8,671	74	.9	11,597
Tailors, seamstresses, designers, furriers	8,571	5,537	64.6	7,411
Barbers, salon stylists, and related workers	3,623	2,554	70.5	12,148
Total	126,683	69,491	54.9	

Source: "Labor Force in Quito," Economic Research Institute, Central University of Quito (supported by CONUEN).

tant factors limiting the growth of microenterprises in the urban informal sector (Ashe 1986), and that women have very limited access to credit in the modern financial markets (Lycette 1984). In response to the first concern, recent years have witnessed the implementation of a series of successful projects in the urban informal sector that extend credit to microentrepreneurs in manufacturing, commerce, and services. Until the implementation of PRODEM in Quito, however, these projects had reached male microentrepreneurs much more successfully than female microentrepreneurs in manufacturing and services. The exceptions to this trend, most of which have been mentioned in this volume, involve extension of credit to women microvendors. For example, only 16 percent of the portfolio of credit to microproducers through PRODEME in Santo Domingo and a BIP project in Lima benefited female owners of microenterprises (Otero and Blayney 1984). In the UNO program in Brazil this figure was 15 percent (Tendler 1983). However, in a Salvadoran program that benefited large numbers of women, most of the borrowers were microvendors (Blayney 1979). In the Progreso project in Lima, Peru, women received 80 percent of the loans for vendors (organized in solidarity groups), but only 14 percent of all individual loans for microproducers (Reichmann 1984b; Chapter 8 of this volume).

In 1984, the Ecuadoran Development Foundation (FED: Fundación Ecuatoriana de Desarrollo) established a microenterprise development program called PRODEM, with technical assistance from Accion International/AITEC and the International Center for Research on Women (ICRW). The program was created with the explicit purpose of providing easy access to credit to both women and men microproducers and microvendors in the city of Quito. To this end a women's component was designed that includes a line of credit for women, technical assistance from the ICRW, and the definition and supervision of specific goals to be achieved through the project. Partly as a result of these actions, and also because of the projected increase in women's participation in the urban informal sector in Quito (see Table 14.2), PRODEM was able to reach significant numbers of women microvendors and microproducers in its first two years of operation (May 1984–May 1986). Some 65 percent of the microvendors who borrowed through PRODEM's solidarity group component were women; more significantly, 35 percent of the microproducers who obtained individual loans from PRODEM were women. This level of women's participation has been maintained as the PRODEM portfolio has grown (see also Table 14.2).

In view of the anticipated high level of women's participation in PRODEM, the ICRW and the FED undertook a study with an experimental design to look into the economic impact of the credit project on men and women microentrepreneurs, in order to answer a series of questions that are raised in the literature on the effectiveness of such interventions on behalf of women. Even though there is consensus that these credit projects are effective (at

TABLE 14.2

PRODEM Loans: Borrowers, Loan Size (in sucres[a]), Arrears Rate, May 1984–May 1986

	Total	Number of Women Borrowers	Percent of Women Borrowers	Total Amount Lent (cumulative)	Average Loan Size (cumulative)	Arrears Rate (percent)
Microproducers						
May 1984[b]	75	17	23	990,000	11,250	—
Oct 1984	414	133	32	17,807,000	18,763	6.67
Oct 1985	634	224	35	64,404,000	22,645	21.05
May 1986	657	232	35	78,859,000	24,212	26.02
Microvendors						
May 1984	58[c]	31	54	164,000	17,400[d]	—
Oct 1984	1,346	859	64	14,886,000	20,481	0.76
Oct 1985	2,196	1,438	65	64,570,000	26,496	15.34
May 1986	2,310	1,508	65	80,485,000	27,840	18.42

[a]   US$1 = 87 sucres in May 1984; 100 sucres in October 1984; 120 sucres in October 1985. Program's first month.
[b]   Program's first month.
[c]   Reflects the total number of individual borrowers, not groups of borrowers.
[d]   Average amount of the group loan. Every group has an average of five or six members.

least in terms of the number of beneficiaries reached and the relatively low default rates), there is less agreement on the economic and social impact of such schemes; in particular, there are no reliable data on their impact on women borrowers.

Without addressing the question of the differential impact on men and women borrowers, a series of studies contend that microenterprise credit projects are among the most effective actions, from an economic standpoint, carried out by private nonprofit development agencies. The indicators of success generally used to measure the impact of these projects include increasing firms' revenues, generating new jobs, improving firms' financial viability, and moving these firms into the formal banking sector. Most of these assessments, however, are case studies that do not use scientific methods for measuring impact. A recent evaluation of five microenterprise credit projects has added methodological rigor to the study of microenterprise credit projects by quantifying economic costs and benefits. The calculations made in that study indicated that benefits outweighed costs for all of the projects analyzed, and that the rates of return were over 100 percent for four of the five projects. However, the evaluation found that none of the projects was successful in terms of self-reliance; instead, the economic benefits were derived both from the direct, visible benefits of firms' increased returns in the most successful projects, and from invisible external economies, particularly for the moderately successful projects (Kilby and D'Zmura 1985).

Another series of evaluations offers a less optimistic view of the economic impact of microenterprise credit projects. One perspective argues that access to credit, especially for the smallest or poorest microentrepreneurs, simply means establishing new channels of dependency and exploitation. An evaluation of credit extended to women microentrepreneurs in Bombay, India, noted that the poorest borrowers simply used the increased incomes they were able to obtain from investing their loans to repay the lender, thereby increasing the latter's income instead of reinvesting the funds in the firm (Everett and Savara 1984). Also, it has been observed that even when obstacles to credit are removed, other factors continue to hinder the growth of microenterprises. These include shifts in demand, difficulties in acquiring raw materials, and entrepreneur attitudes (Tendler 1983). In her evaluation of the UNO program in Brazil, Tendler concluded that credit played an important role in reducing costs (through lower interest rates and cheaper raw materials, purchased wholesale), and thus in increasing the firm's profits, although the volume of sales remained constant.

Instead of facilitating growth in production and employment, the UNO credit seems to have helped the firms survive, and to have held the number of jobs steady, rather than increasing them. The objective of job creation has also been criticized by Kilby (1979). Because work in the informal sector is characterized by low productivity and low levels of income, any improvement implies an increase in the productivity of labor, and thus may reduce the need for additional jobs. Kilby concludes that the main criterion for measuring the impact of projects that assist the informal sector should be maintaining the number of jobs, rather than creating new jobs.

There is also disagreement as to what types of firms benefit most from loans to microenterprises. For some analysts, the structure of loan programs for microentrepreneurs is more appropriate for small-scale merchants, who need little capital but much liquidity, than for firms in the manufacturing sector, which need more capital and long-term loans (Preliminary Report to USAID/Quito 1985). Tendler (1987) finds that "minimalist" credit works better for microvendors than for microproducers in manufacturing and services, as the latter pose a greater risk to the lender. Kilby and D'Zmura (1985), however, believe that microvendors do not generate backward linkages (that is, increments in demand for raw materials and other production inputs), which constitute one of the invisible economies that contribute most to additional positive economic benefits for microenterprises. Finally, channeling credit to microvendors means getting it into the hands of the poorest entrepreneurs. To the extent that distribution criteria are considered to be part of the measurable economic benefits, credit to microvendors may yield more benefits than credit to microproducers.

Studies of credit projects designed for women microentrepreneurs generally agree that such projects have significant economic and social benefits, particularly when evaluated in comparison with the rest of the actions for poor women carried out in the productive sector by development agencies in the Third World (Buvinić 1986). With the exception of the evaluation of the credit program in Bombay cited above, case studies of credit projects for microentrepreneurs in Bangladesh, India, Kenya, the Dominican Republic, and Peru, among others, observe that women borrowers are a good financial risk, and consider credit to bring about economic benefits as well as social or individual ones. Individual benefits are usually described in terms that imply the women feel more sure of themselves and have greater decision-making power within the family (Sebstad 1982; Jain 1980; Berger 1985; Reichmann 1984a, 1984b; Tendler 1987). Nevertheless, these case studies have not used methodologies that would allow them to empirically measure economic and social costs and benefits disaggregated by gender.

To date there is little documented evidence of either the measurable economic impact of microenterprise credit on female borrowers, or the differences in the impact of credit on the firm based on the sex of the microentrepreneur. Nor is there any empirical evidence on the effectiveness of credit provided to female microvendors as compared to female microproducers. The objective of the ICRW/FED study was to begin to throw light on some of these questions. The study was designed to empirically explore the short-term impact of PRODEM credit on the characteristics of the firms and on the welfare of the families of men and women borrowers. The study also added a component that is generally absent from evaluations of development projects: in addition to a baseline measure, or measure of the situation before intervention, it included a control group that was not benefited by the project. This group's behavior yields comparative information that is valuable in evaluating the real benefits of the development interventions.

DESIGN

To assess the impact of PRODEM credit on women microentrepreneurs' incomes and welfare, this research project measured the characteristics of the microentrepreneurs chosen at the outset of the project, in October 1984, and twelve months later, in October 1985, varying the sex and the participation or nonparticipation (status) of microentrepreneurs in the PRODEM project. That is, the design included a control group of nonbeneficiaries or nonborrowers of the PRODEM program, and allowed for comparisons between the initial or baseline measure and the measure twelve months later; between men and women; between borrowers and nonborrowers; and between microproducers and microvendors.

The ability to make these comparisons increases the degree of certainty which we can attribute changes observed between the first and second measures to the project itself, rather than to independent events that may yield the same results and that occur over the same time period. In particular, having a control group of nonborrowers makes it possible to empirically control factors that affect the firms in ways that are not clearly established, such as inflation, which can increase not only raw materials costs, but also the value of sales. In addition, these comparisons make it possible to establish empirically the differences between women's and men's participation in a project that extends credit to the informal sector.

Given the nature of the PRODEM project, the research design subdivided the four groups already mentioned based on the type of activity, that is, whether they were microproducers or microvendors (the microvendors borrowed as members of solidarity groups). This breakdown yields a total of eight factorial groups, each group varying the factors sex, participation, and type of activity. Taking two observations in different years, the combination yields 16 cells (see Table 14.3).

To permit generalizations about PRODEM borrowers, the design was based on a random sample of borrowers. The sample was stratified by entrepreneurial activity and by sex of the microentrepreneur. Because the population (or the size of the informal sector) in Quito is not known, it was not possible to choose a random sample of nonborrowers. As a next best alternative, an attempt was made to select a control group that would match up with the randomly selected group of borrowers in terms of economic characteristics. In the case of microproducers, a control group of entrepre-

TABLE 14.3

Study Design and Sample Size for PRODEM Borrowers and Nonborrowers,[a] 1984–1985

	Borrowers		Nonborrowers	
	1984	1985	1984	1985
No. of Microproducers				
W[b]	42	37	50	41
M	41	41	54	40
No. of Microvendors				
W	42	42	51	39
M	31	25		

[a] Total number of borrowers in the 1984 sample = 311; total number in 1985 sample = 265. The sample of borrowers is random; the control group of nonborrowers is not random but is matched with the sample of borrowers.

[b] W = women; M = men.

neurs was chosen that was similar to the group of borrowers in terms of location of the firm, borrower's sex, type of entrepreneurial activity, and total assets. In the case of microvendors, a group was selected that was similar to the members of the solidarity groups within PRODEM in terms of sales location, vendor's sex, total weekly sales, and type of product sold.

Advantages and Limitations of the Design

The advantages of the research design used are: (1) that it allows an empirical study of changes over time in the characteristics of the borrowers' firms; and (2) that it controls empirically (instead of statistically) for effects or events that are independent of the credit but that overlap in time, a function that may: (a) explain changes in the firm that are mistakenly attributed to credit; or (b) contribute to confound the impact of credit on the firms' growth. The design also yields useful information on the behavior of microentrepreneurs who do not benefit from these specific development interventions.

The greatest limitation of the research design used is the fact that the control group could not be selected randomly. Because this is the case—even though the control group is matched to the borrower group in terms of economic characteristics—the results obtained from the nonborrowers cannot be generalized for the population of microproducers and microvendors in Quito's informal sector. Moreover, the control group of nonborrowers can only be compared to the group of borrowers to the extent that the two groups are similar. If the groups have dissimilar characteristics from the outset, differences found at a later stage may be due to those initial differences, and not to the impact of differential access to credit.

Another less serious limitation of the research design lies in the stratification of the sample which, to guarantee sufficient representation of women microentrepreneurs in a relatively small sample, was not proportional to the make-up of the total population: the proportion of women microproducers was doubled in the sample, as the study's main interest is to compare men and women within each group (and between borrowers and nonborrowers within each generic group).

The design's third limitation is the possibility of bias in the sample due to dropouts between the first and second years of the survey, particularly if the dropout rate is not equal across the different groups.

The fourth limitation is that, to the extent that the credit projects yield invisible economic benefits, use of a control group will always underestimate the loan's net economic benefit. According to Kilby and D'Zmura (1985), who mention this limitation, an increase in sales observed in the control group implies that the control group has had to divert capital from another uses to finance expansion of the firm. Therefore the control group—but not the experimental group—is losing potential revenues from this alternative use of that capital. Because this limitation always works in the same direction within the borrower group, it should not affect comparisons between men and women; but it will have an impact on comparisons between borrowers and nonborrowers.

Sample

To reduce the effects of the holiday season on the economic data, the interviews were held in early November in 1985 and 1986 and elicited information for the previous month (October). Given the initial difficulty of locating the people selected for the sample (especially the group of microvendors, many of whom are street vendors and have no full-time address) and the costs of the survey, it was necessary to work with a relatively small sample. Because of these restrictions, male microvendors who were nonborrowers were not interviewed. The cells left blank in Table 14.3 reflect this decision. Therefore, the final design did not allow for measuring the impact of credit on male microvendors who were borrowers, because no data were collected for the corresponding control group.

The size of the final sample used in 1984 was 311 microentrepreneurs, made up of 156 borrowers and 155 nonborrowers. Table 14.3 shows the original design, as well as the distribution among the different groups included in the design for the 1984 sample. The sample of 156 borrowers accounted for 8.6 percent of all the program's clients in October 1984. It included 32 percent of the female microproducers involved in the program, 14 percent of the male microproducers, and 6 percent of the members of solidarity groups.

Given that the study's main goal was to make comparisons between men and women borrowers, and between both of those groups and the group of nonborrowers, a sample was chosen with at least thirty individuals per group in order to allow statistical analyses rather than to necessitate a proportional sampling of all the borrowers. The initial random selection of borrowers was stratified by sex in the case of microproducers, with the proportional representation of women in this group increased by a factor of 2. Members of solidarity groups were drawn from the list of members, irrespective of sex; the random sample was made up of fifty women and thirty men. Based on the economic characteristics of this sample, staff of the PRODEM program were given guidelines for selecting a control group that would match the group of borrowers.

It was expected that a number of people selected in October 1984 would not be located for the second measurement scheduled for October 1985. In October 1985 forty-six people, or 14.8 percent of the original sample from the previous year, could not be located. The final sample thus included 265 people. As was also expected, a larger number of nonborrowers than borrowers was not located, as the program kept the up-to-date addresses only of borrowers. Some 29 percent of the nonborrowers and only 8 percent of the borrowers from the original 1984 sample were lost; this omission may have biased the sample of nonborrowers, placing greater weight on the more successful ones, who kept the same residence, or the same market stall or stand. Table 14.3 also presents the totals from the final October 1985 sample.

Questionnaire

The questionnaire used in the study had sixty-three questions with precoded alternative responses, and with open questions to expand on some of the preset choices. The questions fall under four main headings: demographic and educational characteristics of the microentrepreneur (18 questions); entrepreneurial activity, including the firm's sales, expenditures, and assets (23 questions); composition and income of the microentrepreneur's household, and characteristics of his or her dwelling (15 questions); and additional questions on credit and savings behavior (7 questions). The period referred to in the questions on income, expenditures, and sales is the month before the survey, that is, October 1984 for the baseline study, and October 1985 for the data for evaluation.

RESULTS

The results presented here include descriptive statistics on the characteristics of the interviewees, comparisons between borrowers and nonborrowers in the initial measurement, measurement of the impact of credit on two independent variables, and preliminary analyses on its impact on employment.

Suspension of Borrowers from the PRODEM Project

Given the unexpected growth in the percentage of defaults in the project in 1985 (due in part to the deterioration of the Ecuadoran economy during this period, and in part to the project's rapid growth and a lack of sanctions for defaulters), PRODEM decided to impose stricter controls on the borrowers and to suspend defaulters from the project. Because of these measures and some voluntary attrition by other clients, an average of 30 percent of the borrowers who were interviewed in 1984 had left the program by 1985. The dropout rate was slightly higher for male microproducers (34 percent) and lower for male microvendors.

When active and suspended borrowers are separated, the average trends in the entrepreneurial activities of these two groups between 1984 and 1985 move in opposite directions: on average, in the course of the year, firms of active borrowers exhibited positive growth, while the average growth for the firms of suspended borrowers was negative. This result, which is repeated for monthly sales, monthly earnings, and total assets for all the suspended borrowers except the male microvendors (who are only six cases), indicates the validity of the questionnaire for measuring data over time; it also points to the need to differentiate between the active and suspended borrowers in all the analyses, in order to obtain reliable data on the project's impact. The statistical analyses eliminated the suspended borrowers even though this step reduces the sample size to less that thirty individuals per group, and limits the possibility of obtaining significant statistical differences. The final sample size for the analyses of variance includes the number of nonborrowers interviewed in 1985 (120 microentrepreneurs) plus the active borrowers in 1985 (95 microentrepreneurs). Thus this sample included the successful borrowers, at least in terms of repayment of the loan and continuation in the program, and probably the most successful nonborrowers, in terms of having maintained their firm or residence in the same location over time.

Comparison of Borrowers and Nonborrowers in the Baseline

In selecting the control group, an attempt was made to choose nonborrowers with characteristics similar to those of the PRODEM borrowers, matching the two groups in terms of location of the enterprise or sales stand, borrower's sex, the type of enterprise or sales operation, and total assets of the firm or total weekly sales. Although demographic and educational characteristics were not controlled for, the groups of borrowers and nonborrowers were quite homogeneous in October 1984 in terms of these characteristics; yet they differed in terms of some characteristics of their firms. Table 14.4 shows the borrowers' and nonborrowers' average demographic and educational characteristics. As the table indicates, the average age of borrowers and nonborrowers varies from thirty-five to thirty-nine years; the number of members of the household, between five and six; and dependents per household, from 2.9 to 3.8 persons. Borrowers and nonborrowers have similar educational levels: they have had an average of 6.8 to 7.5 years

TABLE 14.4

**Average Demographic and Educational Characteristics
for Men and Women Borrowers and Nonborrowers**

	Borrowers		Nonborrowers	
	Men (n = 71)[a]	Women (n = 84)	Men (n = 54)	Women (n = 102)
Age (in years)	36.4	35.3	39.1	37.6
Education (in years)	7.3	6.8	7.5	7.3
No. of household members	5.2	6.1	5.0	5.2
No. of dependents[b] per household	3.3	3.8[c]	3.4	2.9
No. of children 5 years or younger per household	0.8	0.9	0.8	0.5

[a] The "n" indicates the number of cases in each group.
[b] Dependents are household members who do not receive an income.
[c] n = 83.

of formal education. There are no significant differences between these averages.

Among borrowers only microproducers have on average significantly more years of formal education than the microvendors: 8.4 years as opposed to 5.5 years (p < 0.001). This result is consistent with the fact that the vendors who are beneficiaries of PRODEM-type projects are poorer than the microproducers. There are no other significant differences in the average demographic characteristics of microproducers and microvendors included in the project.

When the data on demographic and educational characteristics are analyzed by suspended borrowers versus borrowers still active in the program, no significant differences emerge. More pronounced differences appear if we compare years of operation of these groups' firms: the firms of women microproducers active in PRODEM have been in operation longer than those of the women microproducers suspended from the program, while the opposite was the case for men microproducer borrowers. The male microproducers who were active in the program seem to have been operating their firms for fewer years than did the male microproducers who were suspended. These data suggest that entrepreneurial experience and/or stability of the firm is more important in assuring success for women than for men microentrepreneurs in PRODEM. That is, for women the probability of successfully making use of the credit appears to increase with entrepreneurial experience.

Table 14.5 shows economic data on characteristics of the firms of active borrowers and nonborrowers, with regard to fixed assets and average monthly sales. As the table indicates, there were already differences in the initial measurement in 1984 between men and women, microproducers and

TABLE 14.5

Fixed Assets and Average Monthly Sales[a] for the Businesses of Active Borrowers and Nonborrowers by Sex and Program Area

		Borrowers		Nonborrowers	
		1984	1985	1984	1985
Microproducers					
Fixed Assets	W[b]	290,064(25)[c]	289,830	137,222(38)	128,182
	M	216,400(27)	265,630	171,964(40)	225,525
Monthly Sales	W	60,626(25)	76,832	25,670(36)	26,873
	M	108,148(27)	128,607	30,041(37)	40,224
Microvendors					
Fixed Assets	W	24,326(23)	8,456	8,892(36)	15,680
	M	11,800(19)	23,458		
Monthly Sales	W	37,493(24)	38,046	41,797(36)	54,987
	M	52,620(19)	73,130		

[a]   US$1 = 110 sucres in October 1984; 120 sucres in October 1985.
[b]   W = women; M = men.
[c]   Indicates the number of interviewees for both years.

microvendors, and borrowers and nonborrowers. The baseline differences between men and women and between microproducers and vendors replicate the general pattern according to which men's firms are larger than women's firms, and microproducers are in a more secure entrepreneurial position than microvendors. The difference in the initial measurement between the borrowers and nonborrowers, in contrast, is more problematic: it may reflect real differences between the PRODEM borrowers and the nonborrower population. Specifically, the PRODEM credit may attract entrepreneurs and vendors with greater sales volumes than average for the informal sector. Or differences between borrowers and nonborrowers may be artificial, because of a bias in the sample of nonborrowers, or because they did not answer the questions on economic variables truthfully.

Impact of PRODEM Credit on the Net Business Incomes of Borrowers

Two variables were used to measure the impact of the PRODEM credit: the monthly net income of the firms, calculated as monthly sales minus costs, wages, and salaries; and hourly net income, calculated as monthly net income divided by the number of hours per month that the entrepreneur worked in his or her business. For these two dependent variables, data from the active PRODEM borrowers—who were the most successful in terms of repaying the loan and continuing in the project—were compared with the data from the most successful nonborrowers, that is, those who had maintained the same business location, sales stall, or residence in the course of the year. Although changes of address may indicate upward mobility in a

favorable economic environment, these changes were interpreted as generally indicating downward mobility given that Ecuador was affected by an
economic crisis during the period covered by the study. Therefore, all references to borrowers in the following discussion regard only active borrowers.

Table 14.6 and 14.7 show the average monthly net income and net income per hour for the different groups studied. To analyze the impact of the
credit on these dependent variables in the different groups, analyses of variance were performed on mixed factorial designs that varied factors *between*

TABLE 14.6

**Average Net Monthly Income for Borrower and Nonborrower
Businesses by Sex, Type of Program, and Year (in sucres)**

	Borrowers		Nonborrowers	
	1984	1985	1984	1985
Microproducers				
W[a]	8,783	11,303	5,972	8,108
M	15,807	22,943	11,969	18,112
Microvendors				
W	6,550	9,029	10,281	9,983
M	8,737	9,910		

[a] W = women; M = men.

the interviewees (in this case, the factors varied were the sex of the entrepreneur, whether the entrepreneur was a borrower or nonborrower, and
whether he or she was a microproducer or a microvendor); and also measured each response twice, once in 1984, and once in 1985. That is, the time
factor is varied *within* subjects.

TABLE 14.7

**Average Number of Hours Worked per Month and
Average Hourly Net Income for Borrower and
Nonborrower Businesses by Sex, Type of Program, and Year**

	Borrowers				Nonborrowers			
	1984		1985		1984		1985	
	H[a]	I/H[a]	H	I/H	H	I/H	H	I/H
Microproducers								
W[b]	251	38	208	83	181	39	169	60
M	262	64	263	84	238	51	239	81
Microvendors								
W	197	35	169	62	205	50	197	50
M	253	45	205	52				

[a] H = hours; I/H = income/hour.
[b] W = women; M = men.

Differences Between Borrowers and Nonborrowers

In order to attain a crossed factorial design, the first analysis of variance compared borrowers and nonborrowers only within the microproducer program. The microvendors were excluded from the analysis because of the lack of observations for male microvendors who were not borrowers.

Table 14.8 presents the results of this analysis for the two dependent variables. First, across all the groups, and over the course of the year, borrower's sex is a determining factor in monthly net income ($p < 0.0001$) and hourly net income ($p < 0.05$). Women earn less than men, independent of whether or not they are PRODEM borrowers. Second, across all groups and for both measurements, being a borrower explains the change in monthly net income: the monthly net business incomes of borrowers are greater than those of the nonborrowers ($p < 0.01$). The differences in hourly net income are not significant. Comparing the averages of borrowers and nonborrowers using a t-test shows that there are already significant differences ($p < 0.04$) between the two groups in the initial monthly net income measured in 1984; the same differences occur with the data obtained for fixed assets and monthly sales (see Table 14.5), limiting the validity of comparing the results of the random sample of borrowers with the nonrandom sample of nonborrowers. Because the borrowers' initial values are lower, it is to be expected statistically that their net monthly incomes would increase more than those of the borrowers with higher initial values.

It is therefore highly likely that these results underestimate the impact of credit on increasing the monthly net business incomes of borrowers. In the analysis, borrowers and nonborrowers increased monthly net income ($p < 0.0009$) and hourly net income ($p < 0.0001$) from one year to the next, but being a borrower does not appear to contribute to explaining these variations in monthly or hourly net income (the interaction between the participation factor and the time factor is not significant). It is possible that with a group of nonborrowers whose firms have returns similar to those of the borrowers included in the baseline measure, the impact of the credit would have been more visible or significant. The general increase from one year to the next in the net business incomes of interviewees, across all the groups, reflects in part real growth in microenterprises in the city of Quito; but it might also be due in part to inflation in Ecuador. From October 1984 to October 1985 it is estimated that the consumer price index increased 26 percent. The average increase in monthly net income of the businesses studied was 29 percent, and for hourly income, 38 percent. The following analyses clarify this point; they deal only with the groups of borrowers, for whom the data posed no problems of reliability.

Differences Between Microproducer and Microvendor Borrowers

Table 14.9 shows the analysis of variance for the borrowers, varying both sex and program (that is, microproducer or microvendor), and comparing the

TABLE 14.8

Analysis of Variance for Microproducers Varying Sex (A) and Borrowers Status (B) and Comparing Effects Across Time for Monthly and Hourly Net Income

Source of Variance[a]	Net Monthly Income[b]				Net Hourly Income[c]			
	Degrees of Freedom	Mean Squares	F	p	Degrees of Freedom	Mean Squares	F	p
Between Subjects								
Sex (A)	1	4,399,730,640	31.24	0.0001	1	12,853	3.68	0.05
Status (B)	1	885,858,620	6.29	0.01	1	5,121	1.46	
A × B	1	53,914,144	—		1	142	0.04	
Error (S/AB)	121	140,841,954			116	3,497		
For Each Subject								
Time (C)	1	1,094,859,078	11.70	0.0009	1	48,528	20.87	0.0001
A × C	1	207,504,367	2.22		1	785	0.34	
B × C	1	7,876,316	0.08		1	813	0.35	
A × B × C	1	2,735,688	0.03		1	4,285	1.84	
Error (SC/AB)	121	93,552,554			116	2,325		

[a] The analysis of variance is a mixed factorial design where sex (A) and borrower status (borrower or nonborrower) (B) are varied between interviewees (or subjects). Also, for each subject the year the dependent variables were measured (1984, 1985) were varied in the time factor (C).

[b] Analysis based on a total of 130 observations of which 5 were eliminated because of lack of information (n = 125).

[c] Analysis based on a total of 130 observations of which 10 were eliminated because of lack of information (n = 120).

TABLE 14.9

Analysis of Variance for Borrowers Varying the Sex and Borrowers' Activity (Microproducers or Microvendors) and Comparing the Effects Across Time for Monthly and Hourly Net Income

Source of Variance[a]	Net Monthly Income[b]				Net Hourly Income[c]			
	Degrees of Freedom	Mean Squares	F	p	Degrees of Freedom	Mean Squares	F	p
Between Subjects								
Sex (A)	1	1,372,274,432	9.111	0.0003	1	3,283	1.10	
Status (B)	1	1,635,510,439	10.86	0.001	1	14,491	4.87	0.03
A × B	1	630,319,911	4.19	0.04	1	1,964	0.66	
Error (S/AB)	84	150,605,692			82	2,973		
Within Subjects								
Time (C)	1	285,072,497	2.51		1	10,881	4.96	0.03
A × C	1	113,694,274	1.00		1	967	0.44	
B × C	1	109,375,839	0.96		1	2,818	1.28	
A × B × C	1	88,632,839	0.78		1	4,285	0.03	
Error (SC/AB)	84	113,505,885			82	2,194		

a The analysis of variance is a mixed factorial design where sex (A) and borrower activity (microproducers or microvendor) (B) are varied between borrowers. Also, two measurements of the dependent variables (1984, 1985) in the time factor (C) were varied for each borrower.

b Analysis based on a total of 94 observations of which 6 were eliminated because of a lack of information (n = 88).

c Analysis based on a total of 94 observations of which 8 were eliminated because of lack of information (n = 86).

results for 1984 and 1985. For both dependent variables, and across sex and time of measurement, as is to be expected the microproducers' revenues were significantly greater than those of the microvendors. More interesting, the sex factor explains the variation in monthly net income ($p < 0.0003$); but this effect disappears for hourly net income. This result is explained below. Furthermore, the time factor exercises a major effect only for hourly net income, which for the borrowers increased significantly from 1984 to 1985 independent of sex and the type of program ($p < 0.03$). As Table 14.7 indicates, this difference is due in part to the fact that the borrowers reduced the number of hours worked in 1985 as compared to the previous year.

Differences Within the Groups of Microproducer and Microvendor Borrowers

Because the initial differences in revenues between microproducers and microvendors may mask the effect of the sex and time factors, Tables 14.10 and 14.11 show the analysis of variance separately for the two groups, to discern the more "pure" effect of borrower's sex and time on monthly and hourly net business income. The problem with these analyses is that the small sample size may mask effects that would be significant with a larger sample.

Nonetheless, Table 14.10 shows that the net monthly incomes of male microproducers are greater than those of women, independent of the year ($p < 0.0003$), and that, independent of the borrower's sex, the microproducer borrowers have higher monthly ($p < 0.09$) and hourly ($p < 0.008$) net incomes one year after entering PRODEM. The same sex effect appears in Table 14.11 for microvendors; sex explains variations in monthly net income ($p < 0.007$), but not in hourly net income. For this group, however, one year after entering the PRODEM program there is only a significant increase in hourly net income ($p < 0.02$), and there appears to be a significant interaction between sex and time ($p < 0.06$) for hourly net income: beginning with lower revenues, female microvendors increased their hourly revenues more than male microvendors, as illustrated in Table 14.7, because they increased their net income and reduced their working hours one year after entering the PRODEM program.

The average number of hours worked monthly shown in Table 14.7 suggests even more forcefully for the microproducers that women borrowers somewhat increased their incomes and substantially reduced the hours they worked on a monthly basis, whereas men borrowers increased their incomes but did not curtail the total hours they worked. When the analysis of variance eliminates three extreme observations for the groups of microproducer borrowers (with monthly net income greater than 45,000 sucres in 1984 and 50,000 sucres in 1985, or net income of zero in either year), the interaction between the sex factor and the time factor is significant ($p < 0.06$) and in the same direction as the interaction for the microvendors. It is highly likely that this interaction would have been significant with a larger sample without eliminating extreme observations.

TABLE 14.10

Analysis of Variance for Borrowers/Microproducers Varying Sex and Comparing the Effects Across Time for Monthly and Hourly Net Income

Source of Variance[a]	Net Monthly Income[b]				Net Hourly Income[c]			
	Degrees of Freedom	Mean Squares	F	p	Degrees of Freedom	Mean Squares	F	p
Between Subjects								
Sex (A)	1	2,229,119,155	9.60	0.003	1	4,212	0.99	
Error (S/A)	47	232,171,544			45	4,268		
Within Subjects								
Time (C)	1	529,159,531	2.88	0.09	1	25,342	7.59	0.008
A × C	1	105,913,833	0.58		1	3,578	1.07	
Error (SC/A)	47	184,034,128			45	3,340		

[a] The analysis of variance is a mixed design where sex (A) is varied between microproducers and where two measurements of the dependent variable (1984, 1985) in the time factor (C) were varied for each microproducer.

[b] Analysis based on a total of 51 observations of which 2 were eliminated because of a lack of information (n = 49).

[c] Analysis based on a total of 51 observations of which 4 were eliminated because of lack of information (n = 47).

TABLE 14.11

Analysis of Variance for Microvender Borrowers Varying Sex and Comparing the Effects Across Time for Monthly and Hourly Net Income

Source of Variance[a]	Net Monthly Income[b]				Net Hourly Income[c]			
	Degrees of Freedom	Mean Squares	F	p	Degrees of Freedom	Mean Squares	F	p
Between Subjects								
Sex (A)	1	762,891,258	7.90	0.007	1	418	0.11	
Error (S/A)	43	96,620,627			42	3,784		
Within Subject								
Time (C)	1	70,559,801	1.34		1	14,135	5.40	0.02
A × C	1	30,262,201	0.58		1	9,459	3.62	0.06
Error (SC/A)	43	52,550,252			42	2,616		

[a] The analysis of variance is a mixed design where sex (A) is varied between microvendors and where two measurements of the dependent variable (1984, 1985) in the time factor (C) were varied for each microvendor.

[b] Analysis based on a total of 47 observations of which 2 were eliminated because of lack of information (n = 45).

[c] Analysis based on a total of 47 observations of which 3 were eliminated because of lack of information (n = 44).

Even when the extreme observations are eliminated from the analysis of variance, the results are very similar to those reported here, with the exception of the interaction for the dependent variable "hourly net income." In this analysis, equivalent to the analysis of Table 14.8 but excluding the extreme values, the significant interaction of sex by borrower status and by time ($p < 0.05$) shows that women borrowers increased their hourly incomes relatively more than the men borrowers, as compared to nonborrowers of the same sex. Because eliminating extreme observations may bias the sample, the most conservative analyses, using all the observations, have been reported.

The Impact of PRODEM Credit on Job Stability

One of PRODEM's main objectives is job creation, and—insofar as possible—at a lower cost than in the formal sector. Tables 14.12 and 14.13 present data on the average and total number of workers that correspond to each group included in the sample for both years.

TABLE 14.12
Microproducers:
Total and Average Number of Paid and Unpaid Workers by Year

		Borrowers		Nonborrowers	
		1984	1985	1984	1985
Total no. of paid workers	W[a]	26(25)[b]	26	25(40)	16
	M	49(26)	57	33(40)	58
Average no. of paid workers per business	W	1.04(25)	1.04	0.62(40)	0.40
	M	1.88(26)	2.19	0.82(40)	1.45
Total no. of unpaid workers per business	W	12(25)	16	19(40)	10
	M	6(26)	10	7(40)	3
Average no. of unpaid workers per business	W	0.48(25)	0.64	0.47(40)	0.25
	M	0.23(26)	0.38	0.17(40)	0.07

[a] W = women; M = men.
[b] Numbers in parentheses indicate the number of interviewees.

The data on the number of paid and unpaid workers presented in these tables suggest that the credit did not have the effect of increasing employment. This assumption corroborates data collected by other researchers, according to which credit programs such as PRODEM should not be evaluated solely in terms of their impact on generating employment. The data on workers hired by the borrower and nonborrower firms also suggest that women, probably because of the size of their firms, hire fewer workers on average than the men do, and that microvendors have fewer workers than microproducers.

Table 14.12 suggests that within the group of microproducers, men were able to increase the number of paid workers, while employment gener-

TABLE 14.13
Microvendors:
Total and Average Number of Paid and Unpaid Workers by Year

		1984	1985	Nonborrowers 1984	1985
Total no. of paid workers	W[a]	$1(24)^b$	4	8(34)	1
	M	3(19)	8		
Average no. of paid workers per business	W	0.04(24)	0.17	0(24)	0.17
	M	0.16(19)	0.42		
Total no. of unpaid workers	W	12(24)	8	18(34)	7
	M	11(19)	7		
Average no. of unpaid workers per business	W	0.50	0.33	0.53	0.21
	M	0.58	0.37		

[a]   W = women; M = men.
[b]   Numbers in parentheses indicate the number of interviewees.

ated by women held steady. Table 14.14 attempts to disaggregate these differences by classifying the employment data by economic activity. In two areas that are "nontraditional" for women, leather processing and/or shoe manufacturing, and carpentry/upholstery, the firms are run by women who have

TABLE 14.14
Borrowers/Microproducers:
Job Creation by Branch of Activity and Sex

Branch of Activity	Women No. of Businesses	Total No. of Paid Workers 1984	1985	Men No. of Businesses	Total No. of Paid Workers 1984	1985
Tailor/seamstress	18	14	9	5	6	10
Leather processing and shoe making	3	5	3	8	15	19
Carpentry and tapestry	2	5	3	9	19	20
Weaving and needlecrafts	3	2	7	0	—	—
Bakery	1	0	0	4	10	9
Jewelers	1	0	0	2	2	1
Food preparation	0	—	—	0	—	—
Metalworks	0	—	—	1	2	2
Other manufacturing	2	4	6	4	10	15
Barbershop and beauty salon	1	0	0	1	1	1
Restaurant	3	2	2	0	—	—
Mechanics	0	—	—	1	0	2
Other services	0	—	—	2	2	0
Total	34	32	30	37	67	79

cut back the number of workers, while the firms in these male-dominated areas have slightly increased the number of employees. Even more noteworthy is the pronounced decline in the number of jobs in women's garments businesses, while men tailors have increased the number of workers they hire. These data reflect the great difference between female seamstresses and male tailors in terms of profitability and scale of production, despite the fact that they operate in the same branch of industry.

CONCLUSIONS

The results of this study confirm, first, the not surprising pattern that, on the whole, male entrepreneurs manage larger firms than women, and men's businesses yield higher net incomes. Also to be expected was the significant increase in monthly net income for the sample of entrepreneurs one year after the baseline measure, particularly if we take into account that the sample is biased to successful borrowers within the PRODEM project, who were not suspended because of arrears, and also to the successful entrepreneurs in the control group of nonborrowers, who remained at the same business location or residence throughout the year. Though not surprising, this result confirms the dynamism of the microenterprise sector, where some firms are able to increase net income in the course of a year, despite a lack of access to credit and other inputs available in the formal sector, and in the context of a recessionary economy.

Less expected is the barely visible impact of the PRODEM credit when monthly and hourly net incomes of all borrowers are compared with those of nonborrowers. The absence of significant differences between these groups, nonetheless, can be explained in part by the initial differences in the net incomes of borrowers and nonborrowers, which may lead to underestimation of the impact of credit; the experimental design's limitation in terms of its inability to measure invisible economies; and the possibility that a larger sample of borrowers might have yielded significant effects. In any event, these results suggest that the benefits of credit projects such as the PRODEM one are moderate when increases in the firm's monthly net income are the criterion used for measuring impact. The preliminary tabulations on employment creation also support those studies that find that projects extending credit to microenterprises, contrary to what is expected, do not tend to generate additional employment, but rather preserve jobs, and that their success should not be measured by the generation of new jobs.

The more disaggregated analyses, which consider only the sample of borrowers in the PRODEM project and measure the impact after one year of being in the program in terms of net hourly and monthly income, yield valuable results in terms of the project's differential impact by the sex of the borrower. First, for all microproducer and microvendor borrowers, irrespective of borrower's sex, the significant increase in hourly income from 1984 to 1985 (which is not reflected in monthly income) confirms Kilby's observation (1979) that access to credit increases the efficiency or productivity of microentrepreneurs, as hourly net income can serve as a proxy for labor productivity in microenterprises that have a working owner and few employees. It also rules out the possibility that the increase in net income observed from 1984 to 1985 results solely from inflation. In addition, this finding indicates the importance of including measurements of productivity in impact studies of microenterprise credit projects.

Second, as reflected in the significant interaction between the sex and time factors, this research indicates that, in terms of efficiency measured through hours worked, the positive impact of the PRODEM credit depends on the gender of the entrepreneur: women microproducer and microvendor borrowers increased their hourly net incomes (reducing total hours worked per month) from 1984 to 1985 to a significantly greater extent than did their male counterparts. The fact that this change represents an increase in the female borrowers' productivity, and not a mere reduction in total hours worked from one year to the next, is evidenced by this group's increased net income, and by the significant interaction found among sex, borrower status, and time when the extreme values were eliminated.

This strategy or preference among women microentrepreneurs for using the credit to increase efficiency can be explained by women's twofold responsibility of producing at the workplace and producing in the home. The average number of children in the households of the entrepreneurs included in this study was five to six, and it is women, rather than men, who are mainly responsible for managing the home. The incentive to use credit in order to work more efficiently and thus be able to deal better with their multiple responsibilities of home and work is an understandable strategy for poor women in Latin America. Because men do not share the bulk of these multiple responsibilities, they lack the motivation for shortening their work schedules.

This increased efficiency probably has a very positive impact on the welfare of both the household and the female entrepreneur, as it shortens a very heavy workday and frees time for the entrepreneur to spend at home. For example, women microproducer borrowers who reported the most significant decline in the days and hours dedicated to the firm diminished their workday from 10.3 hours in 1984 to 9.28 hours in 1985.

This explanation has attributed the increase in the productivity of women entrepreneurs to their access to the PRODEM credit, even though strictly speaking this conclusion is not warranted, because there were no significant differences between borrowers and nonborrowers after one year. Given the significant increase in the hourly net income of female PRODEM borrowers from 1984 to 1985, the probable underestimation of the impact of PRODEM loans, and the significant results when we exclude the extreme observations, it does not seem risky to conclude that access to credit was a key factor in the increased productivity observed among women borrowers. This assumption does not imply that without the PRODEM credit women entrepreneurs would not have increased their productivity. It may be that increases in monthly and hourly net income of the nonborrowers from 1984 to 1985 were due to their access to informal credit sources in the city of Quito.

The cost of obtaining credit from informal sources (which is not reflected in these data), women's lack of access to credit sources in the modern financial sector, and the impact of credit in terms of increasing the female entrepreneur's productivity justify PRODEM-style credit projects for women microentrepreneurs. This justification and the benefits of the credit apply to women microproducers in manufacturing and services as well as to women microvendors, even though the latter are poorer. The study also demonstrates the importance of the gender variable in measuring the impact of projects to assist microentrepreneurs, because this variable explains significant variations in short-term results.

Finally, the results of this study should be understood in the broader context of the importance of the urban informal sector and women as participants in this sector of the Latin American economies, particularly in periods of recession, which jeopardize the survival of the poorest families. The fact that a productive-sector credit project was able to reach a large number of low-income women microproducers and microvendors and to keep a considerable number of women active in the project (that is, without defaulting) is in and of itself a success, particularly when these actions are compared with the usual experience of income-generating projects for women in the region, which all too often meet with little or no success.

Bibliography

ACCION International/AITEC. 1986. "Programas de Microempresas Afiliados." Statistical Review of Microenterprise Credit Programs prepared for ACCION. Photocopy.

————. 1985. "The Solidarity Group Programs in Colombia." Cambridge, Mass.: ACCION International/AITEC. Photocopy.

ADEMI. 1983. "Programa." Santo Domingo, Dominican Republic: Asociacion para el Desarrollo de Microempresas, Inc.

Alderfer, Clayton P. 1985. "Changing Race Relations in Organizations: A Comparison of Theories." ONR Technical Reports, no. 4. New Haven, Conn.: Yale School of Organization and Management.

————. 1980. "The Methodology of Organization Diagnosis," *Professional Psychology* 11: 459–68.

————. 1977. "Group and Intergroup Relations." In *Improving Life at Work.* Edited by J.R. Hackman and J.L. Suttle. Santa Monica, Calif.: Goodyear, pp. 227–96.

Alderfer, Clayton P. and Smith, Kenwyn K. 1982. "Studying Intergroup Relations Embedded in Organization," *Administrative Science Quarterly* 27: 35–65.

American Council of Voluntary Agencies for Foreign Service, Inc. 1975. "Criteria for Evaluation of Development Projects Involving Women." New York: ACVAFS, Technical Assistance Information Clearing House.

Arias, Maria Eugenia. 1984. "Peru: Banco Industrial del Perú—Credit from the Development of Rural Enterprise." In *Gender Roles in Development Projects: A Case Book.* Edited by Catherine Overholt, Mary B. Anderson, Kathleen Cloud, and James E. Austin. West Hartford, Conn.: Kumarian Press, pp. 243–82.

Arizpe, Lourdes, and Botey, Carlota. 1987. "Mexican Agricultural Development Policy and its Impact on Rural Women." In *Rural Women and State Policy: Feminist Perspectives on Latin American Agricultural Development.* Edited by Carmen Diana Deere and Magdalena Leon. Boulder, Colo.: Westview Press, pp. 67–83.

Arriagada, Irma. 1987. "Las Mujeres Latinoamericanas y la Crisis: El Impacto en el Mercado de Trabajo." Washington, D.C.: International Center for Research on Women. Photocopy.

Ashe, Jeffrey. 1986. "Sistema de Evaluación del Impacto." Cambridge, Mass.: ACCION International/AITEC.

————. 1985. *The PISCES II Experience: Local Efforts in Micro-Enterprise Development,* Vol. I. Washington, D.C.: U.S. Agency for International Development.

————. 1984. "Assisting the Survival Economy: The Micro-enterprise and Solidarity Group Projects of the Dominican Development Foundation (Revision and Update: 1984)." Cambridge, Mass.: Accion International/AITEC.

————. 1982. "PISCES Phase II. Assisting the Survival Economy: The Microenterprise and Solidarity Group Projects of the Dominican Development Foundation, Volume I." Cambridge, Mass.: Accion International/AITEC.

————. 1981. *The PISCES Studies: Assisting the Smallest Economic Activities of the Urban Poor.* Washington, D.C.: U.S. Agency for International Development.

Asociación de Organizaciónes de Programas de Grupos Solidarios. 1985. "Final Report of the First Latin American Workshop on Solidarity Group Programs." Photocopy.

Babb, Florence. 1985. "Producers and Reproducers: Andean Marketwomen in the Economy." In *Women and Change in Latin America.* Edited by June Nash and Helen Safa. South Hadley, Mass.: Bergin and Garvey, pp. 53–64.

Bàez, Clara, with Dottin, Milagros. 1983. "Participación de la Mujer en el Mercado Laboral en el Distrito Nacional de 1960 a 1980 y en Santo Domingo 1983." Prepared for the seminar on "Población y Sociedad," Santo Domingo, Dominican Republic, October 31–November 4, 1983.

Barro, Rudolf J., and Grossman, Heinrich I. 1971. "A General Disequilibrium Model of Income and Employment," *American Economic Review* (March).

Beneria, Lourdes. 1982. "Class and Gender Inequalities and Women's Role in Economic Development: Theoretical and Practical Implications," *Feminist Studies* 8 (September): 157–76.

————, and Roldàn, Martha. 1987. *The Crossroads of Class and Gender: Industrial Homework, Subcontracting and Household Dynamics in Mexico City.* Chicago: University of Chicago Press.

Berger, Marguerite. 1985. "An Initial Assessment of the Women's Entrepreneurship Development Program." Report prepared for the World Bank, Office of the Advisor on Women in Development. Photocopy.

————, Buvinić, Mayra, and Jaramillo, Cecilia. 1985. "La Participación de la Mujer en el Programa de Crédito PRODEM, Quito, Ecuador: Resultados Preliminares del Estudio Basal." Washington, D.C.: International Center for Research on Women.

Bhat, V.V., and Roe, Alan R. 1979. *Capital Market Imperfections and Economic Development.* World Bank Staff Working Papers, no. 338. Washington, D.C.: The World Bank.

Black, Naomi, and Baker Cottrell, Ann. 1981. *Women and World Change.* Beverly Hills, Calif.: Sage Publications.

Blackwood, Florette. 1986. "Performance of Men and Women in Repayment of Mortgage Loans in Jamaica." In *Learning About Women and Urban Services in Latin America and the Caribbean.* Edited by Marianne Schmink, Judith Bruce, and Marilyn Kohn. New York: The Population Council, pp. 101–15.

Blayney, Robert. 1986. "Micro-enterprise Programs." Report to the Inter-American Foundation. Photocopy.

————. 1979. "El Salvador Second Urban Project: Impact of Small Scale Enterprise (SSE) Credit Program on Women Entrepreneurs." Report prepared for the World Bank, Office of the Advisor on Women in Development. Photocopy.

————, and Lycette, Margaret. 1983. "Improving the Access of Women-Headed Households to Solanda Housing: A Feasible Down Payment Assistance Scheme." Report prepared for USAID/Ecuador. Washington, D.C.: International Center for Research on Women.

————, and Otero, Maria. 1985. "Small and Micro-enterprises: Contributions to Development and Future Directions for AID's Support." Washington, D.C.: U.S. Agency for International Development.

Blumberg, Rae Lesser. 1985. "A Walk on the 'WID' Side: Summary of Field Research on Women in Development in the Dominican Republic and Guatemala." Report prepared for USAID/ Dominican Republic. Photocopy.

Boomgard, James, et al. 1986. "Subsector Analysis: Its Nature, Conduct and Potential Contribution to Small Enterprise Development." International Development Paper. East Lansing, Mich.: Michigan State University.

Boyer, Robert. 1986. *La Flexibilité du Travail*. Paris: Editions La De Couvert.

Bromley, Ray, and Gerry, Chris. 1979. *Casual Work and Poverty in Third World Cities*. Chichester, U.K.: John Wiley and Sons, Ltd.

Brown, Jason. 1981. "Case Studies: India." In *The PISCES Studies: Assisting the Smallest Economic Activities of the Urban Poor*. Edited by Michael Farbman. Washington, D.C.: U.S. Agency for International Development.

Bruce, Judith. 1980. "Market Women's Cooperatives: Giving Women Credit." SEEDS Pamphlet Series, no. 1. New York: The Population Council.

Buvinić, Mayra. 1986. "Projects for Women in the Third World: Explaining their Misbehavior," *World Development* 14 (May): 653–64.

————. 1984. "Projects for Women in the Third World: Explaining their Misbehavior." Report prepared for AID, Office of Women in Development. Washington, D.C.: International Center for Research on Women.

————, and Horenstein, Nadine. 1988. "The Involvement of Women in Projects of PACT Member Agencies: Review and Recommendations." Report prepared for PACT. Washington, D.C.: International Center for Research on Women.

————, and Youssef, Nadia. 1978. "Women-headed Households: The Ignored Factor in Development Planning." Report prepared for USAID, Office of Women in Development. Washington, D.C.: International Center for Research on Women.

————, Berger, Marguerite, and Gross, Stephen. 1984. "Una Mano para la Mujer que Trabaja: The Participation of Women Microentrepreneurs in the Urban Small Enterprise Development Fund of the Industrial Bank of Peru." Report prepared for AID/Peru. Washington, D.C.: International Center for Research on Women.

Carbonetto, Daniel. 1985. "Políticas de Mejoramiento del Empleo en el SIU" In *El Sector Informal Urbano en los Países Andinos*. Edited by Santiago Escobar. ILDIS, CEPESIU, Quito, Ecuador: ILDIS, CEPESIU, pp. 329–62.

Carranza Ordenique, José, and Tucker, William. 1982. *Estudio Preliminar sobre la Situación del Negociante Callejero*. Lima, Peru: Accion Comunitaria/AITEC.

Cartaya, Venessa. 1987. "El Confuso Mundo del Sector Informal," *Nueva Sociedad* 90 (July–August): 76–88.

Carvajal, Jaime. 1985. "Fundación Carvajal: Un Caso de Apoyo a las Microempresas en Cali, Colombia." Reunion Regional Latinoamericano de Agencias Patrocinadores sobre fomento de la Pequeña Empresa. Quito, Ecuador.

Casanovas, Roberto. 1985. "Los Trabajadores por Cuento Propia en el Mercado de Trabajo: El Caso de la Cuidad de La Paz." In *El Sector Informal Urbano en los Paises Andinos.* Quito and Guayaquil, Ecuador: Instituto Latinoamericano de Investagaciones Sociales (ILDIS) y Centro de Formación y Empleo para el Sector Informal Urbano (CEPESIU), pp. 207–45.

CEPAL. 1986. "América Latina: Las Mujeres y los Cambios Socio-Ocupacionales 1960–1980." Santiago, Chile: CEPAL. Documento No. 86-9-905.

———. 1985. "Las Mujeres en el Sector Informal en América Latina: Aspectos Metodológicos." Paper prepared for the Women in the Informal Sector Expert group meeting on participation, income, and production measurements. Santo Domingo, 13–17 October, 1986.

———. 1984. *La Mujer en el Sector Urbano: América Latina y el Caribe.* Santiago, Chile: CEPAL.

Chaney, Elsa. 1984. *Women of the World: Latin America and the Caribbean.* Washington, D.C.: U.S. Bureau of the Census/USAID.

Chen, Marty. 1983. "The Working Women's Forum: Organizing for Credit and Change." SEEDS Pamphlet Series, no. 6. New York: The Population Council.

Chinas, Beverly. 1973. *The Isthmus Zapotecs: Women's Roles in Cultural Context.* New York: Holt, Rinehart & Winston.

Chueca, Marcela, and Vargas de Balmaceda, Vilma. 1982. "Estrategias de Sobrevivencia de la Mujer en la Actual Crisis de la Economía Peruana." Prepared for the Congreso de Investigación Acerca de la Mujer en la Región Andina, Lima, Peru, 7–10 June, 1982.

Chuta, Enyinna, and Liedholm, Carl. 1979. *Rural Non-Farm Employment: A Review of the State of the Art.* Michigan State University Rural Development Papers, no. 4. East Lansing: Michigan State University, Department of Agricultural Economics.

CIDES. 1985. "Programa de Capacitación a Grupos Solidarios para Trabajadores Independientes." Paper prepared for Solidarity Group Programs Workshop, Bogotà, Colombia.

Clower, Robert W. 1965. "The Keynesian Counter-revolution: A Theoretical Appraisal." In *The Theory of Interest Rates.* Edited by F. Hahn and F. Brechling. London: Macmillan.

Cohen, Monique. 1984. "The Urban Street Foods Trade: Implications for Policy." Report prepared for the U.S. Agency for International Development, Office of Women in Development. Washington, D.C.: Equity Policy Center.

Corvalàn Vàsquez, Oscar, in cooperation with Lizarzaburu, Alfonso. 1985. "Los Programas de Capacitación de Trabajadoras del Sector Informal en América Latina." Research Report prepared for IIPE 53. Paris: UNESCO.

Coto, Arnulfo. 1985. "Evaluación sobre el Programa de Generación de Ingreso de los Trabajadores Independientes de la Zona sur Oriental de Cartegena." Photocopy.

Crandon, Libbet. 1984. *Women, Enterprise, and Development: The Pathfinder Fund's Women in Development—Projects, Evaluation and Documentation (WID/PED Program).* Boston: The Pathfinder Fund.

Cross, Larry, Abenoja, Febe, and García, Francial. n.d. "Self-Survey: Towards a New Approach to Conducting Surveys in the Developing World," *Rural Reconstruction Review.*

Deere, Carmen Diana. 1987. "The Latin American Agrarian Reform Experience." In *Rural Women and State Policy: Feminist Perspectives on Latin American Agricultural Development*. Edited by Carmen Diana Deere and Magdalena Leon. Boulder, Colo.: Westview Press, pp. 165–90

De Gómez, Martha Isabel. 1984. "Efectos de la Capacitación Técnica sobre la Situación de la Mujer en el Mercado de Trabajo en Colombia. Report prepared for ICRW study on technical assistance.

de Soto, Hernando. 1986. *El Otro Sendero*. Lima, Peru: Editorial El Barranco S.A.

Development Alternatives, Inc. 1979. *The Development Impact of PVOs: Kenya and Niger*. Washington, D.C.: Development Alternatives.

Doeringer, Peter and Piore, Michael. 1971. *Internal Labor Markets and Manpower Analysis*. Lexington, Mass.: D.C. Heath.

Duarte, Isis. 1983. "Fuerza Laboral Urbana en Santo Domingo: 1980–1983," *Estudios Sociales* no. 53 (September–November).

Dulansey, Maryanne. 1978. "Criteria for the Evaluation of Development Projects Involving Women." In *Approaches to Appropriate Evaluation*. New York: American Council of Voluntary Agencies for Foreign Service, Inc.

————, and Austin, James E. 1984. "Small Scale Enterprise and Women." In *Gender Roles in Development Projects: A Case Book*. Edited by Catherine Overholt, Mary B. Anderson, Kathleen Cloud, and James E. Austin. West Hartford, Conn.: Kumarian Press.

EPOC. 1985. "Final Report: Utilizing the Street Food Trade in Development Programming." Report prepared for U.S. Agency for International Development and the Equity Policy Center.

Escobar, Silvia. 1986. "La Microcomerciante de la Paz, Bolivia: Características y Necesidades." Paper presented to the International Seminar, "La Mujer y su Acceso al Crédito en América Latina: Sugerencias para Programas de Desarrollo," Quito, Ecuador, 12 September, 1986.

Everett, Jane, and Savara, Mira. 1984. "Bank Loans to the Poor in Bombay: Do Women Benefit?" *SIGNS* 10 (Winter): 272–90.

Exprúa, Jose. 1985. "El Acceso al Crédito Formal para la Pequeña Empresa." Trabajo preparado bajo el Convenio BID-INCAI, Programa de Pequeña y Mediana Empresa.

Farbman, Michael, ed. 1981. *The PISCES Studies: Assisting the Smallest Economic Activities of the Urban Poor*. Washington, D.C.: U.S. Agency for International Development, Bureau for Science and Technology.

Farrell, Gilda. 1985. "Los Microcomerciantes del Sector Informal Urbano: Los Casos de Quito y Guayaquil." In *El Sector Informal Urbano en los Países Andinos*. Quito and Guayaquil, Ecuador: ILDIS and CEPESIU, pp. 141–77.

Fernàndez, Blanca. 1982. "Reforma Agraria y Condición Socio-económica de la Mujer: El Caso de dos Cooperativas Agrarias de Producción Peruana." In *Las Trabajadoras del Agro*. Edited by Magdalena León. Bogota, Colombia: Asociación Colombiana de Estudios de Población, pp. 261–76.

Fernàndez, Guillermo. 1984. *Estudio Evaluativo del Programa PROGRESO*. Lima, Perú: Acción Comunitaria del Perú.

Fraser, Peter H., and Tucker, William R. 1981. "Case Studies: Latin America." In *The PISCES Studies: Assisting the Smallest Economic Activities of the Urban Poor*. Edited by Michael Farbman. Washington, D.C.: U.S. Agency for International Development.

Frixone, Cesar. 1985. "La Experiencia Positiva mas Importante de la Federación Nacional de Cámaras de Pequeños Industriales del Ecuador, FENAPI: Creación del Sistema de Garantía Crediticia y la Retrogarantía-plan Piloto de la Cámara de Pequeños Industriales de Pichincha." Paper presented at the workshop for institutions that aid small and medium entrepreneurs. Alajuela, Costa Rica, 1985.

Goldmark, Susan, and Deschamps, Jean-Jacques, with Halvorson, Raundi. 1985. "Promoting Urban Entrepreneurs: An Evaluation of the Peruvian Urban Development Fund." Washington, D.C.: Development Alternatives, Inc.

Goldmark, Susan, and Rosengard, Jay. 1985. "A Manual for Evaluating Small Scale Enterprise Development Projects." AID Program Design and Evaluation Methods Reports, no. 6. Washington, D.C.: U.S. Agency for International Development.

———. 1983. "Credit to Indonesian Entrepreneurs: An Assessment of Badan Kredit Ketamatan Program." Washington, D.C.: Development Alternatives.

Goldmark, Susan, et al. 1982a. "Aid to Entrepreneurs: An Evaluation of the Partnership for Productivity Project in Upper Volta." Washington, D.C.: Development Alternatives, Inc.

———. 1982b. "An Impact Evaluation of the Industrial Bank of Peru's Rural Development Fund." Washington, D.C.: Development Alternatives, Inc.

Gonzàlez Chairi, Jose María. 1984. "Capacitación y Desarrollo de la Población de las Areas Suburbanas de Guayaquil." Report prepared for the Organización Internacional de Trabajo. Guayaquil, Ecuador: CADESURB.

Gonzàlez-Vega, Claudio. 1981. "On the Iron Law of Interest Rate Restrictions: The Rationing Behavior of Financial Institutions Matters." Discussion paper prepared for the Colloquium on Rural Finance, World Bank, Washington, D.C, 1–3 September, 1981.

Gross, Stephen. 1984. "Formulario de Informe Mensual y Notas Explicativas." Cambridge, Mass.: ACCION International/AITEC. Photocopy.

Haggblade, Steve, Defay, Jacques, and Pitman, Bob. 1979. *Small Manufacturing Repair Enterprises in Haiti: Survey Results.* East Lansing: Michigan State University, Off-Farm Employment Project.

Halvorson, Randi. 1985. "Ecuador Small Business Development Project: Credit Component Study." Report prepared for USAID/Ecuador. Washington, D.C.: Partnership for Productivity International.

Harberger, Arnold C. 1971. "The Social Opportunity Cost of Labour," *Revista Internacional del Trabajo* 103.

Harris, J.R., and Todaro, M.P. 1970. "Migration, Unemployment and Development: A Two-Sector Analysis," *American Economic Review* (March).

Harrison, Polly. 1981. "Women in Development Strategy." Report prepared for USAID/Honduras. Photocopy.

Hart, K. 1970. "Small-Scale Entrepreneurs in Ghana and Development Planning," *Journal of Development Planning* (July).

Helzner, Judith, and Overseas Education Fund. 1982. "Improvement of the Socio-Economic Conditions of Low-Income Women Aged 25–50 through the Strengthening of the Union of Moroccan Women." Prepared for the Union des Femmes Morocaines and OEF.

Honadel, George, and Hannah, John P. 1982. "Management Performance for Rural Development: Packaged Training or Capacity Building," *Public Administration and Development* 2: 295–307.

INCAE. 1985. "Programa de Documentación del Seminario-Taller para Instituciones de Apoyo a Pequeños y Medianos Empresarios Celebrado en Alajuela, Costa Rica, julio de 1985."

Instituto Nacional de Estadística (INE), República de Perú. n.d. *Censo Nacional 1981*, Vol. I.

———. 1983. Permanent Household Survey. Peru.

———. 1976. National Population & Housing Census. Peru.

Inter-American Development Bank (IDB). 1987. *Economic and Social Progress in Latin America: 1987 Report.* Washington, D.C.: IDB.

———. 1986. Internal Document on the financial status of the Small and Microenterprise program in Colombia. Cali, Colombia: IDB.

———. 1984. *Ex-Post Evaluation of Two Microenterprise Projects: Small Projects Program, Colombia.* Washington, D.C.: IDB, Operations Evaluation Office.

International Center for Research on Women (ICRW). 1983. "Women's Contribution to Urban Development in Ecuador: Improving Women's Access to Credit." Proposal submitted to the U.S. Agency for International Development, Office of Women in Development.

———. 1982. "Elements of Women's Economic Integration: Project Indicators for the World Bank." Report prepared for the World Bank, Office of the Advisor on Women in Development. Washington, D.C.: ICRW.

———. 1980a. "Policy and Program Recommendations for Enhancing Women's Employment in Developing Countries." Report prepared for the U.S. Agency for International Development, Office of Women in Development. Washington, D.C.: ICRW.

———. 1980b. "The Productivity of Women in Developing Countries: Measurement Issues and Recommendations." Report prepared for the U.S. Agency for International Development, Office of Women in Development. Washington, D.C.: ICRW.

International Labor Office (ILO). 1981. *The Urban Informal Sector in Developing Countries.* Geneva: S.V. Sethuraman, ILO.

———. 1972. *Employment, Income and Equality: A Strategy for Increasing Productive Employment in Kenya.* Geneva: ILO.

Jain, Devaki, assisted by Nalini Singh and Malini Chand. 1980. *Women's Quest for Power: Five Indian Case Studies.* Ghaziabad, India: Vikas Publishing House Pvt. Ltd.

Kahnert, Friedrich. 1987. *Improving Urban Employment and Labor Productivity, World Bank Discussion Papers.* Washington, D.C.: The World Bank.

Kane, Edward J. 1981. "Political Economy of Subsidizing Agricultural Credit in Developing Countries." Discussion paper prepared for the Colloquium on Rural Finance, World Bank, Washington, D.C., 1–3 September, 1981.

Kannappan, Subbiah. 1985. "Urban Employment and Labor Market in Developing Nations." *Economic Development and Cultural Change* 33 (4): 699–730.

Kelley, Marcy. 1987. Phone interview concerning OEF's Women in Business Project in Central America, September, 1987.

————. 1983. "The Administrative Capacity of Economically Productive Women's Groups in the Dominican Republic: The Illusion of Independence." Report prepared for the U.S. Agency for International Development/Dominican Republic.

Kenyon, P. 1978. "Pricing." In *A Guide to Post-Keynesian Economics*. Edited by A. Eichner. New York: Sharpe.

Kilby, Peter. 1979. "Evaluating Technical Assistance," *World Development*, vol. 7, no. 6.

————, and D'Zmura, David. 1985. *Searching for Benefits*. AID Evaluation Special Studies, no. 28. Washington, D.C.: U.S. Agency for International Development.

Kindervatter, Suzanne. 1987. Personal Interview.

————. 1983. "Women Working Together." Washington, D.C.: Overseas Education Fund.

————. 1982. "Striving for an Ideal: The OEF 'Participatory Evaluation System.'" Washington, D.C.: Overseas Education Fund.

King, Elizabeth, and Evenson, Robert. 1983. "Time Allocation and Home Production in Philippine Rural Households." In *Women and Poverty in the Third World*. Edited by Mayra Buvinić, Margaret Lycette, and William Paul McGreevey. Baltimore: Johns Hopkins University Press, pp. 35–61.

King, Kenneth. 1975. "Skill Acquisition in the Informal Sector of an African Economy: The Kenyan Case," *Journal of Development Studies* 11 (January).

Knudson, Barbara, and Yates, Barbara. 1981. "The Economic Role of Women in Small-Scale Agriculture in the Eastern Caribbean: St. Lucia." Report prepared for the University of the West Indies, Women and Development Unit, Barbados.

Ladman, Jerry R. 1984. "Loan Transaction Costs, Credit Rationing, and Market Structure: The Case of Bolivia." In *Undermining Rural Development with Cheap Credit*. Edited by Dale W. Adams, Douglas H. Graham and J.D. von Pischke. Boulder, Colo.: Westview Press, pp. 104–19.

Lembert, Marcella, and Nieves, Isabel. 1986. "Technical Training and Labor Force Participation of Women in Latin America: A Comparative Review." Report prepared for the Ford Foundation and International Development Research Center.

Lewis W. Arthur. 1954. "Economic Development with Unlimited Supplies of Labour." In *The Economics of Underdevelopment*. Edited by A.N. Agarwala and S.P. Singh. London: Oxford University Press.

Liedholm, Carl, and Mead, Donald. 1987. "Small Scale Industries in Developing Countries: Empirical Evidence and Policy Implications." Washington, D.C.: U.S. Agency for International Development.

Lipton, Michael. 1980 (cited in Schmitz, Hubert, 1982). *Manufacturing in the Backyard: Case Studies of Accumulation and Employment in Small Scale Brazilian Industry*. London: Frances Pinter.

Llona, A. and Mezzera, J. 1985. "Mercados Laborales Segmentados y la 'Calidad' del Trabajo," *Socialismo y Participación,* (September).

Looze, Johanna W. 1983. "Credit and the Small Borrower: Bridging the Gap between Borrowers, Lending Programs, and Funding Sources." Washington, D.C.: Creative Associates, Inc.

López Castaño, Hugo. 1985. *Los Programas de Famiempresas de ACTUAR: Contexto Mac-roeconómico e Institucional, Metodología, Realizaciones y Dilemas Estratégicos.* Medel-lín, Colombia: Universidad de Antioquia.

Lycette, Margaret. 1984. "Improving Women's Access to Credit in the Third World: Policy and Project Recommendations." ICRW Occasional Papers, no. 1. Washington, D.C.: International Center for Research on Women.

Lynton, Rolf, and Pareek, Udai. 1978. *Training for Development.* West Hartford, Conn.: Kumarian Press.

March, Kathryn S., and Taqqu, Rachelle. 1982. *Women's Informal Associations and the Organizational Capacity for Development.* Ithaca, N.Y.: Cornell University Press.

Martínez, Nora. 1985. "La Mora en un Programa de Crédito Solidario." Issue paper presented at the Solidarity Group Programs Workshop sponsored by Private Agencies Collaborating Together, Bogota, Colombia, December 1985.

Mazumdar, Dipak. 1976. "The Urban Informal Sector," *World Development* 4 (August).

McDonald, I.M., and Solow, R.M. 1985. "Wages and Employment in a Segmented Labor Market," *Quarterly Journal of Economics,* (November).

McKean, Cressida. 1987. "Small-scale Manufacturing the Potential and Limitations for Growth: the Case of Wood Products in Ecuador." Master's Thesis. Institute of Development Studies. Sussex, United Kingdom.

———. 1985. "Evaluation of the Small and Medium Enterprise Project in the Philippeans." Pragma Corporation.

Merrick, Thomas, and Schmink, Marianne. 1983. "Households Headed by Women and Urban Poverty in Brazil." In *Women and Poverty in the Third World.* Edited by Mayra Buvinić, Margaret Lycette, and William Paul McGreevey. Baltimore: Johns Hopkins University Press.

Mezzera, Jaime. 1981. "Labour Market Segmentation without Policy-Induced Labour Market Distortions," *World Development* 9 (November–December): 1109–14.

Mies, María. 1986. *Indian Women in Subsistence and Agricultural Labor.* Geneva: International Labor Organization.

Mones, Belkis, and Grant, Lydia. 1987. "Agricultural Development, the Economic Crisis, and Rural Women in the Dominican Republic." In *Rural Women and State Policy: Feminist Perspectives on Latin American Agricultural Development.* Edited by Carmen Diana Deere and Magdalena León. Boulder, Colo.: Westview Press, pp. 35–50.

Moser, Caroline. 1978. "Informal Sector or Petty Commodity Production: Dualism or Dependence in Urban Development?" *World Development* 6 (9–10): 1041–64.

Nieves, Isabel. 1980. "Beyond Survival Skills: Providing Basic Services to Satisfy the Needs of Poor Women." In *Priorities in the Design of Development Programs: Women's Issues.* Report prepared for the U.S. Agency for International Development. Washington, D.C.: International Center for Research on Women.

Oficina Nacional de Estadísticas. n.d. "Dimensión Social de Desarrollo," *Plandes,* no. 26.

Osorio Molinski, Fernando. n.d. "Auto-evaluación de Proyectos de Desarrollo."

Otero, María. 1986. *The Solidarity Group Concept: Its Characteristics and Significance for Urban Informal Sector Activities.* New York: Private Agencies Collaborating Together.

————. 1985. "The Small Business Development Project and the Fundación Nacional de Desarrollo Hondureno: A Review of Project Designs with Special Emphasis on Gender Considerations." Report prepared for USAID/Honduras.

————, and Blayney, Robert. 1984. "An Evaluation of the Dominican Development Foundation's Program for the Development of Microenterprises (PRODEME)." Report prepared for USAID/Dominican Republic. Photocopy.

Palmer, Ingrid. 1985. *The Impact of Agrarian Reform on Women.* Women's Roles and Gender Differences in Development, no. 6. West Hartford, Conn.: Kumarian Press.

Patinkin, Donald. 1965. *Money, Interest and Prices,* 2d ed. New York: Rand McNally.

Peattie, Lisa. 1987. "An Idea in Good Currency and How it Grew: The Informal Sector," *World Development* 15, no. 7.

Pezzullo, Susan. 1983. "An Assessment of Five National Development Foundations: A Description of their Credit Programs and their Level of Assistance to Women." Report prepared for the Pan American Development Foundation. Photocopy.

Pinilla, Susan. 1987. "Women in a Peruvian Experience in Support of the Informal Sector." Lima, Peru: Instituto de Desarrollo del Sector Informal.

————. 1985. "Experiencias y Perspectivas de la Promoción Empresarial en el SIU: El Caso Peruano." In *El Sector Informal Urbano en los Paises Andinos.* Edited by Santiago Escobar. Quito, Ecuador: ILDIS, CEPESIU, pp. 301–26.

Pinto, Aribal. 1970. "Notas sobre la Naturaleza e Implicaciones de la 'Heterogeneidad Estructural' en América Latina." In *Dos Polémicas sobre el Desarrollo de América Latina.* Edited by ILPES. Santiago: Editorial Universitaria.

————. 1965. "La Concentración del Progreso Técnico y de sus Frutos en el Desarrollo Latinoamericano," *El Trimestre Económico* (January–March).

Placencia, Maria Mercedes. 1985. "La Promoción en el SIU Ecuadoriano: El Caso del Programa de Apoyo a la microempresa en Guayaquil." In *El Sector Informal Urbano en los Países Andinos.* Edited by Santiago Escobar. Quito, Ecuador: ILDIS, CEPESIU, pp. 275–300.

Portes, Alejandro, and Benton, Lauren. 1984. "Industrial Development and Labor Absorption: A Reinterpretation," *Population and Development Review* 10 (4): 589–611.

Programa Regional del Empleo para América Latina y el Caribe (PREALC). 1985. *Mas Allà del Crisis.* Santiago, Chile: Oficina Internacional del Trabajo, PREALC.

————. 1982. *Mercado de Trabajo en Cifras.* Santiago: PREALC.

————. 1981. *Sector Informal: Funcionamiento y Políticas.* Santiago: PREALC, Oficina Internacional del Trabajo.

————. 1975. *Situación y Perspectivas del Empleo en Paraguay.* Santiago: PREALC.

Quiros, Tito R. n.d. "La Evaluación Participativa de Proyectos de Desarrollo Social."

Rahman, Atiur. 1986. "Consciousness Raising Efforts of the Grameen Bank." Dhaka: Bangladesh Institute of Development Studies.

Ramos, J.R. 1980. "The Influence of Capital-Market Segmentation on the Behaviour of the Labour Market." Monograph Series on Employment. no. 16. Santiago: PREALC.

Ranis, Gustav and Fei, J.C.H. 1961. "A Theory of Economic Development," *American Economic Review* (September).

Reichmann, Rebecca. 1984a. "Women's Participation in ADEMI: The Association for the Development of Microenterprises, Inc." Cambridge, Mass.: Accion International/AITEC.

————. 1984b. "Women's Participation in Progreso: A Microenterprise Credit Program Reaching the Smallest Businesses of the Poor in Lima, Peru." Cambridge, Mass.: Accion International/AITEC.

————. 1984c. "The Dominican Associaton of Tricicleros 'San Jose Obero': A Case Study of Local Empowerment." Cambridge, Mass.: Accion International/AITEC.

Reno, Barbara Morrison, ed. *Credit and Women's Economic Development*. Washington, D.C.: World Council of Credit Unions and the Overseas Education Fund.

Robinson, Joan. 1977. "What are the Questions?" *Journal of Economic Literature* (December).

Rogers, Barbara. 1980. *The Domestication of Women*. New York: St. Martin's Press.

Rosales Villavicencio, Osvaldo. 1979. "La Mujer Chilena en la Fuerza de Trabajo: Participación, Empleo y Desempleo (1957–1977)." Santiago: Universidad de Chile.

Rossini, R.G., and Thomas J.J. 1987. "The Statistical Foundations of *El Otro Sendero*." London, England: Department of Economics, The London School of Economics and Political Science.

Salmen, Lawrence. 1983. "First Phase, Participation-Observer Evaluation of Urban Projects, La Paz and Guayaquil." Draft report to the World Bank. Photocopy.

Sang, Miguel. 1984. "Distribución no Tradicional de Alimentos en Santo Domingo." Instituto de Estudios Dominicanos.

Sanyal, Bishwapriya. 1986. "Informal Sector Revisited: Some Notes on the Relevance of the Concept in the 1980s." In *The Urban Informal Sector and Small-Scale Enterprise*. Washington, D.C.: Inter-American Foundation.

————, and Ferrin, Cynthia. 1986. "Urban Informal Sector and Small-Scale Enterprise. *Grassroots Development*, working paper no. 1. Rosslyn, Va: Inter-American Foundation.

Sassen-Koob, Sashia. 1984. "The New Labor Demand in Global Cities." In *Cities in Transformation: Class, Capital and the State*. Edited by Michael P. Smith. Beverly Hills, Calif.: Sage.

Sawyer, Susan M. 1983. "Dominican Republic: Program for Development of Microenterprises." Case Study and Training Project prepared for the Harvard Institute for International Development.

Schmitz, Hubert. 1982. "Growth Constraints on Small-scale Manufacturing in Developing Countries: A Critical Review." *World Development* 10 (6): 426.

Schumacher, Ilsa, Sebstad, Jennefer, and Buvinić, Mayra. 1980. "Limits to Productivity: Improving Women's Access to Technology and Credit. "Prepared for USAID. Bureau of Program and Policy Coordination, Office of Women in Development. Washington, D.C.: International Center for Research on Women.

Sebstad, Jennefer. 1982. "Struggle and Development Among Self-Employed Women: A Report on the Self-Employed Women's Association, Ahmedabad, India." Report prepared for USAID, Office of Women in Development. Photocopy.

Sethuraman, S.V. 1976. "The Urban Informal Sector: Concept, Measurement, and Policy." *International Labor Review* 114 (1): 69–81.

Souza, Paulo R. 1979. *Emprego e Salarios.* Sao Paulo, Brazil: Hucitec.

Stearns, Katherine E. 1985. *Assisting Informal Sector Enterprises in Developing Countries.* Ithaca, New York: Cornell University Press.

Stern, Naranjo & Co. 1984. "Manual de Crédito para la Fundación Espejo." Paper prepared for la Fundación Espejo en Guayaquil in agreement with a consultancy contract. Quito, Ecuador.

Suàrez, Francisco, and Calatroni, Maria T. n.d. *Evaluación de Programas de Acción Social.* Centro Interamericano para el Desarrollo Social, Buenos Aires, Argentina.

Sylos-Labini, Paolo. 1962. *Oligopoly and Technical Progress.* Cambridge, Mass.: Harvard University Press.

Taylor, Alicia, McFarlane, Donna, and LeFranch, Elsie. 1986. "The Higglers of Kingston." In *Learning about Women and Urban Services in Latin America and the Caribbean.* Edited by Marianne Schmink, Judith Bruce, and Marilyn Kohn. New York: The Population Council, pp. 228–40.

Tendler, Judith. 1987. "What Ever Happened to Poverty Alleviation?" A report prepared for the Mid-decade Review of the Ford Foundation's Programs on Livelihood, Employment and Income Generation.

———. 1983. *Ventures in the Informal Sector, and How They Worked Out in Brazil.* AID Evaluation Special Studies, no. 12. Washington, D.C.: U.S. Agency for International Development.

———. 1982. *Turning Private Voluntary Organizations into Development Agencies: Questions for Evaluation.* AID Program Evaluation Discussion Papers, no. 12. Washington, D.C.: U.S. Agency for International Development.

Till, Naomi, and Chaudhuri, Pinky. 1986. "Participation of Women in Cooperatives and Productive Groups in Honduras." Report of the McNamara Fellows to the Economic Development Institute, World Bank. Photocopy.

Tinker, Irene, and Bo Bramsen, Michele, eds. 1976. *Women and World Development.* Washington, D.C.: Overseas Development Council.

Tippett, B., and McKean, Cressida. 1987. "Evaluation of the Impact of A.I.D. on Small Business and Micro-Enterprise in the Dominican Republic." Report prepared for USAID/Dominican Republic. Washington, D.C.: International Science and Technology Institute, Inc.

Todaro, Michael P. 1969. "A Model of Labour Migration and Urban Unemployment in Less-Developed Countries," *American Economic Review* (March).

Tokman, Victor E. 1978. "An Exploration into the Nature of Informal-Formal Sector Interrelationships," *World Development* (September–October).

Trade and Development International. 1985. Evaluation of the Womens World Banking Program in the Dominican Republic and Colombia. Photocopy.

l'Union des Femmes Morocaines and Overseas Education Fund. 1982. "Improvement of the Socio-Economic Conditions of Low-Income Women Aged 25–50 through the Strengthening of the Union of Moroccan Women." Midpoint evaluation. Washington, D.C.: Overseas Education Fund.

United Nations. 1984. *La Mujer en el Sector Popular Urbano, América y el Caribe.* Santiago, Chile: United Nations.

Universidad de San Buenaventura. n.d. "Evaluación de la Asesoria Brindada a Microempresas en el Marco del Convenio Universidad San Buenaventura." Colombia: Fundación Carvajal.

U.S. Agency for International Development (USAID). 1985. *The PISCES Experience: Case Studies from Dominican Republic, Costa Rica, Kenya and Egypt.* Washington, D.C.: U.S. Agency for International Development.

————. 1980. *Assessing the Impact of Development Projects on Women.* AID Program Evaluation Discussion Papers, no. 8. Washington, D.C.: U.S. Agency for Internaitonal Development.

Valencia Vera, Marcela. 1986. "Proyectos de Crédito para la Mujer." Asociación para el Desarrollo e Intergración de la Mujer.

Vogel, Robert. 1984. "The Effect of Subsidized Agricultural Credit on Income Distribution in Costa Rica." In *Undermining Rural Development with Cheap Credit.* Edited by Dale W. Adams, Douglas H. Graham, and J.D. von Pischke. Boulder, Colo.: Westview Press, pp. 133–45.

————, and Larson, Donald. 1984. "Illusion and Reality in Allocating Agricultural Credit: The Example of Colombia." In *Undermining Rural Development with Cheap Credit.* Edited by Dale W. Adams, Douglas H. Graham, and J.D. von Pischke. Boulder, Colo.: Westview Press, pp. 49–60.

Von Pischke, J.D., and Adams, Dale W. 1980. "Fungibility and the Design and Evaluation of Agricultural Credit Projects," *American Journal of Agricultural Economics* 62 (November): 719–26.

Weeks, John. 1977. "Does Employment Matter?" *International Labor Review.*

————. 1975. "Policies for Expanding Employment in the Informal Urban Sector of Developing Economies." *International Labor Review* 111 (1): 1–13.

White, Karen, et al. 1986. "Integrating Women into Development Programs: A Guide for Implementation for Latin America and the Caribbean." Report prepared for USAID, Bureau for Latin America and the Caribbean. Washington, D.C.: International Center for Research on Women.

World Bank. 1985. *Bangladesh: Employment Opportunities for the Rural Poor: A Feasibility Report.* Washington, D.C.: The World Bank.

Youssef, Nadia H. 1974. *Women and Work in Developing Societies.* Berkeley, Calif.: University of California, Institute of International Studies.

Youssef, Nadia H., and LeBel, Allen. 1981. "Exploring Alternative Employment and Income Generation Opportunities for Honduran Women: Analysis and Recommendations." Report prepared for USAID/Honduras. Washington, D.C.: International Center for Research on Women.

Yudelman, Sally. 1987. *Hopeful Openings: A Study of Five Women's Development Organizations in Latin America and the Caribbean.* West Hartford, Conn.: Kumarian Press.

————. 1987. Personal Interview.

Index